China VAT

Lorenzo Riccardi · Giorgio Riccardi

China VAT

Regulations and Reforms

Springer

Lorenzo Riccardi
Shanghai Jiao Tong University
Shanghai, China

Giorgio Riccardi
RsA Asia
Shanghai, China

ISBN 978-981-15-5966-2 ISBN 978-981-15-5967-9 (eBook)
https://doi.org/10.1007/978-981-15-5967-9

This Springer imprint is published by the registered company Springer Nature Singapore Pte Ltd.
The registered company address is: 152 Beach Road, #21-01/04 Gateway East, Singapore 189721, Singapore

About This Book

This book was written to provide an introduction to the Chinese value-added tax (VAT) system. It is addressed to students, consultants, and managers who are interested in understanding the basics of the VAT regime in the People's Republic of China (PRC).

This guide has the intent to describe the process by which the PRC has introduced VAT and further refined it through the years symbiotically with the parallel development of the economy.

Lorenzo Riccardi wrote, supervised, and edited this book with the cooperation on various chapters of Luigi Wang, Edward Sheehan, Nicola Alessandro Cieri, Alessandro Marincioni, and Tommaso Siniscalchi.

Shanghai, China

Contents

Chapter 1
An Introduction to Taxation in China

1.1 Taxation in China

The Chinese tax system has recently developed closely to the economic growth of the country. The entry of China into the World Trade Organization (WTO) and the economic boom that has characterized past and recent years have made clear the necessity of overhauling a regulatory system in order to provide stability in the administration of the country, even in the tax field. The desire of becoming a leader in the Asian area, keeping up with the major world powers, has led China to make numerous amendments to improve and adapt the tax system to the rapid expansion of the economy and at the same time, to attract an increasing number of foreign companies.

As a result, a significant tax system overhaul was achieved on March 16, 2007 with the enactment of the Enterprise Income Tax Law, which then came into force on January 1, 2008. The new scheme joined together two systems of corporate income tax previously separated, the Domestic Invested Enterprises and the Foreign Invested Enterprises. The main purpose of the reform was to standardize tax treatments for foreign and local companies, removing privileges for foreign companies and formulating new tax legislation in harmony with Western laws.

1.2 Sources of Chinese Tax Law

Competent authorities with the power to legislate within the tax field are the following:

- National People's Congress;
- State Council;
- State Administration of Taxation; and
- Ministry of Finance.

L. Riccardi and G. Riccardi, *China VAT*,
https://doi.org/10.1007/978-981-15-5967-9_1

The National People's Congress (NPC), with its Standing Committee, is the supreme legislative authority in China, while the State Council, which is headed by the Premier, is the main executive organ of government.

The State Administration of Taxation and the Ministry of Finance are the organs empowered to interpret tax laws and regulations and to issue circulars, notices, and rulings about fiscal issues. The State Administration of Taxation is also responsible for tax policy and the administration and collection of taxes.

1.3 Tax Classification

There are different types of taxes levied on individuals and entities, which can be classified into the following categories:

- Direct taxes

  i. Individual Income Tax
  ii. Company Income Tax

- Indirect taxes

  iii. Value Added Tax
  iv. Consumption Tax

- Other taxes

  v. Stamp duty
  vi. Deed Tax
  vii. Land VAT
  viii. Resource Tax
  ix. Vehicles and Vessels Tax
  x. Environmental Protection Tax
  xi. Tax surcharges
  xii. Customs duties
  xiii. Import duties
  xiv. Export duties.

1.3.1 Individual Income Tax

The individual income tax is the income tax levied on Chinese citizens and foreigners residing in China or having a source of income in the country that is subject to taxation.

The tax liability depends on the status of residence in China and on the source of the income.

1.3.2 Enterprise Income Tax

The company income tax is levied on China resident enterprises and China non-resident enterprises with and without a permanent establishment in China.

The standard tax rate is 25%; lower and preferential rates are available for companies engaged in specific sectors and industries.

Taxpayers of the Chinese Company Income Tax are resident enterprises (including companies incorporated in China and companies not incorporated in China but effectively managed and controlled in the country) and non-resident enterprises with permanent establishment in China (which are taxed on their China-sourced income and non-China sourced income effectively connected with the establishment) and without permanent establishment (which are taxed on their income generated in China).

The Company Income Tax is paid on the income generated from the sale of goods, provision of services and transfer of ownership as well as income from dividends, interests, and royalties.

1.3.3 Value Added Tax

The Value Added Tax (VAT) is one of the indirect taxes applied on the purchases and sales of goods, services, intangible and immovable properties.

For small-scale taxpayers, including new established enterprises and companies with an annual sales amount lower than 5 million CNY, the VAT is levied at a rate of 3%, but they are not allowed to offset input VAT with output VAT nor entitled to apply for VAT refund in case of exports.

For general VAT taxpayers, the VAT rates have been amended several times during the past years. Currently, general VAT taxpayers are subject to VAT at rates ranging from 6 to 13%; VAT is considered a neutral tax since general VAT taxpayers are allowed to credit input VAT paid on the purchases of goods and services against the output VAT collected from the sales of goods and services.

A specific announcement jointly issued by Ministry of Finance, State Administration of Taxation and General Administration of Customs have lowered the VAT rates from 16 to 13% and from 10 to 9%, after a previous adjustment introduced in May 2018. The revised VAT rates have been implemented from April 1, 2019.

Taxable item	VAT rate Until 31.03.2019 (%)	VAT rate From 01.04.2019 (%)
Sales of goods	16	13
Leasing of movable property	16	13
Processing and repair services	16	13

(continued)

(continued)

Taxable item	VAT rate Until 31.03.2019 (%)	VAT rate From 01.04.2019 (%)
Transport, postal, basic communication, construction services	10	9
Transfer of land use rights	10	9
Sale of real estate	10	9
Agricultural products, food and edible oil	10	9
Tap water, heating, air conditioning, hot water, gas	10	9
Books, newspapers, magazines, audio and video products, electronic publications	10	9
Feed, fertilizers and pesticides	10	9
Dimethyl ether	10	9
Other goods stipulated by Authorities	10	9
Services not included above	6	6
Export	0	0

1.3.4 Consumption Tax

The Consumption Tax is an indirect tax levied on producers and importers of certain goods classified as "luxury" or "non-essential", such as tobacco, alcohol, fireworks, jewelry, cosmetics, motor-vehicles, etc. There are specific sub-categories with different tax rates and mechanisms for calculating the tax base.

1.3.5 Other Taxes

The other categories of taxes include:

- **Stamp duty tax**, levied on contracts (including sales, purchase and loan contracts), corporate documents and books with rates varying between 0.005 and 0.1%;
- **Deed tax**, calculated and levied on the transfer of ownership rights for land and real properties. The tax is levied on the transferee and the rates vary from 3 to 5%;
- **Land VAT**, calculated on the income resulting from the allocation or transfer of land use rights and buildings;
- **Property tax**, levied on the owner or lender of property and based on the value of the land/buildings and the leases;
- **Resource tax**, imposed on entities engaged in mining, the extraction of natural resources and production of salt within PRC;

- **Vehicle and vessel tax**, levied on the owners of certain categories of vehicles and vessels;
- **Environmental protection tax**, imposed on the entities responsible for emitting pollutants, solid wastes, and noise pollution.
- **Urban construction and maintenance surtax**, a surtax calculated on the amount of indirect taxes payable by the taxpayer. Depending on the location, the surtax rate is 7% (for urban areas), 5% (for county areas) and 1% (for other areas);
- **Education surtax**, a surtax imposed on the amount of indirect taxes payable by the taxpayer at a rate of 3%;
- **Local education surtax**, which is imposed on the amount of indirect taxes payable by the taxpayer at a rate of 2%;

1.3.6 Customs Duties

Customs duties are applied on the goods imported into China and on specific goods exported to other countries. The amount of customs duties on import/export of goods is calculated on the value of the goods multiplied by the corresponding rate; the value of the goods results from the customs declaration. This usually follows a regular check by competent authorities; the single rate is defined from its HS-code (code similar to the INTRASTAT European classification) that identifies the specific product category (Taxable Entities Covered).

1.4 Individual Income Tax

The National People's Congress enacted the Individual Income Tax Law for the first time on September 10, 1980, entering into force on the same day. In the following decades, there have been numerous amendments made to the original text with the last dated August 31, 2018, when the National People's Congress announced the promulgation of a revised text of Individual Income Tax Law of the People's Republic of China to be implemented from January 1, 2019.

The organ carrying out the control and administration of Individual Income Tax (IIT) is the State Administration of Taxation, which is also responsible for the collection and distribution of tax revenue together with local tax offices in provinces and metropolitan cities locally in charge of tax administration. Tax revenue is then divided between central and local governments.

1.4.1 Tax Residence

The revised Individual Income Tax Law divides taxpayers into two categories: resident taxpayers and non-resident taxpayers.

The definition of the resident taxpayer includes individuals who are domiciled in China (for family relationships, economic interests or possession of a home registered under their own name) and individuals who are not domiciled in China but have resided in China for 183 days or more during a tax year.

From the other side, non-resident taxpayers include individuals who are not domiciled in China and that have resided in China for less than 183 days during the tax year.

A tax year begins from January 1 and ends at December 31.

The IIT liability of each individual depends on his/her tax residence status.

1.4.2 Tax Liability

Individual taxpayers who are domiciled in China are subject to IIT on their worldwide income, including income sourced in China and income sourced outside China.

Individual taxpayers who are not domiciled in China but have resided in China for 183 days or more for more than 6 consecutive years, are subject to IIT on their worldwide income starting from the seventh year of tax residence.

Individual taxpayers who are not domiciled in China but have resided in China for 183 days or more during the tax year and are tax resident in China for no more than 6 consecutive years, are subject to IIT on their income sourced in China and their income sourced outside China but paid by a Chinese entity. The portion of income sourced outside China and paid by an overseas entity is exempt from China IIT.

Individual taxpayers who are not domiciled in China and have stayed in China for less than 183 days during the tax year are subject to IIT on their income sourced in China.

Individual taxpayers who are not domiciled in China and have stayed in China for less than 90 days during the tax year are subject to IIT on their income sourced in China and paid by a Chinese entity.

Only the days in which the individual has stayed in China for 24 h are included in the counting, while those days in which the individuals stayed less than 24 h are excluded.

Individuals who have dual employment and work both in China and abroad can determine their income sourced in China and the related tax liability based on the actual working period in days in China. In this case, the days in which the individuals stayed less than 24 h in China are counted as half day.

1.4.3 Worldwide Taxation and Six-Year Rule

According to the revised IIT Law, individuals who are considered tax resident in China shall be subject to China IIT on their worldwide income. However, individuals who are not domiciled in China and that have not been tax resident in China for more than six consecutive years can be exempted from China IIT on their income sourced outside China that is paid by an overseas entity. Individuals who are not domiciled in China shall be therefore subject to China IIT on their worldwide income starting from the seventh year of tax residence.

The six-year period shall be counted starting from January 1, 2019 and shall be counted again if the individual leaves China for more than 30 days on a single trip in any year during which he resided in China for 183 days or more.

1.4.4 Income Classification

The Individual Income Tax Law lists different categories of income subject to the individual income tax:

1. Income from wages and salaries;
2. Income from remuneration for personal services;
3. Income from author's remuneration;
4. Income from royalties;
5. Income from business operation;
6. Income from interest, dividends, and bonuses;
7. Income from lease of property;
8. Income from transfer of property; and
9. Contingent income.

The incomes listed in items 1–4 are aggregated in the comprehensive income and subject to the individual income tax on a consolidated basis.

The incomes listed in items 5–9 are computed separately from the comprehensive income.

1.4.5 Calculation of Taxable Income

For comprehensive income received by a resident individual, the taxable income is calculated as the gross income less the standard deduction (60,000 CNY/yearly), the social contributions, the special additional deductions and any other deduction provided by the law.

For a non-resident individual, the income from wage and salary is taxed after deducting the standard deduction (5000 CNY/monthly).

For income derived from labor services and royalties income, the taxable income shall be the gross amount less the deduction of 20%.

For income from author's remuneration, the taxable income is determined by deducting 20%, with an additional deduction of 30% from the resulting amount.

For business income, the taxable amount is determined as the remainder after deducting costs, expenses, and losses from the gross income generated in the tax year.

For income derived from leasing of property, the taxable income is the remainder after deducting 800 CNY (or 20% of the amount received) from the total amount received.

For income derived from the transfer of property, the taxable income is the capital gain calculated as the difference between the total proceeds and the original cost of the property and reasonable expenses incurred in the transfer.

For interest, dividends and other occasional income, the taxable income is determined based on the amount received each time.

1.4.6 Individual Income Tax Rates

For comprehensive income, progressive rates ranging from 3 to 45% are applied on the taxable income calculated after subtracting all the allowed deductions:

Income tax rate on comprehensive income (yearly basis)			
From	To	Tax rate (%)	Quick deduction
Not exceeding 36,000		3	0
36,000	144,000	10	2520
144,000	300,000	20	16,920
300,000	420,000	25	31,920
420,000	660,000	30	52,920
660,000	960,000	35	85,920
Exceeding 960,000		45	181,920

On a monthly basis, the tax rates are:

Income tax rate on comprehensive income (monthly basis)			
From	To	Tax rate (%)	Quick deduction
Not exceeding 3000		3	0
3000	12,000	10	210
12,000	25,000	20	1410
25,000	35,000	25	2660

(continued)

(continued)

Income tax rate on comprehensive income (monthly basis)			
From	To	Tax rate (%)	Quick deduction
35,000	55,000	30	4410
55,000	80,000	35	7160
Exceeding 80,000		45	15,160

For business operation income, progressive rates ranging from 5 to 35% are applied on the taxable income calculated after deducting costs, expenses, and losses:

Income tax rate on business operation income (yearly basis)			
From	To	Tax rate (%)	Quick deduction
Not exceeding 30,000		5	0
30,000	90,000	10	1500
90,000	300,000	20	10,500
300,000	500,000	30	40,500
Exceeding 500,000		35	65,500

For interest, dividends, income from leasing and transfer of property and occasional income, a rate of 20% shall apply.

1.4.7 Social Contributions

Chinese employees are required to make contributions for social insurance, including pension, medical, unemployment, maternity, and work-related injury insurances and the housing provident funds. Foreign citizens are also required to participate in social security schemes, even if at the moment the implementation varies from city to city.

Both employee and employer shall contribute to social security schemes and the amount of these social contributions is calculated based on the employee's average salary calculated in the previous year and the rates determined by local Authorities.

The rates currently applied in Shanghai and Beijing are as below:

Item	Shanghai		Beijing	
	Employer (%)	Employee (%)	Employer (%)	Employee (%)
Pension	16	8	16	8
Medical	9.5	2	10	2
Work-related injury	0.26	–	0.4	–
Maternity	1	–	0.8	–
Unemployment	0.5	0.5	0.8	0.2
Housing fund	7	7	12	12

1.4.8 Special Additional Deductions

Besides the standard deduction of CNY 5000 monthly (equal to CNY 60,000 yearly), the Individual Income Tax Law and its Implementing Regulations provide additional deductions from taxable income for children's education, continuing education, treatment of serious disease, the caring for the elderly, house loan interest and rents.

Item	Qualifying conditions	Annual deduction
Children's education	Pre-school Compulsory education Intermediate education Higher education	12,000 CNY/child
Continuing education	Formal education Professional education	4800 CNY 3600 CNY
Medical fee for serious disease	Self-paid medical expenses over 15,000 CNY	Actual expense not exceeding 80,000 CNY
House loan interest	Mortgage on first house	12,000 CNY
Housing rental fee	Not owning a property in the city of work	9600–18,000 CNY
Elderly dependent care expenses	Parents and grandparents aged 60 years or elder	12,000–24,000

1.4.9 Tax Allowances for Expats

Foreign employees can be exempted from individual income tax on certain benefits received during their employment in the territory of China. Such deductible allowances include:

- housing, meal and laundry allowances received in a non-cash for or on a reimbursement basis;
- reimbursement of reasonable relocation expenses upon commencement or cessation of China assignment;
- travel expenses for a couple of return flight tickets to home country;
- language training and children education expenses.

All the expenses shall be supported by relevant documentation.

Foreign employees can be allowed to enjoy such allowances until the end of 2021; from January 2022 foreigners can benefit only of the special additional deductions introduced for Chinese employees in 2019.

1.4.10 Withholding and Final Settlement

Employers are required to withhold the individual income tax at the payment of the remuneration: for wages and salaries, the tax shall be withheld on a monthly basis, while for author's remuneration, royalties and remuneration for personal services, the tax shall be withheld at each payment.

The revised IIT Law introduced a new withholding system, according to which the resident taxpayers earning a salary are subject to individual income tax withholding based on the cumulative taxable income.

A final IIT settlement shall be handled by the taxpayers between March 1 and June 30 following the tax year if the withholding tax on their comprehensive income has not been correctly applied at source, if they have earned overseas income, if they have to apply for a refund or if they earned taxable income in two or more working places.

1.5 Company Income Tax

The current Company Income Tax Law and its implementing rules have entered into force on January 1, 2008, responding to the demand of an action able to adapt the wholly foreign owned enterprises taxation with local firms' taxation.

1.5.1 Company Income Tax Rate

The standard rate of the company income tax is 25%; reduced and preferential rates are granted to those enterprises operating in certain industries and geographic areas. For example:

- high-tech enterprises are eligible for a reduced rate of 15%;
- enterprises operating in encouraged industries and established in the Western regions are eligible for a reduced rate of 15%;
- from 2019 to 2021, small low-profit companies with a taxable income up to 3 million CNY, a number of employees not exceeding 300 and total assets not exceeding 50 million CNY are eligible for reduced rate of 20%, to be applied on 25% of the income up to 1 million CNY and on 50% of the income exceeding 1 million CNY and up to 3 million CNY.

1.5.2 Taxable Entities

The company income tax is levied on resident and non-resident enterprises. For the purpose of the taxation, are considered as resident those enterprises that are incorporated in China or incorporated outside China but effectively managed and controlled in China. Resident enterprises are taxed on their worldwide income.

Non-resident enterprises are those not included in the definition of resident enterprises and can be further divided into two categories: non-resident enterprises with a permanent establishment in China. For these entities, the income sourced outside China may be exempt from taxation.

Type of company	Taxable income
Resident company (incorporated in China or effectively managed and controlled in China)	Worldwide income (income sourced in and outside China)
Non-resident company with a permanent establishment in China	Income sourced in China and the income sourced outside China that is connected to the permanent establishment
Non-resident company without a permanent establishment in China	Income sourced in China only

1.5.3 Categories of Taxable Income

The Company Income Tax Law provides a list of revenue considered taxable:

1. Revenue from the sales of goods and provision of services;
2. Proceeds from the transfer of tangible and intangible properties;
3. Dividends received from private and listed companies;
4. Interest, rental, royalties, and revenue from donations; and
5. Other income.

1.5.4 The Source of the Income

A relevant issue is to identify the source or the origin of the profits of a company: non-resident enterprises are subject to tax only on the portion of the income generated within China or effectively connected with the permanent establishment.

The source of the income shall be determined according to the art. 7 of Implementing Rules of Company Income Tax:

1. For revenue from sales of goods and provision of services, the source is determined in accordance with the place in which the activities occur;
2. For income from transfer of immovable properties, the source is determined according to the place where the property is located;
3. For income from transfer of movable properties, the source is determined according to the place of the transferring enterprise;
4. For income from transfer of equity, the source is determined according to the place where the invested enterprise is located;
5. For dividends, the source is the place of the enterprise which makes the distribution;
6. For income from royalties, rental and interest, the source is determined according to the place of the enterprise paying the income;
7. For other income, the source is determined according to the State Council.

1.5.5 Tax Liability and Computation

The taxable income for Company Income Tax is determined by starting from the total income (including all the taxable revenue from sale of goods, provision of services, transfer of goods and related rights, dividends, interest, rental and royalties, along with donations and other non-operating income and deducting the non-taxable or exempt items).

The total income is then deducted by items as not-taxable income and expenditure incurred during the course of business, including costs, expenses, losses on disposal of assets, depreciation and carry-forward losses.

1.5.6 Withholding Tax

Non-Resident companies without a permanent establishment in China are subject to Company Income Tax which is withheld at source on income earned within PRC 's territory. The taxable income may consist of earnings from dividends, royalties, interest, rental, and capital gains. To determine the origin of a source of income it is recommended to consult the art. 7 of EITIR, where the Chinese Legislator has laid down principles to verify the provenance of sources and their possible liability to corporate income tax.

The withholding tax on income from Non-resident companies without a permanent establishment in China is equal to 10% unless otherwise stated.

1.5.7 Withholding Agent

In China, withholding tax is levied on Non-resident companies providing services to China-based business. The income tax payable on such income derived by Non-resident enterprises shall be withheld at source, and the client, becoming a withholding agent, has the responsibility to transfer this amount to the State Treasury in name and behalf of the tax bureau. The process ends with a tax return delivered within seven days after the payment.

1.5.8 Tax Computation and Deadlines

The Company Income Tax is calculated multiplying a tax base by its applicable rate and then subtracting tax credits previously accrued thanks to preferential treatments and taxes already paid abroad. The annual CIT declaration must be filed within 5 months after the closing of the fiscal year which always coincides with the calendar year as stated in the Company Income Tax Law. Advance payments are finally required, based on quarterly interim financial statements released every three months and followed by a net balance adjustment sum paid by the Authority after the submission of the annual CIT declaration.

1.5.9 Anti-avoidance Rules

The Company Income Tax Law provides a series of anti-avoidance rules aimed at designing a general framework in line with the principles adopted in the legal systems of Western countries:

- standard on transfer prices between related parties;
- standard on Controlled Foreign Companies;
- standard on Advance Pricing Agreement between a Firm and Financial Administration about transaction prices between related parties;
- standard on Cost Sharing Agreement that involves the deductibility of common costs charged to intra-group companies;
- legal obligation to document ongoing transactions between the entity and its affiliated companies ("Related Party Transaction Annual Report").

The tax authority has also introduced a general anti-avoidance clause that enables local officials to make adjustments in a wide range of cases:

> If an enterprise engages in a business arrangement without bona fide commercial purposes that results in reducing its taxable revenue or taxable income, the tax authorities in charge have the right to make adjustments based on reasonable methods.

1.6 Transfer Pricing

1.6.1 General Framework

The Circular no. 42 issued in 2016 by the SAT introduces a three-tiered documentation framework providing a new landscape for transfer pricing practice in China, in line with the main guidelines provided by OECD.

The transfer pricing documentation includes a master file, a local file, and a special issue file.

Enterprises having only domestic related-party transactions are not required to prepare the above files.

1.6.2 Related-Party Definition

An enterprise is a related party to another enterprise, organization or individual if one of the following conditions is met:

- one party directly or indirectly owns at least 25% of the equity of another party or a third party directly or indirectly owns at least 25% of both parties;
- one party takes a loan from another party (other than an independent financial institution) in an amount equal to or more than 50% of the borrower's actual paid-in capital, or 10% or more of the total debts are guaranteed by another party (other than an independent financial institution);
- more than half of the senior management or at least one senior member of the board of directors who may control the board of one party is appointed by another party, or at least half of the senior management or at least one senior member of the board of directors who may control the board of both parties is appointed by the same third party;
- more than half of the senior management of one party are also senior management of another party, or at least one senior member of the board of directors who may control the board of one party is also a senior member of the board of directors of another party;
- the normal operation of production or business of one party is dependent on the industrial property or proprietary technology licensed by another party.

1.6.3 Master File

The requirement of the master file applies to enterprises that during the year have carried out overseas related-party transactions for an aggregate value exceeding

1 billion CNY or to enterprises that have carried out transactions with overseas related parties and which financial statements are consolidated by an ultimate holding company that has prepared a master file. In the second case, the master file is prepared by the ultimate holding company and shall be provided to the Chinese subsidiary.

1.6.4 Local File

The enterprises required to prepare the local file are those with:

- An annual sum of related-party transactions related to tangible assets exceeding 200 million CNY;
- An annual sum of related-party transactions related to intangible or financial assets exceeding 100 million CNY; or
- An annual sum of other related-party transactions exceeding 40 million CNY.

The related-party transactions covered by an advanced pricing agreement shall not be included in the local file.

1.6.5 Special Issue File

A special issue file is required if the enterprise has entered or has implemented a cost-sharing agreement or falls under the thin capitalization requirement, with a debt-to-equity ratio exceeding 2:1 (for non-financial enterprises) and 5:1 (for financial enterprises).

1.6.6 Country-by-Country Reporting

The Chinese resident enterprises that are the ultimate holding company of a multinational group with consolidated revenue over 5.5 billion CNY or that have been nominated as the CbC reporting entity by their group are required to prepare a CbC report.

1.7 Tables

Double Tax Agreements Signed by China

Jurisdiction	Belt Road	Dividends (%)	Interest (%)	Royalties (%)
Standard		10	10	10
Albania	•	10	0–10	10
Algeria	•	5–10	0–7	10
Armenia	•	5–10	0–10	10
Australia		10	10	10
Austria	•	7–10	0–10	10
Azerbaijan	•	10	0–10	10
Bahrain	•	5	0–5	10
Bangladesh	•	10	0–10	10
Barbados		5–10	0–10	10
Belarus	•	10	0–10	10
Belgium		5–10	0–10	7
Bosnia and Herzeg.	•	5	0–10	10
Botswana		5	0–7.5	5
Brazil		10	0–10	10
Brunei	•	5	0–10	10
Bulgaria	•	10	0–10	7–10
Canada		10	0–10	10
Croatia	•	5	0–10	10
Cuba		5–10	0–7.5	5
Cyprus		10	10	10
Czech Republic	•	5–10	0–7.5	10
Denmark		5–10	0–10	7–10
Ecuador		5	0–10	10
Egypt	•	8	0–10	8
Estonia	•	5–10	0–10	10
Ethiopia	•	5	0–7	5
Finland		5–10	0–10	10
France		5–10	0–10	10
Georgia	•	0–5–10	0–10	5
Germany		5–10	0–10	6–10
Greece	•	5–10	0–10	10
Hong Kong		5–10	0–7	7
Hungary	•	10	0–10	10

(continued)

(continued)

Jurisdiction	Belt Road	Dividends (%)	Interest (%)	Royalties (%)
Iceland		5–10	0–10	10
India	•	10	0–10	10
Indonesia		10	0–10	10
Iran	•	10	0–10	10
Ireland		5–10	0–10	6–10
Israel	•	10	7–10	10
Italy	•	10	0–10	10
Jamaica	•	5	0–7.5	10
Japan		10	0–10	10
Kazakhstan	•	10	0–10	10
Korea, South	•	5–10	0–10	10
Kuwait	•	0–5	0–5	10
Kyrgyzstan	•	10	0–10	10
Laos	•	5	0–10	10
Latvia	•	5–10	0–10	7
Lithuania	•	5–10	0–10	10
Luxembourg	•	5–10	0–10	6–10
Macau		5–10	0–7	7
Macedonia	•	5	0–10	10
Malaysia	•	10	0–10	10–15
Malta		5–10	0–10	7–10
Mauritius		5	0–10	10
Mexico		5	0–10	10
Moldova	•	5–10	0–10	10
Mongolia	•	5	0–10	10
Montenegro	•	5	0–10	10
Morocco	•	10	0–10	10
Nepal	•	10	0–10	15
Netherlands		0–5–10	0–10	6–10
New Zealand	•	10	0–10	10
Nigeria		7.50	0–7.5	7.50
Norway		10	0–10	10
Oman	•	5	0–10	10
Pakistan	•	10	0–10	10
Papua New Guinea	•	10	0–10	10
Philippines	•	10	0–10	10
Poland	•	10	0–10	7–10

(continued)

(continued)

Jurisdiction	Belt Road	Dividends (%)	Interest (%)	Royalties (%)
Portugal		10	0–10	10
Qatar	•	10	0–10	10
Romania	•	10	0–10	7
Russia	•	5–10	0–5–10	6–10
Saudi Arabia	•	0–5	0–10	10
Serbia	•	5	0–10	10
Seychelles		5	0–10	10
Singapore	•	5–10	0–10	6–10
Slovenia	•	5	10	10
South Africa	•	5	0–10	7–10
Spain		10	10	10
Sri Lanka	•	10	0–10	10
Sudan	•	5	0–10	10
Sweden		5–10	0–10	10
Switzerland		0–10	0–10	9–10
Syria	•	5–10	0–10	10
Tajikistan	•	5–10	0–8	8
Thailand	•	10	0–10	10
Trinidad and Tobago	•	5–10	0–10	10
Tunisia	•	8	0–10	5–10
Turkey	•	10	0–10	10
Turkmenistan	•	5–10	0–10	10
Uganda		7.50	0–10	10
Ukraine	•	5–10	0–10	10
United Arab Emirates	•	0–7	0–7	10
United Kingdom		0–5–10	0–10	6–10
United States		10	0–10	10
Uzbekistan	•	10	0–10	10
Venezuela		5–10	0–10	10
Vietnam	•	10	0–10	10
Zambia		5	0–10	5

Note According to the Vision and Actions on Jointly Building the Silk Road Economic Belt and 21st-Century Maritime Silk Road, the Belt and Road covers—but is not limited to—the area of the ancient Silk Road. It is open to engagement with all countries, and international and regional organizations

1.8 Main Tax Updates

1.8.1 China Imposes Tariff as Countermeasures to US Trade Restrictions

In order to safeguard China's trading interest, the Ministry of Finance announced, with the Circular 13 (2018), the imposition of duties on 128 products from United States, in response to the tariffs on steel and aluminum imports decided by Trump.

The new measures, that apply starting from April 2nd, shall impose a tariff of 15% on 120 items and a tariff of 25% on other 8 products imported from United States.

The main goods hit by the duties are fruits and related products, along with pork meat, steel and aluminum products.

1.8.2 Additional Tax Cuts Package 2018

The State Council announced on April 25th, 2018 additional tax cuts, in order to further stimulate the development of small and micro businesses and the creation of new jobs, by reducing the cost for innovation and entrepreneurship, facilitating the access to finance and reducing the overall tax burden.

In accordance with the guidelines set out by the Central Economic Work Conference and the Government Work Report, the State Council introduced the following tax measures:

- the annual taxable income threshold of small and microbusiness eligible for halved income tax have been be raised from 500,000 CNY to 1,000,000 CNY. The measure are effective for three years, from January 1, 2018 to December 31, 2020 and reduce the corporate tax burden for a number of small enterprises;
- the per unit value of newly—purchased R&D equipment eligible for one—time tax deduction have been raised from 1,000,000 CNY to 5,000,000 CNY. The measure are implemented for three years, from January 1, 2018 to December 31, 2020, and shall raise the ceilings on deductible purchases of equipment;
- the pilot preferential tax policies for venture capital firms and angel investors, implemented in eight innovation and reform experimental zones, shall be extended nationwide. These investors enjoy a tax incentive that deducts the 70% of their investment from the taxable income of early stage high tech start up. The tax incentive have been implemented from January 1, 2018 for corporate income tax and from July 1, 2018 for personal income tax;
- the precedent preclusion of the expenses of commissioned overseas R&D from additional tax deductions have been abolished from January 1, 2018

- the time limit for the capital loss carry-over of high-tech enterprises and technological small and medium enterprises are extended from five to ten years. The measure entered in force from January 1, 2018.
- the tax deduction for the employee training expenses raised from 2.5 to 8% for all the companies. The measure are in force from January 1, 2018.
- The stamp duty relief for books of account starting from May 1, 2018.

Customs announced further tariff cut from July 1 on consumer goods

In order to give a further boost to the domestic consumption, the Customs Tariff Commission of the State Council announced that MFN (most-favored-nation) tariffs on almost 1500 articles of daily consumer goods have been cut from July 1st 2018, including food preparations, pharmaceutical products, cosmetics, articles made of plastic, rubber, leather, apparel, clothing accessories and footwear.

Moreover, MFN provisional duties rates on 210 items are abolished and replaced by lower custom duties rates.

China personal tax reform

On June 19, 2018 the draft amendment to the Individual Income Tax Law has been submitted to the National People's Congress Standing Committee for reviewing.

In order to achieve a better income distribution, reduce the tax burdens for taxpayers and increase the consumption expenses, the draft amendment includes significant changes to the current IIT law, as the increase of the no tax area, the consolidation of some categories of income, the deductibility of certain expenses and anti-tax avoidance rules.:

The amendment may greatly affect the definition of tax residency, since it may introduce a new personal tax residence rule, from 365 to 183 days, even if at the present time it is still unclear how this new rule apply.

Currently, according to the Art. 1 of the Individual Income Tax Law, an individual is considered resident in China for IIT purpose if he has lived in China for one full year or more. In this case the individual is subject to tax on his China—sourced income plus any non-China—sourced income paid by individual or enterprise located in China. Moreover, individuals who have lived in China for more than five full consecutive years are subject to tax on their worldwide income. The five-year period of residence can be broken and the taxation on the worldwide income prevented if the individual leaves China for a certain period, referred to as "tax break"; this period can be an aggregate of 91 days or more during a year or a single period of at least 31 days.

If the new residence test is applied annually, the foreigner workers may be subject to China tax on their worldwide income starting from their first year of tax residence; if the five-year concession still remains, it may be more difficult to be in compliance with tax break rules, since an absence of 183 days may be required.

Extension of loss carry-forward period to 10 years for high-tech companies

China's Ministry of Finance (MOF) and the State Administration of Taxation (SAT) jointly released on July 11, 2018 the "Circular on Extending the Length of

Years for High-tech Enterprises and Technology-oriented Small- and Medium-sized Enterprises to Carry Forward Their Losses" Caishui [2018] No. 76

According to the Circular 76, the 5-year-loss carry forward period is extended to 10 years for High Tech and New Technology Enterprises (HNTEs) and Technology-based Small and Medium-sized Enterprises (TSMEs).

Under the Corporate Income Tax Law, tax losses can be carried forward for five years. Circular 76 extends the current 5-year loss carryforward period to 10 years for an enterprise identified as an HNTE or TSME in the current year, if the entity has tax losses incurred within the 5 preceding years. Circular 76 benefits foreign-invested enterprises that make substantial investments in technologies developments, as these enterprises typically sustain large losses in the initial investment periods. Allowing a longer loss carryforward period enables the enterprises to utilize more losses against future profits.

However, there are some uncertainties regarding the implementation of Circular 76, such as whether a change/cessation of HNTE status for the enterprise affects the utilization of tax losses in the years after the status change, requiring clarification by the SAT.

The Circular takes effect retroactively, as of January 1, 2018

Preferential income tax policy for small low-profit companies

China's Ministry of Finance (MOF) and the State Administration of Taxation (SAT) jointly released on July 11, 2018 the "Circular on Further Expanding the Coverage of the Preferential Income Tax Policy for Small Low-profit Enterprises" Caishui [2018] No. 77.

In order to further support the development of the small low-profit companies, the Circular No. 77 provides that during the period starting from January 1, 2018 and ending in December 31, 2020, the upper limit of the annual taxable income of a small low-profit enterprise is set to CNY 1 million (from the previous CNY 500,000). This means that if the annual taxable income of a small low-profit enterprise is lower or equal to CNY 1 million, its income is counted in the taxable income at the half-reduced rate and the company income tax is calculated and paid at the rate of 20%.

A small low-profit enterprise is an enterprise engaged in an industry not restricted or prohibited by the State and meeting the following conditions:

In the case of industrial enterprise, it is regarded as a small low-profit enterprise if its annual taxable income does not exceed CNY 1 million, the number of persons employed is lower than 100 and the total assets is not more than CNY 30 million;

In the case of other kinds of enterprise, it is regarded as a small low-profit enterprise if its annual taxable income does not exceed CNY 1 million, the number of persons employed is lower than 80 and the total assets are not more than CNY 10 million.

The number of persons employed by the enterprise, as mentioned above, refers to the staff members with a labor relationship with the enterprise and the dispatched workers.

If the enterprise starts or quits its activities during the year, the above indicators shall be calculated according to the actual business period during the tax year.

The measure provides relief to smaller companies, reducing the tax burden and boosting their development.

China to improve its export tax rebate system

During the meeting held on October 8, 2018, the China State Council decided to improve the export tax rebate policy granted to the Chinese companies engaged in foreign trade, by cutting the number of export tax rates brackets and raising some rates.

From November 1, 2018, the number of export tax rebate brackets have been be cut from seven to five. Moreover, some rates have been raised to a higher percentage. Specifically, the 15% bracket and part of the 13% bracket have been raised to 16% (full refund); the 9% bracket have been adjusted to 10% or 13%, while the 5% bracket increased to 6 and 10%.

On the contrary, the export rebate rates for high energy consumption and seriously polluting goods remain unchanged, along with those involved in the cuts of industrial production capacity.

The procedures for obtaining the tax rebate are simplified and shortened especially for companies with good credit record and paperless declarations have been fully implemented in order to improve the efficiency of the whole process.

The new measure help those companies which are export-oriented and that have been affected by the duties levied by US government on imports from China.

Interim measures for special additional deductions to IIT

The Ministry of Finance and the State Administration of Taxation have issued on October 20, 2018 a draft of the Interim Measures for Special Additional Deduction of Individual Income Tax, unveiling the measures on special additional deductions from personal taxable income.

Besides the standard deduction of CNY 5000 monthly (equal to CNY 60,000 yearly), the interim measures provide additional deductions from taxable income for children's education, continuing education, treatment of serious disease, the caring for the elderly, house loan interest and rents. Moreover, the special deductions shall be fair, reasonable, simple and practical in order to actually reduce the burden on the taxpayers.

The expenses for children's education can be deductible for an amount up to CNY 12,000 yearly (or CNY 1000 monthly). These expenses include pre-school education, compulsory education, high school, university and PhD.

The continuing education expenses incurred by the taxpayer for professional qualification can be deducted up to CNY 3600 yearly, if the relating qualification is obtained during the year.

The expenses incurred for the treatment of serious diseases can be deductible for the portion exceeding CNY 15,000 (and limited to CNY 60,000).

The rental expenses incurred by the taxpayer in the city in which he works are deductible for an amount limited to CNY 14,400 yearly (CNY 1200 monthly) based on the city and the area in which the taxpayer lives.

Elderly care expenses refer to the costs incurred by the taxpayer for parents and grandparents aged 60 or above. These expenses would be deductible for an amount limited to CNY 24,000 yearly (CNY 2000 monthly).

Loan interest paid for the purchase of the first home are deductible up to CNY 12,000 yearly (CNY 1000 monthly) from commercial or housing fund loans.

Foreign individuals meeting the requirements for the special additional deductions can choose to continue to enjoy the current tax benefits related to deductible allowances or to deduct the special additional deductions according to the new Interim Measures.

A final version entered in force from January 1, 2019.

Foreign workers and China five-year rule from 2019 onwards

According to the current Individual Income Tax Law, individuals domiciled in China and expatriates who have lived in China for more than five full consecutive years are subject to personal tax on their worldwide income. For the expatriates, the taxation on the worldwide income starts in the subsequent year after the five full consecutive years.

The so-called five-year rule provides that a foreign individual is considered to have lived in China for five full consecutive years if he has been residing in the country for a full year in each of the past five consecutive years. Individuals who have lived in China for 365 days in a tax year are regarded as having lived in China for a full year; it shall be noted that a single temporary absence from China not exceeding 30 days or multiple absences not exceeding a total of 90 days within a tax year are not deducted from the total days spent in China.

If the five-year rule is established, the taxpayer is subject to income tax on his worldwide income sourced within and outside China if he lives in China for one full year in any of the years from the sixth year onwards.

Currently, a foreign worker employed in China can avoid being subject to Chinese individual income tax on his or her worldwide income by leaving the country for more than 90 days (in case of cumulative multiple absences) or than 30 days (in case of single absence) during the five years period.

The new Implementing Regulations of the Individual Income Tax Law issued for comments on October 20th, 2018 confirms that the five-year rule shall be applied after the entry into force of the new IIT Law, with some important changes.

According to the Implementing Regulations, for individuals who do not have a domicile in China but that have lived in China for a total of 183 days but less than five years or for five years and having a single departure for more than 30 days, the income derived outside China is be subject to individual income tax for the part paid by Chinese enterprises, individuals and institutions. If the taxpayer has lived in China for a total of 183 days in a row for five consecutive years and has not a single departure for more than 30 days within the five years, from the sixth year onwards, if the residence in China is over 183 days, he or she is be subject to personal income tax on any income derived outside China.

The five-year rule has been an important tax benefit in order to attract foreign talents in China and the authorities seem to be determined to continue down this path. The Implementing Regulations adjusted the time standard for residents from the one year to 183 days, making easier for expat workers to be considered tax resident in China.

The Implementing Regulations of the new Individual Income Tax is be available for comments and discussions until November 4, 2018 and is expected to enter in force from January 1, 2019.

China tax: special additional deductions for tax residents

A draft issued on October 20, 2018 of the "*Interim Measures for Special Additional Deductions of Individual Income Tax*" has introduced some itemized categories of expenses that can be deducted by the taxpayer when calculating the personal income tax starting from January 1, 2019.

In order to clarify the implementation of the special additional deductions, the State Council has issued on December 13, 2018 the Circular Guo Fa [2018] no. 41 on "*Issuing the Interim Measures for Additional Special Deductions for Individual Income Tax*", followed few days after by the Announcement no. 60 [2018] of the State Administration of Taxation on "*Operating Measures for Additional Special Deductions for Individual Income Tax (for Trial Implementation)*"

From January 1, 2019 every China tax resident can, if certain conditions are satisfied, reduce his/her tax burden by deducting additional expenses related to children's education, continuing education, critical illness medical care, housing mortgage interest, house rent and elderly care.

Taxpayers can enjoy the additional special deductions in two alternative ways:

- through the employer, who acts as a withholding agent. In this case, the taxpayer shall provide the employer with information related to additional special deductions using the "deduction information sheet"; or
- by claiming the deductions in the yearly final settlement (from March 1 to June 30 of the following year), providing the tax bureau with the relevant form.

The deduction information sheet shall contain relevant information that are required in order to enjoy the deductions and shall be submitted by the taxpayer to the employer, who cannot refuse to apply the deductions during the withholding of the individual income tax.

The taxpayer shall also keep the relevant materials and documentation, along with the deduction information sheet, for a period of five years for any future inspection. The employer is also required to keep the deduction information sheet provided by the taxpayer for the same amount of time.

The special additional deductions represent a further measure in order to reduce the tax burden of the Chinese tax residents and is implemented from January 2019 along with the new individual income tax law. A foreign employee who is a China tax resident can enjoy the special additional deductions (if he/she is entitled) or can continue to enjoy the existing deductions provided to foreign citizens.

Year-end bonus and treatment of deductible allowances for expats from 2019
The Ministry of Finance and the State Administration of Taxation have jointly issued, on December 27, 2018, the Circular Cai Shui [2018] no. 164 about the "*Convergence of preferential policies after the revision of the Individual Income Tax Law*".

The Circular provides important clarifications about two issues that mainly concern the foreign employees working in China after the amendments to the Individual Income Tax Law, which are the tax treatment of the year-end bonus and the deductible allowances for expats.

Year-end bonus
According to the Circular, the preferential tax treatment for the year-end bonus in compliance with Guo Shui Fa [2005] no. 9 "*Notice of the State Administration of Taxation on Adjusting the Method of Calculating and Imposing Individual Income Tax on Annual One-off Bonuses and other Benefits Obtained by Individuals*" can be enjoyed until December 31, 2021.

The taxpayer can enjoy the preferential tax calculation dividing the year-end bonus by 12 and determining the applicable tax rates, without including the bonus amount into the comprehensive income.

Alternatively, tax residents can also choose to include the bonus into the comprehensive income.

From January 1, 2022 tax residents receiving the year-end bonus shall include the amount received into the comprehensive income of the year and calculate the personal income tax accordingly.

Deductible allowances for foreign individuals
From January 1, 2019 to December 31, 2021 the foreign employees who are tax resident in China may choose to enjoy the special additional deductions of personal income tax or, alternatively, to continue to follow preferential allowances for housing, language training, children's education, etc.... as provided by Caishui [1994] no. 20 "*Circular of the Ministry of Finance and the State Administration of Taxation on Issues concerning Individual Income Tax Policies*", Guo Shui Fa [1997[no. 54 "*Circular of the State Administration of Taxation on Imposing and Exempting Individual Income Tax on Qualifying Subsidies Granted to Foreign Individuals*" and Cai Shui [2004] no. 29 "*Circular of the Ministry of Finance and the State Administration of Taxation on Exempting the Hong Kong or Macao Housing Subsidies Received by Foreign Individuals from Individual Income Tax*".

From January 1, 2022 the foreign employees shall no longer be allowed to enjoy the preferential allowances currently granted to them; these employees may instead start to enjoy the special additional deductions if they are entitled.

Yearly final settlement of the individual income tax
The Announcement of the State Administration of Taxation on "*Issues concerning the self-declaration of Individual Income Tax*" [2018] no. 62 issued on December 21, 2018, provides detailed information about the cases in which a taxpayer shall

handle the yearly final settlement of the individual income tax, to be done between March 1 and June 30 of the year following the tax year.

According to the announcement, a resident taxpayer shall handle the yearly final settlement in the following circumstances:

- he/she receives comprehensive income from two places or more, and the balance of the comprehensive income minus deductions exceeds CNY 60,000;
- he/she receives one or more income from remuneration for personal services, income from author's remuneration and royalty income and the balance of the comprehensive income minus special deductions exceeds CNY 60,000;
- he/she paid an amount of tax in advance during the tax year that is lower than the amount of tax payable;
- he/she applies for a tax refund;
- he/she receives overseas income (specific provisions to be announced separately);
- he/she receives income, but the withholding agent does not withhold tax; and
- he/she earns income from interest, dividends, from property leases and transfers or contingent income.

Moreover, a non-resident taxpayer shall handle the final settlement in case he/she receives income included in the comprehensive income (wages and salaries, remuneration for personal service, author's remuneration or royalty) and the withholding agent does not withhold tax.

The taxpayer shall handle the final settlement and submit the self-declaration form for annual individual income tax with the competent tax authority in the place where his/her employer is located or in the place of domicile or habitual residence in case the taxpayer is not employed by an entity.

The Announcement also provides requirements for yearly final settlement for taxpayers receiving business income (before March 31 of the year after the year in which the income is received) and in case of house-hold deregistration.

The State Administration of Taxation shall announce further specific measures for taxpayers' handling of the final settlement and the payment of tax on comprehensive income.

Six-year rule

The new Individual Income Tax Law (Order of the President of the People's Republic of China no. 9 2018) and the related Implementing Rules (Order of the State Council of the People's Republic of China no. 707 2018) that is fully implemented from January 2019 provide a new definition of tax resident and introduced the so-called six-year rule.

According to the new Individual Income Tax Law, "the *individuals who have a domicile in China or individuals who do not have a domicile in China but have resided in China for an aggregate of 183 days or more within a single tax year shall be deemed as resident individuals.*"

However, individuals who have resided in China for 183 days or more within the single tax year can avoid being taxed in China for their worldwide income following the six-year rule as provided by the amended Implementing Rules of the Individual

Income Tax, according to which taxpayers without a domicile in the territory of China and have not been tax resident in China for more than six consecutive years can continue to be exempted from the individual income tax on their foreign-sourced income that is not paid by a Chinese resident company or individual:

> An individual who has no domicile in China but has resided in China for not more than six consecutive years in each of which he resided for 183 days or more accumulatively shall be exempted from individual income tax on his income derived outside the territory of China and paid by any overseas entity or individual, subject to record –filing with the competent tax authority; where an individual left China for more than 30 days on a single trip in any year during which he resided in China for 183 days or more accumulatively, the consecutively years in each of which he resided in China for 183 days or more accumulatively shall be counted again.

The six-year rule introduces a put-on-record filing required to claim tax exemption of the foreign-sourced income and further clarifications are expected to be provided.

Preferential CIT rate for small companies

On January 9, 2019 China's State Council announced further tax cuts and wider implementation of preferential tax policies, in order to support companies and provide additional incentives for small enterprises.

On January 17, 2019 the Ministry of Finance and the State Administration of Taxation have jointly issued the Circular Caishui no. 13 [2019] on "*Implementing the Policy on Inclusive Tax Reliefs for Small and Micro Businesses*", which introduced a preferential Company Income Tax rate for small and micro companies with a taxable income up to 3 million CNY. In particular:

- small scale and low-profit enterprises with taxable income lower than 1 million CNY can enjoy a CIT rate of 20%, that would be applied on 25% of their income, leaving the residual 75% tax-free and leading to an effective rate of 5%;
- small scale and low-profit enterprises with taxable income between 1 million CNY to 3 million CNY can enjoy a preferential CIT rate of 20%, that would be applied on 50% of their income, leaving the residual 50% tax-free and leading to an effective rate of 10%.

The above-mentioned small scale and low-profit enterprises refer to companies engaged in non-restricted and non-prohibited industries and meeting all the following conditions:

- annual taxable income less or equal to 3 million CNY;
- number of employees not exceeding 300; and
- total assets not exceeding 50 million CNY.

Moreover, the Circular provides that

- small-scale taxpayers with monthly sales less or equal than 100,000 CNY is exempted from the payment of VAT;
- local authorities may, according to the actual conditions of the area and the needs of macro-economic regulation and control, reduce the resource tax, property tax,

urban land use tax, stamp duty, farmland occupation tax, urban maintenance and construction tax, education surcharge, and local education surcharge; technology-based start-up companies with a number of employees not exceeding 300 and total assets and annual sales not exceeding 50 million CNY can be eligible to apply the preferential policy provided by the Circular Caishui no. 55 [2018], according to which the 70% of the investments made and completed between January 1, 2019 and December 31, 2021 can be deducted from the taxable income.

The provisions of the Circular is implemented for a period of 3 years, from January 1, 2019 to December 31, 2021 and grants significant tax benefits for a large number of taxpayers.

Chinese companies benefit new tax cuts in 2019

In order to face a more complicated and challenging economic and financial environment, with the Chinese economy under slight downward pressure, Premier Li Keqiang has introduced, during the annual legislative sessions held by the National People's Congress in March 2019, several measures so that the country could meet the economic target of 6.5% GDP growth and the social development goals.

According to the work report provided by the government, China has reduced the tax burden for enterprises and the social insurance contributions. The tax cuts are mainly enjoyed by manufacturing companies and small businesses and include:

- a further decrease of the value added tax rates following the cut already introduced in 2018. The rates are reduced from the current 16 and 10% to respectively 13 and 9% and mainly involve enterprises operating in the manufacturing, transportation and construction industries;
- a decrease of the social contributions borne by the employers, in particular, the pension insurance rate for urban employees may be cut down to 16% (currently the rates in TIER 1 cities as Shanghai and Beijing are respectively 20 and 19%).

The measures, to be implemented, reduce the tax burden in 2019 by an expected amount of 2 trillion RMB, higher than the 1.3 trillion RMB of tax cuts achieved in 2018.

China SAT clarifies how to calculate the length of residence of individuals

The Ministry of Finance and the State Administration of Taxation have jointly issued the Circular no. 34 (2019) on "*The Criteria for the Determination of the Length of Residence of Individuals having No Place of Abode in China*", in order to implement the revised Individual Income Tax Law and its Implementing Rules and to clarify the criteria for the calculation of the six-year period and the number of days spent in China by a non-domiciled individual.

The Article 1 of the Individual Income Tax Law provides that the individuals who have a domicile in China or the individuals who do not have a domicile in China but have resided in China for an aggregate of 183 days or more within a single tax year, shall be deemed as resident individuals. Income derived by resident individuals from inside and outside China shall be subject to individual income tax according to the provisions of this Law.

According to the Circular, only the days in which the individual has stayed in China for 24 h are considered in the calculation; those days in which the individuals stayed less than 24 h are not counted.

In addition, the Article 4 of the Implementing Rules of the Individual Income Tax Law provides that an individual who has no domicile in China but has resided in China for not more than six consecutive years in each of which he resided for 183 days or more accumulatively shall be exempted from individual income tax on his income derived outside the territory of China and paid by any overseas entity or individual; where an individual left China for more than 30 days on a single trip in any year during which he resided in China for 183 days or more accumulatively, the consecutive years in each of which he resided in China for 183 days or more accumulatively shall be counted again.

According to such provision, if the individual stays in China for accumulated 183 days during the tax year and if the accumulated number of days in the previous six years has exceeded 183 days, and there is no single absence of more than 30 days during a single tax year, he/she would be subjected to China individual income tax on his/her worldwide income.

The Circular clarifies that the above six-year period shall be counted starting from the tax year 2019 (included).

The provisions included in the Circular came into force from January 1, 2019.

China implements new VAT rates from April 1, 2019

The PRC Ministry of Finance, the State Administration of Taxation and the General Administration of Customs have jointly issued, on March 20, 2019, the Announcement on "Deepening the policies related to the VAT reform." The Announcement implements the decision to reform further the VAT policy taken during the annual legislative sessions held by the National People's Congress and announced by the Premier Li Keqiang earlier this month.

According to the provisions, the VAT rates for general VAT taxpayers are lowered from 16 to 13% and from 10 to 9%. Consequently, the highest export VAT refund rate, which grants a full recovery of the input VAT, have been also lowered to 13%.

The revised VAT rates have been implemented from April 1, 2019 and represent the second reform involving the value-added tax in less than one year.

Belt road initiative and new tax treaties

China and Italy signed on Saturday 23rd a Memorandum of Understanding (MoU) on the Belt and Road Initiative. Italy's Prime Minister Giuseppe Conte signed the New Silk Road MoU with Chinese President Xi Jinping in Rome, endorsing the global infrastructure-building project.

Conte and Xi shook hands after 29 separate sections of the MoU were signed by members of both governments.

Among the agreements signed, there is also a new Double Tax Agreement (DTA) replacing the previous DTA signed in 1986.

Regarding DTAs, nowadays China signed 107 treaties, while Italy signed 98 tax treaties. Economy Minister Giovanni Tria and the Foreign minister Wang Yi signed the new tax treaty at Palazzo Madama on 23rd March.

Previous China-Italy tax treaty was signed on 1986.10.31, effective from 1989.11.14 and applicable since 1990.1.1. The new tax treaty updates the previous one and includes OECD/G20 BEPS recommendations.

As regards dividends, a reduction in the withholding tax rate has been introduced compared to the previous DTA signed in 1986, from 10 to 5%, in case of qualified dividends, therefore with direct participation of at least 25% of the equity held for not less than 365 days.

This rate reduction grant a tax benefit to Italian companies that receive dividends from their subsidiaries. Besides, the beneficial rate of 5% for qualified shareholdings increases the equity ratio allocation for investments in both countries.

Dividends non-qualified (equity lower than 25%) shall be taxed with ordinary rate of 10%.

With reference to interests, the measure of the withholding tax applicable in the State of the source may not exceed a rate of 10% of the gross interest amount; A reduced rate of 8% on interest paid to financial institutions is granted in relation to loans with a minimum duration of three years aimed at financing investments projects and tax exemption for interests paid or received by public institutions.

Concerning royalties, the new tax treaty confirms a standard rate of 10% and introduces an effective rate of 5% for payments related to the use or right to use industrial, commercial or scientific equipment. This new rate on royalties is lower than the royalty rates of main European countries where 6% is the rate on similar royalties for DTA with Germany, France, United Kingdom, and Spain.

This new DTA probably needs a few years to be ratified and enter into force. If we look at the recent experiences of France and Germany for example, the new DTA between China and France signed in November 2013 was ratified one year later and entered into force in January 2015; in the case of Germany, the double taxation agreement was signed in March 2014, ratified in April 2016 and became applicable in January 2017. The new Agreement signed in Rome for the Avoidance of double taxation and the prevention of fiscal evasion grants an advantage in doing business between China and Italy.

This is an agreement that clearly show how tax treaties may reflect diplomatic and political cooperations between countries and how Belt Road members may enjoy a special treatment also in term of international taxation.

China–USA trade war

During 2018 the two world largest economies, USA and China, which are also strong trade partners, started to implement tariffs and duties on goods sourced from the other side, that quickly escalated in what is now known as China–USA Trade War.

USA's President Donald Trump has triggered the trade war by announcing a series of China-specific measures hitting goods imported by the USA from China.

Despite several high-level trade talks in the previous months and a temporary truce that has been declared to reduce tensions, in May the US President Donald

Trump announced that the increase from 10 to 25% tariff previously expected to be effective on January 1, 2019, shall take effect starting from May 10, 2019, hitting USD 200 billion of goods imported from China.

The response from China has been announced on May 13 by Customs Tariff Commission of the State Council, according to which China has implemented new tariffs from June 1, 2019, hitting USD 60 billion of imports from the US. According to the new measures, a 25% tariff imposed on 2493 goods, a 20% tariff on 1078 goods, a 10% tariff on 974 goods and keeping the 5% tariff on 595 goods.

Chapter 2
The Historical Development of Value Added Tax in China

Value Added Tax (VAT) is a tax imposed upon the added value, (or the increase in value), of a commodity as it goes through each stage of the production and supply chain from production to the point of final sale. VAT is the most common form of consumption tax globally having been adopted in 166 countries and every OECD country with the notable exception of the United States, as of 2019. VAT is a relatively easy tax to administer when contrasted with other forms of consumption taxes as VAT places the obligation upon businesses at each stage of the production and supply chain to remit the tax to the tax authority. Each business pays on its ‘value added’, which is the total sales value subtracted the cost of the any goods or services (inputs) used in the production of the product.

As VAT is imposed upon a sale at every stage in the production process the tax paying party is entitled to deduct the tax paid at the preceding stage. This is enabled under the credit-invoice method, which is a mechanism that enables a registered business to formulate the tax on the taxable goods every time they supply a product to a consumer, the registered business is then permitted to subtract the amount of VAT paid to other registered businesses in purchasing inputs. The sum of VAT credit available to a registered business to offset its VAT liability is calculated based upon the printed invoices received by a registered business when it purchases inputs from another registered business. These invoices stipulate the quantity of VAT collected on a sale, and also include the VAT registration numbers of both parties. Therefore, double taxation is avoided, and tax is paid only on the value added at each stage of production and supply chain. The tax authority can through the invoices confirm the VAT paid by the supplier and the input tax deducted by the purchaser, this enables that the correct VAT can be paid in stages and prevents a potential default of the total VAT by a supplier in the chain if they fail to fulfil their liabilities. This process means that VAT can be considered a self-policing tax policy as registered businesses demands invoices in order to offset their own liabilities. This leads us to a problem however, for VAT to be fully effective the best practice for tax authorities is to apply it to the supply every, or virtually every good and service. However, this is seldom done in practice so as to mitigate the regressive nature of VAT, as it consumes a

L. Riccardi and G. Riccardi, *China VAT*,
https://doi.org/10.1007/978-981-15-5967-9_2

larger %age of low-income consumers income than high income consumers. Once a VAT regime has been altered this way it increases the implementation costs and provides opportunities for unscrupulous businesses to attempt evasion. One method tax authorities use is to provide tax credits or exempt certain goods such as those regarded to be necessities like schoolbooks, bread and milk, children's clothing etc., and apply a higher value of VAT to luxury goods such as jewellery, electronics and automobiles to reduce the inequality inherent in VAT.

2.1 Turnover Taxes in the Early People's Republic of China

Prior to the unification of China under the Chinese Communist Party (CPC), the regions controlled by the CPC during the war with Japan and during the civil war had emergency tax rates to aid in the war efforts. These tariffs included a tax on production and sale of goods, and also a turnover tax on few businesses which were not co-opted into the war efforts. To achieve parity in tariffs across China, the CPC upon the cessation of the war held their very first tax conference between the 24th of November and 9th of December 1949 in Beijing. Following the conference, the draft Enforcement Guidelines of National Taxation was promulgated in January 1950, which introduced several taxes which were to be introduced nationwide. Some of the taxes included in the draft guidelines were a salt tax and customs tariffs along with product, industrial and business taxes. The product taxes were applied to a range of goods including cosmetics, cigarettes, industrial products, building materials, and agricultural products at rates varying widely from 3% up to 120%. The commercial and industrial taxes consisted of a business tax and an income tax on the few commercial entities which existed in Communist China.

The framework for the business tax originated from the nationalist era, whereby provincial governments levied taxes on goods passing internal customs checkpoints. This led to instances of double taxation when goods were transported through different provinces. To the CPC this was an untenable situation and they amended the business tax to suit the needs of the new government. There were two means of calculating the business tax, the first based upon the turnover of the business at a rate of 1–3% or the second method where the tax was applied to the profits of the business at rates of 1.5–6%. Private businesses paid both turnover taxes, business and income along with joint state-private businesses. Wholly state-owned businesses paid business tax and were not subject to the income tax. Exemptions were granted to state owned monopolies, household businesses and non-profit entities. All proceeds from the industrial and commercial taxes were remitted to the central government rather than the provincial government bodies. This new method of taxation was reflective of the CPC's desire to have a centrally planned economy and reduce regional independence by denying them sources of revenue.

In 1952 there were several changes made to the taxation system, which was spurred on by the declining tax revenues despite the economic boom which was occurring after nearly two decades of war. The decreasing tax revenue was exacerbated by the dramatic shift in China's economy, the substantial rise of the state-owned economy with the contraction of the private economy. The scope of the business tax was expanded to include taxes on cultural and entertainment bodies, which was inclusive but not limited to music and dance halls, operas and cinemas. This addition was coupled with restaurants and hotels being moved to a new tax bracket of 5–15%. The last significant change to the business tax was to switch the remittance of the tax from wholesale to production. Aside from the amendments to the business tax, a new commodity tax was promulgated towards the end of 1952. The commodity tax was applied to several goods both basic and luxurious items such as fabrics, spirits and cigarettes to raw materials such as steel, coal and processed oils, much like the product tax introduced in 1949 there was a widely ranging tax bracket from 7 to 66%. Goods on which the tax was already paid were not subject to any other tax when they were sold at the retail stage nationwide.

The switching of the tax from wholesale to production proved to be controversial however as it led to increases in the price of goods from private businesses which were incentivised to pass the cost on to the consumer, state owned businesses had fixed prices and were subsidised by the government which was to lead to further tax reforms later on following the reform and opening up. The controversy resulted from the fact that there was no distinction was made between state-owned and private economic entities, which was contrary to the CPC belief that taxation should be a measure to control the private economy. This political disquiet had a great influence on later tax developments and the government's tax policies.

2.2 Turnover Taxation During the 1958 and 1973 Tax Reforms

Between 1958 and 1978 China underwent significant political and economic change, which was reflected in two taxation overhauls. The reforms were undertaken on an ideological standpoint rather than with consideration for sensible fiscal planning due. This was due to the hardening of the communist policies and the view that taxation was an exploitative tool of capitalist economies which robbed the people of their work. The 1958 tax reform was greatly influenced by Soviet tax planning of the period, despite the fact that unlike the heavily industrialised Soviet economy, China's economy was still agrarian in nature. The Soviet tax regime was heavily reliant on turnover taxes which was unfortunately not fit for purpose in China and did not generate significant revenue for the state. The industrial and commercial taxes were amalgamated into a new "consolidated industrial and commercial tax" (CICT). This consolidation was influenced by the belief that the preceding taxation system was too complicated as goods were subjected to taxation at multiple stages. The CICT was passed by the standing committee of the National People's Congress in September 1958 and the old regulations dating back to the foundation of the state and nationalist era were abolished. The CICT changed the subjects of the tax, exemptions were granted for state institutions in the financial sectors, health care providers, scientific bodies and some agricultural entities while manufacturers, importers and service providers were the taxpayers. There were over 100 items subject to the CICT at rates from 1.5 to 69% based upon the sales value of the goods or services. CICT was the first time in China where a turnover tax was applied to both goods and services, it also granted a degree of autonomy to the provincial governments with regards to the implementation of the tax and the granting of exemptions.

The next great tax reform occurred in 1973 in the midst of the Cultural Revolution, greatly influenced by Maoist theory taxation was ever more firmly believed to be representative of capitalist markets and unsuitable for a truly socialist economy. The aim of the reformation was further consolidation of taxes in a simplified form for ease of collection. There were three stages to the reform, the first where a single rate was applied on individual businesses and the integration of all taxes on businesses; the second a single rate on sectors of industry; and finally the third reform a new industrial and commercial tax which absorbed all previous iterations and applied uniformly to private businesses and state-owned enterprises. The provinces gained even more autonomy as they were granted the power to administer and collect the remitted taxes independently of the central government. The greater autonomy granted to the provinces resulted in little standardisation of tax policies and collection, this coupled with the decrease in taxable items from over 100 to 44 lead to a significant reduction in tax revenue as a share of total fiscal revenue.

2.3 Taxes on Goods and Services from 1979 to 1993

China began a series of economic reforms in December 1978 under Deng Xiaoping, the most pressing goal was the reformation of the centrally planned economy towards a supervised market economy. The loss of revenue occurred by the 1973 consolidation of the CICT led to tax reform being considered essential by government strategists to balance the fiscal deficit and thereby strengthen the economic outlook for the country. As with other reforms, the government implemented a piecemeal trial by error tax policy. Certain regions were selected in 1979 to trial the newly introduced taxes, which proved to be successful. Following on from the successful trials, in 1984 the first recognisable version of VAT was promulgated in China, but only for a limited list of 24 specified goods.

The list was further expanded upon in a series of announcements which greatly complicated the tax regime, necessitating a large reformation undertaking in 1994. Prior to this reform in 1994, there were four distinct turnover taxes; VAT, a product tax, a business tax, and a consolidated industrial and commercial tax. The product tax was applied to cigarettes, alcohol, chemical and petrochemical goods, electrical and light industrial products, and agricultural products whereas VAT applied to every other category of goods. This regime was considered unwieldy and unfit for purpose; in 1992 there were 31 categories with 143 subcategories of goods with specified VAT rates, only 66 of the subcategories were subject to the standard 14% rate. The 1994 reforms were marked with the promulgation of "The Provisional Regulation of the People's Republic of China on Value Added Tax". The provisional regulations also coincided with a renegotiation of the tax sharing between the provinces and the central government.

The tax sharing agreement between the provinces and the central government was introduced in the early 1980s with the transition of the centrally planned economy to the supervised market economy. Under the tax sharing agreement of the early 1980s, the provincial governments were responsible for revenue collection and were required to remit fixed figures to the central government. Any collected revenue which exceeded the fixed amount could be used by the provinces at their own discretion. Following the opening up and reform, the eastern coastal provinces quickly grew, with the sums being remitted to the central government accounting for a negligible sum of the total revenue generated by these coastal provinces. This proved untenable for the central government, which lead to a series of negotiations between the provinces and central government on proposed reform in the revenue sharing scheme based on a principle of adequate centralisation. Although the regional governments had strong negotiating positions due to their wealth and gained some concessions from the central government, the ultimate goal of the central government was achieved with a shift from fixed figure to a %age-based remittance of tax revenue. The division of income tax revenues was relatively straightforward, with the central government entitled to 60% and the provinces to 40% of the revenue from income taxes on enterprises and individuals. The multiple enterprise income tax laws were consolidated into two regimes, one applying to domestic-owned companies and another to foreign-owned companies. The two tax systems were then combined into a single corporate income tax in 2007, effective from 2008.

A more complex division was applied to indirect taxes. Four distinct taxes were agreed on and placed in three legislative instruments. The simplest of the four indirect tax regimes was an excise tax (called the "consumption tax") which replaced the products tax. It was similar to conventional excise taxes elsewhere, applying to standard negative goods such as petroleum products, cigarettes, and alcohol. Probably reflecting the socialist instincts of the law's designers, the excise tax also extended to a range of luxury goods such as jewellery or those associated with leisure or recreational activities that the designers presumably associated with higher-income individuals. The provinces agreed that the central government could retain 100% of the consumption tax revenue. The second indirect tax regime was a turnover tax, known as the business tax, that applied to transfers of real and intellectual property and to supplies of services other than those directly related to the repair, processing, or replacement of goods. Those excluded services were subsumed into the third indirect tax regime, a so-called VAT on the sale of goods by larger enterprises. A fourth regime, labelled the simplified VAT and included in the VAT legislation, imposed a turnover tax on sales of goods by small businesses. The provinces and the central government agreed that 100% of the revenue from the Business Tax (apart from BT paid by railway companies and banking or insurance companies) and 25% of the VAT would be allocated to the provincial governments. The central government received 75% of the VAT revenue as well as all BT paid by railway companies and banking or insurance companies. Authority for the enactment of those taxes was delegated to the State Council, and all were levied by way of provisional regulations pending adoption of replacement legislation by the National People's Congress.

This consolidated VAT code greatly simplified the VAT regime in China and is still in effect as of 2019 albeit with many iterations. Formal legislation has yet to be adopted almost two and a half decades later. The taxes continue to be levied by way of executive and implementing regulations, as well as by circulars or rulings by the Ministry of Finance, the State Administration of Taxation (SAT), or both jointly. From a reform perspective, one advantage of the non-legislative basis for the taxes is the flexibility, it affords for piecemeal changes to the system. Another key outcome of the 1993 negotiations between the central and provincial governments was an agreement to operate parallel tax administrations and divide responsibility for collecting different taxes between the SAT, the central government's tax administration body, and provincial offices. The provincial government offices were given responsibility for collecting the BT (unless paid by railway companies and banking or insurance companies), personal income tax (un lesson loan interest), and company income tax imposed on privately owned and collectively owned companies. The SAT collected consumption tax, VAT, the BT paid by railway companies and banking or insurance companies, and enterprise income taxes paid by state-owned enterprises and banks. Nationally, the provincial tax bureaus established and operated by the provincial governments were subject to joint oversight by the SAT and provincial authorities. They were in theory to base their interpretations upon SAT guidelines, although, in practice, they reported primarily to the provincial governments.

Chapter 3
Business Tax and Value Added Tax

To readers from other jurisdictions the idea of a separate tax for goods and services may seem strange, however it is important to remember the context in which the Chinese taxes were promulgated. Although the taxes were newly enacted they were influenced by those who had been educated in a highly socialist orthodoxy which less than 11 years previously had stressed distinguishing between consumer taxation, which was to be discouraged, and heavy industry taxation, which was to be encouraged.

3.1 VAT with Chinese Characteristics

When implementing VAT in 1994, China followed European precedent and enacted a two-rate model with a standard rate and a reduced rate. Almost all services were placed outside the scope of the VAT regime. While VAT is intended to act as a tax on final consumption by individuals, the base of the tax is the value of taxable supplies made by registered businesses—with the supplier and not the customer responsible for remitting the tax. The object of a tax on final consumption is achieved by providing intermediary businesses with credits for tax included in the cost of acquisition, effectively eliminating the tax burden throughout the production chain until final consumption. This however was not evident in the Chinese VAT, as it included no general input tax credit entitlement. Instead, a limited credit was available for VAT to be included in the cost of inventory. No credits were available for the cost of other assets—most notably, capital equipment. Seeking to place the unique design of the Chinese VAT, essentially a turnover tax with limited input tax credits, under the umbrella of a VAT-type tax, officials labelled it as "production-type VAT," suggesting it was a viable alternative to the conventional, consumption-type VAT.

The Chinese approach to VAT also treated exports differently than VAT in other jurisdictions. Other jurisdictions generally zero-rate exports, meaning that no tax is imposed on the suppler to foreign purchasers, to achieve this the exporter can

L. Riccardi and G. Riccardi, *China VAT*,
https://doi.org/10.1007/978-981-15-5967-9_3

recover all input tax incurred on acquisitions used to make the good for export. This policy ensures there is no domestic tax burden on consumption which occurs outside the exporting country, thereby enhancing national competitiveness. In contrast, the Chinese VAT system had no general zero-rating rule. Instead, a VAT export credit system was administered separately from the general VAT regime. This was reflective of the government's desire to an ability to strong influence, if not directly control the direction of investment and business activity, by using the export VAT credit system to encourage investment in the sectors deemed important for economic development. Different rebate rates were established for different industries, and which changed regularly as officials altered their views on what sectors should be supported.

The treatment of small business also differed from that of jurisdictions. While there are some exceptions to the general rule, most VAT regimes include a registration threshold which exempt businesses with turnovers below the threshold from any requirement to become a VAT payer. As these businesses are wholly outside the VAT system, they are also not entitled to input tax credits. Therefore, their sales are effectively input-taxed. This means that the sale price includes the embedded VAT they paid on acquisitions but no VAT on their value added. However, most regimes normally allow for optional registration by small businesses regardless of whether they meet the threshold requirement as registered businesses shall not buy from a supplier unable to provide a tax.

Similar to other jurisdictions the Chinese approach used a small business threshold albeit it was not a registration threshold. Instead, the Chinese approach applied to specific businesses limited input credits for tax imposed upon acquisitions of inventory or instead subjected small businesses to a separate turnover tax labelled as "simplified VAT". Prior to reforms in 2008, the small businesses turnover tax had two rates of 4 and 6%, which were ultimately replaced with a single 3% rate.

3.2 Business Tax

The Business Tax was applied to transfers of both tangible and intangible property, and to the supply of services which were not subject to VAT. It was promulgated in 1993 through Decree No. 136 of the State Council, with further amendments made in 2008 with the Interim Regulations on Business Tax of the People's Republic of China (IRBT) before being amalgamated with the VAT in May 2016. The business tax introduced the concept of "mixed" sales whereby a business, which sells goods, engaged in services that were not subject to VAT (car rental, hotels, client meals, staff entertainment and staff meals), the activity resulting from this combination of goods and services was to be considered to be "mixed" sales activity, and to be subject to either Business Tax or Value Added Tax depending on the dominant operation type of business. The tax base for the business tax was decided by the volume of business generated by the business. With the exception of freight forwarding and construction companies costs were not considered deductible, freight forwarding, and construction companies were allowed to deduct for expenses related to subcontracting actives.

If in instances a businesses' turnover was deemed to be unjustifiably low the tax authorities were capable of seeking the average tax remittance which was gathered from comparable service providers in the sector. The business tax rate ranged between 3 and 5% (construction, sports and culture) and 20% (entertainment businesses).

3.3 The VAT Reform Projects (2004–2019)

The VAT regime introduced in 1994 implemented a standard rate of 17% and a reduced rate of 13%. Smaller businesses were eligible to pay a reduced rate of just 6% on outputs but were not given any credits towards inputs.

The next major round of reformation of China's VAT regime occurred in 2004, where VAT shifted from a production-based to a consumption-based tax. The main objective of the reformation was to adapt the tax regime to an extensive and growing consumer-based market. The 2004 reformation involved the promotion of a more egalitarian market environment, incentivized technological advancements, and a projection to allow an easier environment for competition between domestic and foreign companies.

In 2007, subsequent VAT reformation was extended to the 26 cities of six provinces in central China; Shanxi, Anhui, Jiangxi, Henan, Hubei and Hunan and following the devastating Sichuan earthquake in 2008 the scheme was rapidly expanded into southern China.

The greater availability of tax credits to Chinese businesses saw a shift in the structure of the economy from vertically integrated enterprises to a more efficient and less expensive specialist external supply enterprises (with no effect on revenue) and increased investment and economic activity as the tax savings were used as capital for investment.

In 2008 the next round of reforms was enacted which enabled businesses to deduct input VAT credits for the purchase of fixed assets. The definition of fixed assets under the VAT law excludes "real property" such as buildings, and also provided an exclusion for motor vehicles. The goal of the 2008 reform was to provide assistance to domestic enterprises in facing the global financial crisis, the new input credits were devised to stimulate the investment by Chinese enterprises into more technologically advanced sectors. The simplified VAT rate was reduced from 6 and 4% to a flat rate of 3%.

In 2011, there were two major VAT reformations, the first was a reformation of Land VAT, which was then followed by a localized tax reform in Shanghai, aimed at phasing out Business Tax in favour of VAT. This pilot projects goal was to resolve the double taxation issues under the existing system and to foster the development of specific service industries in Shanghai. This pilot program was initially applied to certain industries such as transportation and a number of "modern services". Following its successes, the reform was expanded to other sectors of the economy, including postal services, before the project was expanded to other pilot regions and an eventual national wide roll out in August 1, 2013. Finally, in 2016 the consolidation of the two turnover taxes, the VAT and the Business Tax, was completed.

In May 2018, further reformations of the VAT occurred, there majorly three significant changes to the VAT regime. (i) VAT rates were lowered from 17 and 11% to 16 and 10% respectively, with the base level of 6% for the service sectors unchanged. (ii) the annual turnover thresholds of RMB 500,000 and RMB 800,000 for the small-scale VAT payers in the manufacturing and trading sectors were consolidated and significantly raised to RMB 5,000,000. (iii) the scope of the excess input tax refund was expanded.

In 2019 further reductions of the VAT occurred, the 16% rate for the manufacturing sector was reduced to 13%, the 10% rate which applied to the construction and transport sectors was lowered to 9%, and in the 6% bracket more deductions were introduced.

3.4 The Initial Reform Program (2004–2008)

Reform of China's production-type VAT into a consumption-type VAT started as an attempt to subsidize the modernization of industry in less-developed and rust belt regions struggling to adjust to modern market pressures.

In July 2004, three north eastern provinces were selected to trial the development of a consumption-based VAT. These pilot areas included six, specifically chosen industries, namely agricultural production, equipment manufacture, automobile manufacture, petrochemicals, and metallurgy. With the VAT base implemented, these companies were given the ability to deduct expenditures on fixed assets. One of the key goals of the 2004 reform was to reduce instances of double taxation and to relieve the tax burdens placed upon businesses. These savings would then be passed on to consumers via lower pricing and encourage investment into fixed assets.

In the context of the production style VAT, the input tax credits were regarded as a concession which officials decided were a useful subsidy for industries in the designated regions. The reform program began in 2004 with the extension of input tax credits to the acquisitions of capital goods in eight industries, including the oil, chemical, and automobile industries, in three northeast provinces. The approach taken to the initial reform became the standard for all subsequent reform of the VAT. This process of reformation which was both regional and sectoral was regarded by the state as the preferred means of introducing new regulations. This approach was possible due to the fragmented administration of VAT which treats each branch of a business as an independent taxpayer for VAT purposes to be collected in the regional tax administration office.

The pilot projects proved to be successful and by 2008, had been expanded to eight central and southern provinces. The tax administration offices having developed sufficiently advanced systems to accommodate the expanded input tax credits approved for the nation-wide rollout of input tax credits for all acquisitions of assets when VAT was imposed on supply with the exceptions of motor vehicles and boats.

In contrast to the VAT, the Business Tax which was applied to the supply of services and the transfer of intangible and tangible property, underwent little reform from its enactment. Like all turnover taxes, the Business Tax had a cascading effect which was not mitigated by input tax credits unlike those granted to VAT in the reformations. Providers of services were unable to claim credits for tax on services they had acquired, and customers were unable to claim credit for tax imposed on the supplies made to them.

3.5 A Comparison Between VAT and Business Tax

Tax Comparison Table Between VAT and Business Tax in Different Kinds of Services.

Services	BT (%)	VAT (%)
Construction services	3	11
Real estate	5	11
Financial and insurance	5	6
Hospitality	5	6

Business Tax (BT):

- applied to each transaction in the supply chain.
- collected and administered by local tax bureaus.
- applied to both the domestic market and the export of services.

Value Added Tax (VAT):

- effectively only taxes the final price paid by the end-consumer, however it is applied to each transaction in a supply chain.
- collected and administered by State tax bureaus.
- usually is zero rated for export.

The Business Tax was applied to the services which were outside the remit of the VAT; the VAT applied to the sale of all goods, except for intangible and immovable property, as well as to the provision of processing, repair, and replacement services, resulting in the BT being applied to the supply of all other services and the transfer both of intangible and real property. VAT and BT were mutually exclusive to prevent the same transaction being subjected to both taxes. When compared to most turnover taxes the BT had a much larger base at two tax brackets; at three % it applied to transportation, construction, postal, telecommunication, cultural, and sports industries; and at the higher rate of five % it subjected financial services, real estate rental, and the transfer (sale and resale) of real property.

Chapter 4
Consolidation of the Busines Tax and Value Added Tax

4.1 Reforms Between 2012–2016

While VAT revenues had grown in absolute terms as the economy grew in the recovery period after the 2008 global recession, vat revenue growth was not reflective of the growth of the economy which was shifting toward the consumption of services. The relative contribution of the BT on services to total tax revenues remained steady while the contribution of the VAT on goods declined. In 1994, VAT accounted for 45% of tax revenue; but by 2012, its contribution had declined to 26%. Over the same period, the contribution of the BT had climbed from 13% of tax revenue to 15.6%.

The central government's concern was not the overall level of revenue it received relative to the provinces, but rather with the effect of changes on the BT and VAT. While VAT revenues had declined as a % age of the total revenues, the taxes which went mostly to the central government had increased. Therefore, the central government's overall position relative to that of the provinces improved significantly. In 1993, prior to the adoption of VAT and the BT, the central government received 22% of tax revenues, while the provincial governments received 78%. In 2011, when the State Council considered proposals for a consolidation of the two taxes, the shares of tax revenue received by the central and provincial governments were roughly equal, a change attributable to the growth of taxes with higher % ages of revenue going to the central government. As the economy shifted from goods to service among consumer consumption, revenues of the central government would decline, and the provincial revenues rise. While the central government was in a far stronger position relative to the provinces both economically and politically in 2011 than in 1993, there was a realisation that it could not simply appropriate almost one-fifth of the provinces' tax revenue by shifting the BT into the VAT without some sort of compensatory arrangement.

In late 2011, the State Council directed the MOF to proceed with a pilot program to shift supplies of services from the business tax to VAT regime. Soon after, the MOF and SAT released details of the first pilot program; The pilot program would take place in Shanghai from the beginning of 2012 and cover a selected range of

L. Riccardi and G. Riccardi, *China VAT*,
https://doi.org/10.1007/978-981-15-5967-9_4

services, including most forms of transport, leasing (both financial and operating), some modern services (for example, research and development), and professional services.

In mid-2012, the State Council approved the progressive extension of the pilot program to eight more jurisdictions over the last three months of the year. On August 1, 2013, the VAT pilot reform was implemented nationalwide. It directed the MOF and SAT to roll out the program across the rest of the country. Directions, issued in late 2013, brought railway transportation and postal services into the VAT reform pilot program beginning in January 2014; The telecom sector was included in the reform beginning in June 2014. By the end of 2014, the number of pilot taxpayers had increased from 2.73 million to 4.1 million, including 760,000 general taxpayers and 3.34 million small-scale taxpayers.

Three practical issues had to be resolved in the context of the pilot scheme and permanent shift

The first was the VAT rate for transferred services. While higher rates would have been of limited concern to business customers claiming input tax credits for a new VAT on services, a jump from a rate of 5–17% on services commonly used by unregistered people would have been dramatic and almost certainly would have led to a public outcry. There would have been similar disapproval from business customers unable to obtain tax invoices from small service providers.

The Chinese government decided to add four more rates (11, 6, 3, and 0%) to the 17 and 13% VAT tax rates. The standard 17% rate applied to lease arrangements. The new reduced 11% rate applied to transportation services. The 6% rate applied to modern services and 3% applied to professional services. The new 0% rate that applied to a range of exported services brought China into line with the international practice of zero rating exported goods and services.

The second practical issue to be resolved was determining which tax administration would be responsible for the VAT on services, which was ultimately determined to be the SAT resulting in provincial tax bureaus having significantly lightened workloads.

The third was how to appease the provincial governments if an important part of their revenue moved to the central government. Under the pilot scheme, responsibility for collecting VAT on services previously subject to the BT was transferred to the local SAT branches. Yet, the central government agreed that during the pilot program, the VAT revenue collected from the shifted services would have been transferred wholly to the relevant provincial governments. The arrangement was unsustainable in the long run because the transferred amount was based on a gross tax imposed on supplies. This left the central government to bear 100% of the cost of input tax credits in business-to-business transactions.

By May 2014, a large portion of supplies formerly subject to tax under the BT was in theory, subject to VAT. Actual implementation moved much more slowly in some areas of the country, particularly where smaller and remote offices were located. But in principle, by mid-2014, only four types of supplies remained subject to the BT: construction; real estate; financial and insurance services; and consumer services, such as hotels, restaurants, and entertainment. However, those were the most important elements of the BT, accounting for more than 70% of its total revenue in 2015.

Throughout 2015, official announcements issued an end-of-year deadline complete the transfer of the tax base from the BT to the VAT. The deadline came and went; however, national and provincial officials and business interest groups were unable to agree on appropriate VAT rules for the remaining sectors. Construction and consumer services raised the same problems as services previously shifted to the VAT: how to avoid rate shock for consumers and how to compensate provincial governments for lost revenue. Furthermore, financial services and supplies of real property raised different and conceptually far more difficult issues.

4.2 Consolidated BT and VAT

On May 1st, 2016, the Business Tax was integrated into the VAT regime to form a comprehensive tax encompassing all goods and services. The inclusion of the supply of real estate and financial services the Chinese VAT has one of the broadest tax bases globally. There were three notable changes which came about as a result of the consolidation of the turnover taxes.

(i) *The consolidated rates and revenue sharing*

The final transfer rules did not establish any new rates in the transition from the BT to VAT other than those present in the pilot program, with the standard 17% VAT rate applied to leasing arrangements, an 11% rate to transportation services, and a 6% rate to modern services. The 3% rate which applied to consumer services was removed and subsumed into the new 6% rate. The 11% rates on construction services and supplies by way of sale or lease of real property interests and 6% on financial supplies were maintained in the consolidating rules and finally export services were granted a zero-rate bringing them in line with international norms. The supply of services transferred from the BT to VAT were moved to the higher VAT brackets from 5 to 17% for leases; from 3 to 11% for transportation, postal, basic telecommunication, and construction services as well as the sale and leasing of real property and real property rights; from 5 to 6% for financial services; and from 3 to 6% for other services.

There was a notable change in the revenue sharing the central government in the pilot program transferred all VAT revenues from services which were previously subject to the business tax to the provincial governments. This approach yielded a fiscal windfall for the provincial governments in two respects. The first, these services were now taxed at the higher rates of the VAT; Secondly, the BT payments to provincial governments were based on the gross receipts, not the net tax after the cost of offsetting input tax credits claimed by business customers acquiring the services.

(ii) *New anti-avoidance rules*

The implementing documents for the transition from the BT to the combined VAT established new anti-avoidance rules which apply to the VAT regime. If the local tax bureau considers the price used in a transaction to be abnormal "without a reasonable business purpose," the tax authority is entitled to impose a market value price. A price shall be considered to be without a reasonable business purpose if the transaction is "*for the main purpose of obtaining tax benefits, through carrying out artificial arrangement to reduce, exempt or defer the payment of VAT or increase the refundable VAT amount.*" This VAT anti avoidance regulation is comparable to similar regulations found in China's Corporate Income Tax Law. The tax office applies a sequential three-step process to determine market value. The initial step looks at the average price of recent supplies in a comparable supply. The next step is the comparison of the average price of recent supplies made by other competing businesses which are the same as or similar to the disputed supplies. The final step applies a formula based on the cost and a presumed profit margin as established by the SAT in order to determine the market value of a supply.

(iii) *Concessions and exemptions*

The BT contained many concessions a number of which were transferred to the VAT regime. These concessions include reduced tax burdens for supplies by retired soldiers; and tax exemptions for kindergarten services, supplies by schools, aged-care institution services, funeral services, and medical care. As these businesses are treated as exempt supplies, no input tax credits are available to the suppliers, in effect making the supplies input-taxed supplies—that is, the input tax incurred by the suppliers shall be incorporated into the price of their supplies. Two groups of taxpayers—users of financial lease services and users of pipeline transportation services—are entitled to a unique concession: an immediate refund of the excess input tax credits without the need to wait for a full reconciliation in a VAT return. The calculation of refundable credits is based on a presumed entitlement to credits as a percentage of the turnover.

The consolidation of the BT into the VAT addressed the most significant structural issue in China's turnover taxation system, there are still many reforms to be made to the VAT as evidenced by the fact that the implementing documents for the VAT are called the Provisional Rules.

4.3 The 2018 Reforms

In May 2018, further reformations of the VAT occurred, there majorly three significant changes to the VAT regime. (i) VAT rates were lowered from 17 and 11% to 16 and 10% respectively, with the base level of 6% for the service sectors unchanged.

(ii) the annual turnover thresholds of RMB 500,000 and RMB 800,000 for the small-scale VAT payers in the manufacturing and trading sectors were consolidated and significantly raised to RMB 5,000,000. (iii) the scope of the excess input tax refund was expanded.

Item	VAT rate (%)	VAT rate (%)	Changed
	Until 2018.4.30	From 2018.5.1	
Movable property leasing	17	16	Yes
Transport services	11	10	Yes
Postal services	11	10	Yes
Basic telecommunication services	11	10	Yes
Construction services	11	10	Yes
Transfer of land use rights	11	10	Yes
Sale of real estate	11	10	Yes
Sales of goods	17	16	Yes
Processing and repair services	17	16	Yes
Export	0	0	No
R&D and technology services	6	6	No
Information and technology services	6	6	No
Culture and creative services	6	6	No
Logistics supporting services	6	6	No
Authentication and consulting services	6	6	No
Radio, film and television services	6	6	No
Business supporting services	6	6	No
Other modern services	6	6	No
Value added telecommunication services	6	6	No
Loan services	6	6	No
Direct financial services	6	6	No
Insurance services	6	6	No
Financial product trading	6	6	No
Cultural and sports services	6	6	No
Education and medical services	6	6	No
Catering and accommodation services	6	6	No
Daily services	6	6	No
Other lifestyle services	6	6	No
Sales of intangible assets	6	6	No
Agricultural products	11	10	Yes
Food and edible vegetable oil	11	10	Yes
Tap water, heating, air conditioning, hot water, gas	11	10	Yes
Books, newspapers, magazines	11	10	Yes

(continued)

(continued)

Item	VAT rate (%)	VAT rate (%)	Changed
	Until 2018.4.30	From 2018.5.1	
Feed, fertilizers, pesticides	11	10	Yes
Audio and video products	11	10	Yes
Electronic publication	11	10	Yes
Dimethylether	11	10	Yes

This expansion of the input tax refunds now includes qualified enterprises engaging in modern services (e.g. research and development) and advanced manufacturing, as well as enterprises operating in the energy sector. The aforementioned three VAT reform measures were enacted to improve the supply-side structural reform and facilitate the growth the targeted business environments, based upon the governments strategic policies following a comprehensive analysis of the developmental trends of the global and domestic economies. These measures mark significant leap in the journey to establishing a fit for purpose VAT system which observes the fundamental principles of tax neutrality, efficiency, fairness and simplicity as advocated by the OECD International VAT/GST Guidelines. These reform measures demonstrate a harmonisation between China's VAT system with the international standards on VAT design and China's commitment and contribution to the development of consistent and effective international VAT policies.

4.4 The 2019 Reforms

The first half of 2019 was marked by many further reductions in VAT rates in the face of a worsening global outlook and an escalating Sino-American trade war. The most significant VAT decrease was the VAT at 16% for taxable sales being reduced to a 13% VAT rate. In addition, general VAT taxpayers who were subject to a 10% VAT rate for taxable sales or importation now enjoy a reduced rate of 9%.

Item	VAT rate (%)	VAT rate (%)	Changed
	From 2018.5.1	From 2019.4.1	
Movable property leasing	16	13	Yes
Transport services	10	9	Yes
Postal services	10	9	Yes
Basic telecommunication services	10	9	Yes
Construction services	10	9	Yes
Transfer of land use rights	10	9	Yes
Sale of real estate	10	9	Yes
Sales of goods	16	13	Yes

(continued)

(continued)

Item	VAT rate (%)	VAT rate (%)	Changed
	From 2018.5.1	From 2019.4.1	
Processing and repair services	16	13	Yes
Export	0	0	No
R&D and technology services	6	6	No
Information and technology services	6	6	No
Culture and creative services	6	6	No
Logistics supporting services	6	6	No
Authentication and consulting services	6	6	No
Radio, film and television services	6	6	No
Business supporting services	6	6	No
Other modern services	6	6	No
Value added telecommunication services	6	6	No
Loan services	6	6	No
Direct financial services	6	6	No
Insurance services	6	6	No
Financial product trading	6	6	No
Cultural and sports services	6	6	No
Education and medical services	6	6	No
Catering and accommodation services	6	6	No
Daily services	6	6	No
Other lifestyle services	6	6	No
Sales of intangible assets	6	6	No
Agricultural products	10	9	Yes
Food and edible vegetable oil	10	9	Yes
Tap water, heating, air conditioning, hot water, gas	10	9	Yes
Books, newspapers, magazines	10	9	Yes
Feed, fertilizers, pesticides	10	9	Yes
Audio and video products	10	9	Yes
Electronic publication	10	9	Yes
Dimethylether	10	9	Yes

General VAT taxpayers are also be subject to a 9% input credit rate for the purchase of agricultural products, which previously have had a 10% rate. In addition, purchases of agricultural products for manufacturing or processing of goods shall be subject to a 10% credit rate instead of a 13% rate. The export of goods which were previously subject to VAT and a VAT refund rate at 16%, shall now face a decreased refund rate of 14%. Similarly, for the export of goods which were previously subject to VAT and a VAT refund rate at 10%, the export refund rate was reduced to 9%.

A new tax credit was introduced for a limited period until 31st December 2021, taxpayers in certain industries are eligible for a 10% credit on their input VAT. This credited amount is deductible from VAT payable, and any surplus amount is transferable to the next filing period as credit.

VAT taxpayers from the following industries are be eligible for this new tax credit:

- Postal services;
- Telecommunication services;
- Modern services (such as R&D, information technology services, logistics services and certification and consulting services among others);
- Lifestyle services (including cultural/sports services, education and healthcare, travel and entertainment as well as F&B).

To be eligible for this credit however taxpayers must obtain more than 50% of their total revenues from the specified industry category in the 12 months prior to their claim, if a business was founded after 1st April 2019, they shall be evaluated based upon the first 3 months of their operations.

The 2019 China VAT reform also expanded the scope of creditable input VAT for service providers and for the purchase of certain items such as real estate and construction services. These purchases can now be directly deducted from the output VAT. Along with expanding the scope of the input VAT credit, the 2019 reforms allowed for general VAT taxpayers to claim input VAT credit for domestic passenger transport services which can be credited against output VAT.

Finally, a pilot scheme for claiming incremental VAT credits is being trialled. Previously businesses were unable to claim refunds for excess input VAT rather they were only able to carry the excess input VAT forward to offset future output VAT. However, under this pilot scheme taxpayers who have incremental uncredited input VAT are entitled to see a refund. Taxpayers are entitled to a VAT refund only if they meet the following criteria;

(i) The VAT for six consecutive months (two consecutive quarters if taxed quarterly) is a positive number, and the incremental overpaid VAT in the sixth month greater than RMB 500,000;
(ii) The taxation credit is rated as A or B;
(iii) The taxpayer has not been convicted of VAT fraud in the last 36 months prior to claim;
(iv) The taxpayer has not been penalised by the tax authorities in the preceding 36 months before they claim for VAT refund.

The following table outlines the percentage changes in VAT during the period of 2018–2019.

Item	VAT rate (%)	VAT rate (%)	VAT rate (%)	Change %
	Until 2018.4.30	From 2018.5.1	From 2019.4.1	
Movable property leasing	17	16	13	4
Transport services	11	10	9	2
Postal services	11	10	9	2
Basic telecommunication services	11	10	9	2
Construction services	11	10	9	2
Transfer of land use rights	11	10	9	2
Sale of real estate	11	10	9	2
Sales of goods	17	16	13	4
Processing and repair services	17	16	13	4
Export	0	0	0	0
R&D and technology services	6	6	6	0
Information and technology services	6	6	6	0
Culture and creative services	6	6	6	0
Logistics supporting services	6	6	6	0
Authentication and consulting services	6	6	6	0
Radio, film and television services	6	6	6	0
Business supporting services	6	6	6	0
Other modern services	6	6	6	0
Value added telecommunication services	6	6	6	0
Loan services	6	6	6	0
Direct financial services	6	6	6	0
Insurance services	6	6	6	0
Financial product trading	6	6	6	0
Cultural and sports services	6	6	6	0
Education and medical services	6	6	6	0
Catering and accommodation services	6	6	6	0
Daily services	6	6	6	0
Other lifestyle services	6	6	6	0
Sales of intangible assets	6	6	6	0

(continued)

(continued)

Item	VAT rate (%)	VAT rate (%)	VAT rate (%)	Change %
	Until 2018.4.30	From 2018.5.1	From 2019.4.1	
Agricultural products	11	10	9	2
Food and edible vegetable oil	11	10	9	2
Tap water, heating, air conditioning, hot water, gas	11	10	9	2
Books, newspapers, magazines	11	10	9	2
Feed, fertilizers, pesticides	11	10	9	2
Audio and video products	11	10	9	2
Electronic publication	11	10	9	2
Dimethylether	11	10	9	2

Chapter 5
VAT Overview (2019)

5.1 Goods and Services Subject to VAT

The Value Added Tax is levied on taxable transactions carried out in the territory of the P.R.C which includes:

- Supply of goods against payment transferring the ownership of assets;
- Services of processing, repairing or replacement upon payment;
- Transportation services to deliver goods or passengers to destination through use of means of transportation, including land transportation, waterway transportation, air transportation and pipeline transportation., modern services like manufacturing, cultural, modern logistics etc. industries, including R&D and technology services, information technology services, culture and creative services, logistic supporting services, leasing of tangible and movable assets, advisory services.

VAT is also levied on the sale of commodities and precious metals futures, the sale of silver and gold, stamp products for stamp collection by units/individuals other than the Ministry of Post and Telecommunication, and the sale of consignment goods on behalf of a consignor.

With regards to finance lease operations without prior approval from the People's Bank of China and Ministry of Commerce, VAT is applicable if ownership of the leased product has been transferred to the lessee; VAT is applied to the issuance of newspapers and journals by units and individuals other than Post Units, the production and distribution of silver contained in concentrated silver mines or other concentrated non-ferrous metal mines, medium refinery products and finished silver products, and the fees charged by electric power enterprises on electricity generation enterprises to enter the power grid are all subject to the VAT regime.

Taxable item	VAT rate (%)
Sales of goods	13
Leasing of movable property	13

(continued)

L. Riccardi and G. Riccardi, *China VAT*,
https://doi.org/10.1007/978-981-15-5967-9_5

(continued)

Taxable item	VAT rate (%)
Processing and repair services	13
Transport, postal, basic communication, construction services	9
Transfer of land use rights	9
Sale of real estate	9
Agricultural products, food and edible oil	9
Tap water, heating, air conditioning, hot water, gas	9
Books, newspapers, magazines, audio and video products, electronic publications	9
Feed, fertilizers and pesticides	9
Dimethyl ether	9
Other goods stipulated by Authorities	9
Services not included above	6
Export	0

5.2 Taxable Subjects—Small-Scale and General Taxpayers

Only entities which exceed a specific threshold of income from taxable transactions are required to pay VAT. The government does not precisely state thresholds but, suggests a range in address of the maximum limit. Provincial tax authorities determine the limit—making the variation based on location. In January 2019 the SAT issued the *Notice on the Collection and Management of Small-scale Taxpayer Exemption from VAT Policy*, which outlined that small-scale VAT taxpayers with monthly sales under RMB 100,000 are exempt from paying VAT on a number of items, up from RMB 30,000 previously. Small-scale taxpayers with monthly sales under RMB 100,000 and quarterly sales under RMB 300,000 do not need to pay VAT on such sales. Furthermore, general VAT taxpayers with less than RMB 5 million in sales over the last 12 months are entitled to be included in the small-scale taxpayer bracket. The provincial governments are entitled to cut local tax items for small-scale taxpayers by up to 50%, and the tax authorities shall expand tax breaks for venture capital firms and angel investors that invest in high-tech start-ups.

General taxpayers are enterprises or enterprise units whose annual taxable sales value exceeds the threshold stipulated for small-scale taxpayers.

The annual taxable sales value is the sales volume achieved by the VAT taxpayer in an operation period of no more than 12 consecutive months, on which VAT shall be levied. VAT-exempted sales volume is also inclusive.

VAT taxpayers with an annual taxable sales value below the stipulated threshold for small-scale taxpayers and newly established VAT payers may apply to the competent tax authority to be recognized as general taxpayers if the taxpayer can prove sophistication in account management. Thus, have the ability to provide and establish accurate tax information.

General taxpayers have the ability to deduct inputs; unless, the sophistication of their accounting system is deemed unsatisfactory. Ultimately if the taxpayer cannot provide and establish accurate tax information or sales revenue to exceeds the threshold, yet do not register as a general taxpayer, they are deemed a general taxpayer under the VAT.

A VAT rate authorized as an input deduction may not match the VAT purchase rate. The taxpayer's deduction may be limited on the discrepancy of the category of good or time of input purchase.

VAT subjects

The VAT applies to the following transactions in the Chinese territory by individuals and/or production units:

- Supply of goods;
- Services (processing), general services (Pilot Reform), repairs or replacement;
- Imports of goods.

Small Scale Taxpayers and requirements

The Small-Scale Tax Taxpayers are generally small companies with a simplified book-keeping system which meet the following requirements and satisfy certain rules.

Kind of companies	Level of turnover
Manufacturing companies	Turnover <5,000,000 CNY
Commercial companies	

Rules

- VAT is non-deductible on purchases (=higher cost for the company);
- Sales and billing through the tax bureau;
- VAT equals to 3% of the value of sales.

General Taxpayers

The General Taxpayer are normal enterprises with a sophisticated internal accounting system. Which satisfy the following requirements and rules.

Kind of company	Level of turnover
Manufacturing companies	Turnover >5,000,000 CNY
Commercial companies	

Rules

- VAT at 13% of sales;
- Deductible VAT on purchases from VAT on sales;
- VAT payable = output VAT − input VAT;
- VAT refund on exports.

5.3 Goods Exempt from VAT

Not all goods and services are subjected to VAT—some are exempted from the VAT (Legislature in Article 15 of the IRVAT and 35 of IRVATIR). Among those products, there are agricultural commodities, contraceptive drugs, ancient books, goods imported to be used in scientific research, experiments and education, goods imported by foreign governments for humanitarian purpose, and second-hand goods, etc. No refund is given for the exportation of gold or any jewelry containing gold — But, there is a refund for processing fees.

In 2008, The Circular GuoShuiHan ruled that the production and sales of silver, made from wastes, are also exempted from the VAT. VAT taxpayers who produce or sell goods/services which are listed as exempt are obligated to submit a waiver declaration to the tax authorities in order to request a waiver of the exemption. The month following the submission of the claim, the taxpayer is then obliged to calculate and pay VAT according to the prevalent rules. Taxpayers who chose to waive tax exemptions, have the opportunity to be considered a general taxpayer, but has not been recognized as such, is authorized to apply for the recognition of a VAT general taxpayer, in addition to the rules applied to general taxpayers. Therefore, the taxpayer is permitted to issue VAT invoices for goods and services sold.

The VAT applies at applicable rates to all compatible goods and/or services that are sold/produced by the taxpayer once the tax exemption is waived. For specific customers, the tax exemptions cannot be waived. According to the PRVATIR Art. 36, a taxpayer cannot apply for tax exemption within 36 months after the tax authority accepts the tax exemption waiver declaration filed by the taxpayer. During the tax exemption period, obtained input VAT invoices or claim certificated, or taxable services purchased for the exempted items cannot be used for an input VAT credit claim.

5.4 Non-taxable Services

Many export services are exempt from VAT, such as the leasing of tangible movable property where the property is outside China, unlicensed international transportation, engineering and exploration services where the project or mineral resources are overseas, technology transfer services, technology consulting services, energy management services, software services, circuit design and testing services, business process management services, convention and exhibition services outside China, trademark and copyright transfer services, intellectual property services, advertising services where the advertisement is outside China, logistics and ancillary services, certification, verification and consulting services, and international telecommunications services provided by Chinese providers to overseas and fully consumed outside China.

The service recipient of a Chinese provider has to be located outside the mainland and the good or service provided cannot be related to immovable property in China, or the intangible asset must be in use entirely outside the mainland and have no relation to goods or immovable property in China to be considered "fully consumed outside China". This may limit the scope of eligible exported services when applying for VAT exemption, creating difficulty for VAT taxpayers to prove full consumption outside of the mainland.

VAT taxpayers which are engaged in non-taxable services, as well as taxable activities shall account separately for the sales value of goods, taxable services, and non-taxable services. Without separate accounting, or where accurate accounting cannot be made, the competent tax authority shall access the sales amount of goods and taxable services separately.

5.5 VAT Rebates for Exporters

For licensed manufactured and commercial imported and exported goods, there is a guaranteed partial refund of the VAT. Rates vary among 13, 9 and 6% according to the type of product and the Harmonized Item Description and Coding System (HS-code) specific to the category of product.

In relation to exports, there are two methods for calculating the VAT. Production companies use exemption, credit, and refund method (ECR method). Commercial companies use the exemption and refund method (ER method). The ECR method is generally applicable only to production enterprises qualified as general taxpayers. Exemption means that goods which are exported by production enterprises either directly or on consignment through foreign trade companies are exempt from output VAT. Credit means that, for enterprises whose self-produced goods are both exported and sold domestically, the input VAT credit on materials purchased for the production of export goods is offset against the output VAT on domestic sales. Refund means that, after offsetting the input VAT against the VAT payable, any excess amount of input VAT is refundable. The ER method is applied to the export of goods or service by export enterprises or other enterprises with no manufacturing capabilities. Under the ER method, output VAT of the exported goods is exempted, and a certain portion of input VAT is refundable, but not creditable. To secure a refund for exports, the company is required to submit the proper requisition within 90 days of exporting—including client shipping receipt and attached documentation.

Export VAT refund

- Partial or total refund of VAT paid on the purchase of exported goods;
- Trading and Manufacturing companies have different export VAT refund calculation method;
- Refund rates vary depending on the type of product: it is necessary to check the HS customs codes to confirm the % export VAT refund (Customs Tariff Code).

Requirements and terms

- Relevant applications must be submitted within 90 days from the export day;
- Together with documentation and receipt of payment from the customer.

Chapter 6
Future Developments

6.1 The Consulation Draft of the VAT Law of the People's Republic of China

While this primer on the VAT regime in the PRC was being researched and published, the NPC released "the Consultation Draft of the VAT Law of the People's Republic of China" (hereinafter referred to as "the Draft") on the 27th of November 2019. This Draft was published for comment by various industry representative groups and by national chambers of commerce which have a presence in China.

This chapter shall include a brief overview of the Draft and highlight the key changes with the current *Interim Regulations of the People's Republic of China on Value-added Tax*.

6.2 Taxable Thresholds Changes

Legal entities and individuals whose sales turnover is under RMB 300,000 are not considered to be taxpayers under the Consultation Draft. It is permissible for these entities and individuals to elect to pay VAT in accordance with the VAT Law on a voluntary basis.

This taxable threshold is the same amount as the VAT exemption amount of VAT small-scale taxpayer as defined in the current VAT Law. Regardless the Consultation Draft specifies that legal entities and individuals whose sales turnover is below the taxable threshold are not taxpayers.

Further information should be forthcoming on whether existing general VAT payers are covered in this taxable threshold, in what manner non-taxpayers can be managed and the applicability of this tax threshold to foreign entities.

The Consultation Draft has amended the definition of conducting a taxable transaction from "*the sale or purchase of services (excluding leasing of immovable properties) and intangible assets (excluding the right to use natural resources) from*

L. Riccardi and G. Riccardi, *China VAT*,
https://doi.org/10.1007/978-981-15-5967-9_6

an entity domiciled in China" to the "*sale of services, intangible assets (excluding the right to use natural resources) by domestic organisations and individuals, or the services and intangible assets are consumed in China*". The following excerpt "*purchaser is domiciled in China*" has been removed from the definition.

This change is particularly relevant for legal entities or individuals outside of China which sell services or intangible assets which to other entities or individuals outside of China which are then subsequently consumed within China.

6.3 Taxable Scope Under the Draft VAT Law

The definition of taxable scope has been expanded by the inclusion of "*processing, repair and installation services*" into "*services*" scope and through the listing "*trading of financial products*" in a new sub-category in the "*services*" scope. There is however no proposed change to the relevant applicable tax rate, so the proposal consultation draft shall not bring substantial changes to the current VAT regulations.

The Consultation Draft removes a number of non-taxable items such as "*provision of services by an organisation or sole proprietor to its employees*", "*provision of railway and aviation services for no consideration in accordance with the State's directives*", "*insurance claims received by insured person*", and "*housing special maintenance fund collected by housing authorities or designated organisations, provident fund administration centres, development enterprises and property management organisations*". The Consultation Draft also removes the transfer of goods, immovable assets and land use rights which are involved in the asset restructuring from the non-taxable item category. This is in line with the narrowing of the scope of deemed transactions discussed below.

The Consultation Draft does not include consignment transactions, investment, distribution to investors, consignment sales or the provision of services without receipt of consideration as within the scope of taxable transactions.

With regards to the consignment sales and transfer of goods between entities under the same taxpayer deemed sales treatment concerning these items shall rarely apply. Concerning distribution to investors or shareholders, the deemed sales treatment is less significant for two reasons, the current regulations already enable the transfer of assets during a restructuring transaction if the entity being transfer is exempted from VAT, and secondly, if the transfer of the entity's assets is subjected to VAT, the transferee can claim input VAT credit.

The provision of services without receipt of consideration is not particularly important for the deemed sales treatment. Due to the intangible nature of services combined with the lack of consideration, it can prove very difficult for the tax authorities to determine whether there are services provided for no consideration. As such the removal of these transactions from the scope of deemed transactions does not result in a considerable practical change.

6.4 Miscellaneous Changes

Continuance of the concept of adopting the main business in mixed sale transactions

The Consultation Draft continues with the concepts of "*concurrent operation*" and "*mixed sale*" which are found in the current VAT Law, and further stipulates that if a single taxable transaction consists of more than two tax rates, the tax rate which is applicable to the core of the transaction shall apply.

There is the possibility that it may be difficult to ascertain whether a transaction is a "*single transaction*" or "*multiple transactions*" under a concurrent operation. In addition to this, when an enterprise is engaged in different categories of business, determining what the "main" or core business transaction is can prove difficult. Does the core transaction refer to the main business of the enterprise, or to the item with the highest value in the specific transaction?

Expansion of conditions for non-creditable VAT items

Under the current VAT Law, input VAT generated from entertainment and catering services are not creditable. In the Consultation Draft, the condition applied to a good of "*acquired and consumed directly*" was added to assist in the determining of non-creditable input VAT items. This may result in a change whereby the input VAT generated from the purchase of catering and entertainment services, which are a part of a final product of an enterprise could be credited. This may have a significant beneficial impact on enterprises which are engages in catering or exhibition services.

New criteria for input VAT

The Consultation Draft has further developed the criteria for input VAT whereby it now should be "*related to the taxable transactions*". This maybe difficulty to accurately determine in practice whether the input VAT is related to taxable transactions. The Consultation Draft also introduces input VAT for "*VAT paid or borne in acquiring financial products*", this suggests that there may be a change regarding VAT concerning the trade of financial products, so they shall now be considered under the gross basis with input VAT credit method.

VAT credit balance refunds

The Consultation Draft provides clarity on the process for managing excess input VAT. In scenarios where the volume of input VAT is larger than the volume of output VAT in a filing period, the excess volume can either be refunded or carried forward to the next filing period. This is a continuation of the pilot scheme which was rolled out in 1st of April 2019 regarding the incremental input VAT refund for all industries.

Changes for the assessable value of import goods

There is a change in the Consultation Draft regarding the calculation of the assessable value of an import goods. The term "*duty paid value*" is amended to '*dutiable value*", and there is additional clarity given whereby the consideration related to trade of services shall not be included in the dutiable value.

The change is aimed at the removal of potential instances of double taxation, although in practice, at the moment the tax bureaus usually permit businesses to claim credit for both input VAT. Under the current VAT law, the custom value of a good includes warranty fees and/or royalties, which provide the basis for calculating custom duty and payable import VAT, while concurrently requiring the purchaser to withhold VAT for services provided from abroad. The new Consultation draft aims to rectify this issue.

Tax filing period extensions

For small scale taxpayers, the three VAT assessment periods of one-, three- and five-day periods from the current VAT law are removed in the Consultation Draft, and are replaced by a half year period. The Consultation Draft shall provide for 10 days, 15 days, one month, a quarter or half a year assessment periods. This reduction of the frequency of filing should significantly reduce the burden on small scale taxpayers. This is not applicable however to general taxpayers.

Further clarity given regarding withholding agent

Currently, if a foreign enterprise is conducting a taxable activity in China without a taxable presence in China, the purchaser shall withhold the VAT. The Consultation Draft has amended this to remove the need for the purchaser to ascertain whether or not the supplier has a taxable presence in China with the following text "*for foreign organisations or individuals conducting taxable transactions in China, the Purchaser will be the withholding agent*".

This clarification of the duties of the Purchaser should reduce potential liabilities on the purchaser by removing the possibility where the purchaser may mistakenly not withhold the VAT payable from the supplier if they mistakenly believed the supplier had a taxable presence in China.

Information exchange

The Consultation Draft has promoted the transfer of information between different administrative organs of the state. The Customs authorities shall now share information regarding VAT collection and the export declaration of goods with the tax bureau, banks, the state administration of foreign exchange and the Market supervision authority. The Consultation Draft states that there shall be a mechanism established to facilitate the VAT information exchange and coordination between these different administrative bodies to further strengthening VAT collection and administration.

Chapter 7
Regulation and Circulars

7.1 Circulars of the MOF and SAT from 2004 to 2008

Circular of the Ministry of Finance and the State Administration of Taxation Concerning Stopping Regulating the Export Enterprises Purchasing Export Goods from General Value-added Taxpayers with Tax Payment Notice Used Specially for Value-added Tax Cai Shui.

No. 101 June 4, 2004.

The financial departments (bureaus) and state taxation bureaus of all provinces, autonomous regions, municipalities directly under the central government, and cities specifically designated in the state plan, as well as the financial bureau of the Xinjiang Production and Construction Corps.

For the purposes of promoting the efficiency of export tax refund, simplifying the procedures while strengthening the administration, accelerating the progress of tax refund, and further supporting the foreign trade export of our nation, the Ministry of Finance and the State Administration of Taxation, on the basis of the growing perfection of tax project and the continuous reinforcement of value-added tax administration, determine to stop regulating the export enterprises purchasing export goods from general value-added tax payers with Tax Payment Notice (used specially for export goods) for value-added tax or Tax Payment Division Voucher for Export Goods (hereinafter referred to as Special Tax Receipt for VAT). We hereby notify the details as follows:

Article 1

When an export enterprise applies for export tax refund for goods that were declared to the customs for export (the export date shall be ascertained by the date indicated in the customs declaration for export, the same as follows) after June 1, 2004, with special value-added tax invoices issued after June 1, 2004, it shall be exempt from providing the Special Tax Receipts for VAT, in addition to Article 5 of this Circular.

L. Riccardi and G. Riccardi, *China VAT*,
https://doi.org/10.1007/978-981-15-5967-9_7

Article 2

With respect to the electromechanical products making use of loans from foreign governments and international financial institutions which have adopted international bidding and win bids at home, as well as domestic equipment purchased by foreign-funded companies, where their special VAT invoices or general invoices were issued after June 1, 2004, the enterprises winning bids and the foreign-invested companies shall be exempt from providing the Special Tax Receipts for VAT when applying for tax refund, in addition to Article 5 of this Circular.

Article 3

From June 1, 2004 (based on the date of invoices issuance), goods exported by foreign trade enterprises after June 1, 2004, electromechanical products sold by the enterprises (not including the production enterprises) winning the bids as well as domestic equipment purchased by foreign-funded companies may be applied for tax refund based on provisions, on condition that they were purchased from non-production enterprises and have complete tax refund documents. The taxation authorities in charge of export tax refund may approve hereof according to provisions. The tax refund scope for production enterprises exporting non-self-made goods shall be carried out pursuant to the Circular of the State Administration of Taxation on Issues Concerning Tax Refund on Export Products Deemed as Self-Produced Products (Guo Shui Han [2002] No. 1170).

Article 4

The extra tax payments made by production enterprises owing to the Special Tax Receipt for VAT issued before May 31, 2004 may offset the VAT payable of the month of July 2004. Therefore, meaning amount after offset, the tax authorities shall handle exchequer returning from the original treasury after confirming that there are no receipt invoice problems and excluding the possibility of tax evasion of the enterprises.

Article 5

The export tax refund for export goods purchased from small-scaled taxpayers by the export enterprises shall continue to adopt the Special Tax Receipt for VAT administration. With respect to the consumer tax payable goods exported by the export enterprises, the administration measures for Special Tax Receipt for VAT shall continue to be carried out in accordance with the Circular of Adopting Measures of Administration of Special Tax Payment Notice for Consumer Tax of Export Goods by the State Administration of Taxation (Guo Shui Ming Dian [1993] No. 71).

Article 6

With respect to the goods exported before May 31, 2004 required to be issued the Special Tax Receipt for VAT, the state taxation authorities of various levels shall issue thereof in time based on provisions, and shall not reject the requests of goods-offering enterprises on issuing the Special Tax Receipt for VAT for any reason.

Article 7

The state taxation authorities of all levels shall strengthen the administration on the collection of VAT, strengthen the administration on VAT receipt offset vouchers without being brought into the surveillance range of VAT anti-fake control and audit system, as well as formulate practical and workable measures to collect all the receivable tax and prevent tax in arrears. Meanwhile, they shall monitor and control closely the enterprises purchasing and processing agricultural products, and the sales information of waste and used materials recovery companies as well as enterprises using general invoices for waste and used materials, customs receipts and transport invoices as major offset vouchers for VAT. With respect to the goods with abnormally growing sale as well as goods sold by the above-mentioned three types of enterprises newly applied, the state taxation authorities of various levels shall extend the enforcement in checking, prevent the criminals from carrying out tax fraud by using false offset vouchers to issue invoices, conversing circulation enterprises into foreign trade enterprises and so on.

Circular of the Ministry of Finance and the State Administration of Taxation on Making Proper Preparations for Fully Implementing the Pilot Program of Replacing Business Tax with Value-added Tax Cai Shui.

No. 32 March 7, 2016.

The finance departments (bureaus) and state and local tax bureaus of all provinces, autonomous regions, municipalities directly under the central government and cities under separate state planning, and the Finance Bureau of Xinjiang Production and Construction Corps, The State Council proposes in the Report on the Work of the Government submitted for deliberation at the Fourth Session of the 12th National People's Congress to replace business tax with value-added tax in an all-around way. As of May 1, the pilot program of replacing business tax with value-added tax ("Pilot Program") can be expanded to cover the construction, real estate, financial and consumer service sectors. In order to ensure the smooth implementation of the Pilot Program and achieve the objectives as scheduled, the finance and tax authorities at various levels shall immediately make good preparations within the scope of their respective functions. Relevant matters are hereby announced as follows:

I. To fully implement the Pilot Program is an important strategic arrangement of the CPC Central Committee and the State Council for deepening reform in an all-around manner, a significant strategic move of creating an upgraded version of China's economy, and also a significant political task. The finance and tax authorities at various levels shall attach great importance to and assume responsibilities to implement the Pilot Program under a tight schedule and a heavy workload. Under the leadership of the local Party committees and governments, the finance and tax authorities shall, with a strong sense of responsibility, mission and urgency, rely on the working mechanism of the leading group for the Pilot Program and take effective measures to coordinate with each other to formulate roadmaps and timetables for the Pilot Program, and set schedules in reversed order, with detailed division of responsibilities and duties, in order to accomplish the tasks under the Pilot Program as scheduled.

II. After the Pilot Project is fully implemented, all business taxpayers under the current tax system shall be incorporated into the Pilot Program and pay value-added tax instead of business tax. As of the date of issuance of this Circular, the state and local tax authorities of all provinces shall organize the handover of taxpayer records and make other necessary preparations to ensure the tax system conversion on May 1 as scheduled. Related policies and documents regarding the full implementation of the Pilot Program shall be separately promulgated.

III. The finance authorities at various levels shall conduct overall coordination and strengthen communication with the tax authorities, industrial administrative departments and departments within the finance system to coordinate with all parties concerned to make proper preparations for the Pilot Program, in order to create a favorable environment for the reform and provide necessary support and guarantee for tax authorities to carry out their work.

IV. The state tax authorities at various levels shall take the initiative and submit comprehensive and detailed requirements for the transfer of taxpayer data; make overall plans for the allocation of information hardware resources, optimize the software system, conduct online testing for information systems and put them into use when conditions permit, in order to provide technical support for the reform; scientifically establish tax service halls, reasonably allocate human resources, further optimize tax services, enhance tax-related consultation, guidance and assistance, and create an efficient and convenient service environment and conditions for taxpayers.

V. The local tax authorities at various levels shall reflect their consciousness of the overall situation, clear up, establish and hand over taxpayer records in a complete and accurate manner to ensure that all data are correct without the need for any tedious reprocessing steps, and in the meantime, continue to collect business tax before the date of tax system conversion, so as to ensure the smooth transfer of taxpayer data and normal collection of taxes.

VI. After the issuance of relevant policies and documents on fully implementing the Pilot Program, all regions shall place emphasis on the publicity, training and interpretation of the policies. The publicity work shall be in strict accordance with the rules of journalism, with uniform publicity plans and uniform release of information, in order to correctly lead the public opinion, illuminate the positive significance of the reform in various aspects, boost the recognition of the reform by all sectors of the society, and create a favorable public opinion atmosphere for the smooth implementation of the Pilot Program. All regions shall help taxpayers understand, observe and benefit from the new tax system through training and policy interpretation to achieve positive interactions between the tax authorities and enterprises and smooth tax system conversion. Any problem encountered in the implementation of the reform shall be reported to the Ministry of Finance and the State Administration of Taxation in a timely manner.

Circular of Ministry of Finance and State Administration of Taxation on Several Issues Relevant to Nationwide Implementation of Transformation Reform of Value-added Tax Cai Shui.

No. 170 December 19, 2008.

All provinces, autonomous regions, municipalities directly under the central government, cities specifically designated in the state plan, State Administration of Taxation, Finance Bureau of Xinjian Production and Construction Corps, To facilitate the improvement of the value-added tax (VAT) system and promote the steady and speedier development of national economy, the State Council has decided to implement VAT transformation reform nationwide with effect from January 1, 2009. To ensure the implementation of reform is in place, the relevant issues are hereby notified as follows:

I. With effect from January 1, 2009, the purchase tax incurred by general taxpayers of VAT (hereinafter referred as to "taxpayers") for purchase (including accepting donation and investment in kind, hereinafter the same) or production of (including extension and installation, hereinafter the same) fixed assets (hereinafter referred to as "purchase tax on fixed assets" may be offset and deducted from output tax on the strength of VAT special invoice, customs import VAT special demand of payment and delivery charge settlement receipt (hereinafter referred to as "VAT deduction receipts") in accordance with the Interim Regulations of the People's Republic of China on Value-added Tax (State Council Decree No. 538, hereinafter "Regulations") and the Implementing Rules for the Interim Regulations of the People's Republic of China on Value-added Tax (Decree of Ministry of Finance and State Administration of Taxation No. 50, hereinafter "Implementing Rules"), and the purchase tax shall be put under the subject of "payable tax¡ªpayable value-added tax (purchase tax)".

II. The purchase tax on fixed assets that is allowed to be offset and deducted by taxpayers shall refer to the VAT indicated on VAT deduction receipt issued after January 1, 2009 or the VAT calculated with reference to VAT deduction receipt that is actually incurred by taxpayers after January 1, 2009 (inclusive, hereinafter the same).

III. In respect of the taxpayers of old industrial bases in northeast China, cities of old industrial bases in six provinces in central area and eastern area of the Inner Mongolia Autonomous Region that have been included in the trial of enlarged scope of VAT offsetting and deduction, the purchase tax on fixed assets incurred after January 1, 2009 may not be rebated and the balance of purchase tax on fixed assets pending offsetting and deduction incurred before December 31, 2008 (inclusive, hereinafter the same) shall be transferred to the subject of "payable tax¡ªpayable value-added tax (purchase tax)" in January 2009 at one time.

IV. With effect from January 1, 2009, taxpayers who sell the fixed assets that have been used by themselves (hereinafter "used fixed assets") shall be levied VAT pursuant to different circumstances:

1. In respect of sale of used fixed assets purchased or self-produced after January 1, 2009, VAT shall be levied at applicable tax rate;
2. Taxpayers who have not been included in the trial of enlarged scope of VAT offsetting and deduction before December 31, 2008 that sell used fixed assets purchased or self-produced before 31 December 2008, VAT shall be levied at half of the 4% rate;
3. Taxpayers who have been included in the trial of enlarged scope of VAT offsetting and deduction before December 31, 2008 that sell used fixed assets purchased or self-produced prior to the trial of enlarged scope of VAT offsetting and deduction in the locality shall be levied VAT at half of the 4% rate. The sale of used fixed assets purchased or self-produced after the trial of enlarged scope of VAT offsetting and deduction in the locality shall be levied VAT at applicable rate.

   For the purposes of this Circular, the term "used fixed assets" shall refer to fixed assets in which provision for depreciation is made by taxpayers with reference to the financial and accounting system.

V. Where purchase tax on fixed assets has been offset and deducted in the circumstances of Items (1)–(3) of Article 18 of the Regulations, the purchase tax that may not be offset and deducted shall be calculated with reference to the following formulas in the same month:

$$\text{Purchase tax that may not be offset and deducted} = \text{net value of fixed assets} \times \text{applicable tax rate}$$

For the purposes of this Circular, the term "net value of fixed assets" shall refer to the net value of fixed assets calculated after provision for depreciation is made by taxpayers with reference to the financial and accounting system.

VI. The fixed assets as stipulated in Article 4 of the Implementing Rules by taxpayers shall be deemed as sales. Where the sale price of used fixed assets cannot be determined, the net value of fixed assets shall be deemed as the sale price.

VII. With effect from January 1, 2009, the policies of exemption of VAT on imported facilities and VAT rebate on domestically produced facilities procured by foreign investment enterprises shall cease to be implemented. The specific measures shall be specified otherwise by the Ministry of Finance and the State Administration of Taxation.

VIII. This Circular shall go into effect as of January 1, 2009. The Circular of the Ministry of Finance and the State Administration of Taxation on Issue of (Cai Shui [2004] No. 156), the Circular of the Ministry of Finance and the State Administration of Taxation on Issue of (Cai Shui [2004] No. 168),the Urgent Circular of the Ministry of Finance and the State Administration of Taxation on Further Implementation of the Enlarged Scope of Value-added Tax Offsetting and Deduction of Northeast China (Cai Shui [2004] No. 226), the Circular of the Ministry of Finance and the State Administration of Taxation on Issues

Relevant to Implementing Enlarged Scope of Value-added Tax Offsetting and Deduction by Enterprises of Military Products and High and New Technology Products in Northeast China (Cai Shui [2004] No. 227), the Circular of the State Administration of Taxation on Launching the Task for the Recognition of Business Enterprises By Expanding the Scope of Value-added Tax Deduction (Guo Shui Han [2004] No. 143), the Circular of the Ministry of Finance and the State Administration of Taxation on Issues Relevant to the Enlarged Scope of Value-added Tax in Northeast China for 2005 (Cai Shui [2005] No. 28), the Circular of the Ministry of Finance and the State Administration of Taxation on Rebate of Purchase Tax on Fixed Assets in the Enlarged Scope of Value-added Tax in Northeast China for 2005 (Cai Shui [2005] No. 176), the Circular of the Ministry of Finance and the State Administration of Taxation on Issues Concerning the Expansion of the Scope of Value-added Tax Deduction for the Production Manufacturers of Military and Hi-tech Products in Northeast China (Cai Shui [2006] No. 15), the Circular of the Ministry of Finance and the State Administration of Taxation on Rebate of Purchase Tax on Fixed Assets in the Enlarged Scope of Value-added Tax in Northeast China for 2006 (Cai Shui [2006] No. 156), the Circular of the Ministry of Finance and the State Administration of Taxation on Printing and Distributing the Interim Measures for Expanding the Scope of Value-added Tax Deduction in Central Regions of China on Issue of the (Cai Shui [2007] No. 75), the Supplementary Circular of the Ministry of Finance and the State Administration of Taxation on Issues Relevant to Offsetting and Deduction (Tax Rebate) of Fixed Assets for 2007 in the Locality in the Enlarged Scope of Value-added Tax Offsetting and Deduction (Cai Shui [2007] No. 128), the Circular of the State Administration of Taxation on Printing and Distributing the Interim Administrative Measures for Expanding the Scope of Value-added Tax Credits on Issue of (Cai Shui [2007] No. 62), the Circular of the Ministry of Finance and the State Administration of Taxation on Issue of (Cai Shui [2008] No. 94), the Circular of the Ministry of Finance and the State Administration of Taxation on Printing and Distributing the Interim Measures for Expanding the Scope of Value-added Tax Deduction in Areas Severely Damaged by the Wenchuan Earthquake on Issue of (Cai Shui [2008] No. 108), and the Circular of the Ministry of Finance and the State Administration of Taxation on Tax Rebate Issues of Purchase Tax on Fixed Assets in the Enlarged Scope of Value-added Tax Offsetting and Deduction in Northeast, Central and Eastern Area of Mongolia (Cai Shui [2008] No. 141) shall be repealed simultaneously.

Circular of Ministry of Finance and the State Administration of Taxation on the Discontinuation of the Rebate Policy on the Purchase of Domestically Manufactured Equipment by Foreign Investment Enterprises Cai Shui.

No. 176 December 25, 2008.

All financial departments (bureaus) and offices of the State Administration of Taxation of provinces, autonomous regions, municipalities directly under the Central

Government and cities separately designated in State Plan, and Financial Bureau of Xinjiang Production and Construction Corp.

In order to cooperate with the national transformation and reform of value-added tax, it is decided to discontinue the implementation of the policy of value-added tax rebate on the purchase of domestically manufactured equipment by foreign investment enterprises upon the approval by State Council. The relevant issues are hereby notified as below:

I. The policy under which foreign investment enterprises that purchase domestically manufactured equipment within the aggregate investment may have the value-added tax on such domestically manufactured equipment rebated shall be discontinued to implement as of January 1, 2009. The following documents and the clauses contained therein shall be repealed simultaneously:

   1. The Circular of the State Administration of Taxation on the Print and Issuance of the 'Trial Measures for the Rebate Administration on the Purchase of Domestically Manufactured Equipment by Foreign Investment Enterprises' (Guo Shui Fa [1997] No. 171);
   2. Article 1 of the Circular of Ministry of Finance and the State Administration of Taxation on Several Specific Issues on the Rebate (Exemption) of Exported Goods (Cai Shui [2004] No. 116);
   3. The Circular of Ministry of Finance and the State Administration of Taxation on the Adjustment of the Scope of Rebate Policy on the Purchase of Domestically Manufactured Equipment for the Projects with Foreign Investment (Cai Shui [2006] No. 61);
   4. The Circular of the State Administration of Taxation and National Development and Reform Commission on the Print and Issuance of the 'Tentative Measures for the Rebate Administration on the Purchase of Domestically Manufactured Equipment for the Projects with Foreign Investment'(Guo Shui Fa [2006] No. 111); and
   5. The Circular of the State Administration of Taxation on Tax Refund for the Tax Imposed on the Purchase of Domestic Equipment by Construction Enterprises Providing Labor and Materials to Foreign-invested Enterprises by Contract (Guo Shui Han [2007] No. 637).

II. In order to guarantee successful transition of policy adjustment, foreign investment enterprises that purchase domestically manufactured equipment prior to June 30, 2009 (including June 30, hereinafter the same) may, where the auditing information of the exclusive value-added tax invoices are correct after auditing, select to continue the implementation of the rebate policy on value-added tax in accordance with the previous provisions, provided that the following requirements are met simultaneously:

   1. Such enterprises have obtained the Letter of Confirmation of the Projects with Foreign Investment Conforming to the State Industry Policy prior to November 9, 2008, and have registered with competent tax authorities for reference prior to December 31, 2008;

2. Such enterprises have actually purchased domestically manufactured equipment and produced exclusive value-added tax invoices prior to June 30, 2009, and applied for rebate with competent tax authorities; and
3. The domestically manufactured equipment purchased by such enterprises have been included in the List of Domestically Manufactured Equipment for Project Procurement.

III. The amount of value-added tax on the domestically manufactured equipment purchased by foreign investment enterprises and covered by the rebate policy on value-added tax may not deduct output tax as input tax.

IV. The domestically manufactured equipment purchased by foreign investment enterprises and covered by the rebate policy on value-added tax shall be under the supervision and administration by competent tax authorities for 5 years. Within such period, foreign investment enterprises shall, in case of changing into enterprises with domestic investments, or transferring, donating the ownership of equipment, or leasing, or re-investing, supplement the rebated tax to competent taxation authorities. The tax amount to be supplemented shall be calculated based on the following formula:

$$\text{Tax amount to be supplemented} = \text{net value of domestically manufactured equipment} * \text{applicable tax rate}$$

The net value of domestically manufactured equipment is the net value of equipment calculated after depreciation in accordance the financial accounting systems by enterprises.

Circular of the Ministry of Finance and the State Administration of Taxation on Issues concerning Value Added Tax Policies for the Shareholding Reform of Defense Industry Enterprises Cai Shui.

No. 172 January 21, 2008.

The financial departments (bureaus), the Offices of the State Administration of Taxation of all provinces, autonomous regions, municipalities directly under the Central Government and cities specifically designated in the state plan, and the financial bureau of Xinjiang Production and Construction Corp.

With a view to meeting the requirement of the state on further deepening the investment system reform of the industry of defense-related science and technology, guaranteeing the smooth implementation of the policy of value-added tax exemption on military items and maintaining the equity of tax bearing, the relevant policy of value-added tax on military items relevant to the shareholding reform of defense industry enterprises is hereby notified as follows:

Where a wholly-owned subsidiary enterprise of the defense industry group which at first enjoys the policy of value-added tax exemption from military products is restructured into a limited liability company or stock limited company solely funded by the state (wholly-owned by the state), with shares absolutely controlled by the state or relatively controlled by the state pursuant to the Circular of the State Commission of Science and Technology for National Defense Industry on Printing and Issuing the Tentative Measures for the Implementation of the Shareholding Reform of Defense Industry Enterprises (Ke Gong Gai [2007] No. 1366), the military products manufactured and sold by it shall continue to be exempted from value-added tax in accordance with the Circular of the Ministry of Finance and the State Administration of Taxation on Collection of Turnover Tax and Resource Tax from the Military Units and Defense Industry Units (Cai ShuiZi [1994] No. 11).

This Circular shall come into force as of January 1, 2008. The departments in all areas shall report promptly to the Ministry of Finance and the State Administration of Taxation the problems encountered during policy implementation.

Please implement accordingly.

7.2 Circulars and Announcements from 2007 to 2012

Announcement of the General Administration of Customs on the Issues Concerning to the Refund after the Collection of Import Duties and Value-added Tax on Some Key Spare Parts Imported for Development and Manufacture of Large Sectional Tunnel Boring Machines by Domestic Enterprises.

Announcement of the General Administration of Customs [2007].

No. 54 October 15, 2007.

According to the relevant provisions of the Circular of the Ministry of Finance, the National Development and Reform Commission, the General Administration of Customs, and the State Administration of Taxation on Implementing the Relevant Import Tax Policies in the Opinions of the State Council on Accelerating the Development of Equipment Manufacturing Industry (Cai Guan Shui [2007] No. 11), from January 1, 2007 (subject to the date on which the customs authority accept the application of the enterprises), duties and value-added tax on some key spare parts imported for development and manufacture of large sectional tunnel boring machines by domestic enterprises shall be refunded after the collection. The relevant issues in the implementation are hereby announced as follows:

Article 1

A large sectional tunnel boring machine mentioned in this Announcement refers to a large sectional tunnel boring machine with the diameter of the cutter is equal or more than five meters, including four types, namely, Earth Press Balancing Shield Machine, Tunnel Boring Machine, Mud.

Press Balancing Shield Machine and Combined Tunneling Shield Machine.

Article 2

Details of the List of Tax-refund Commodities of Imported Key Spare Parts (hereinafter referred to as "the List of Levying First and Refunding Later") are specified in Appendix. As for Imported Key Spare Parts on the List of Levying First and Refunding Later to which Interim Duty Rate is applicable, Interim Duty Rate shall prevail.

The relevant ministries or commissions (offices or bureaus) shall adjust the List of Levying First and Refunding Later from time to time according to the application of the enterprises, the implementation effect of the policy and the domestic capacity of coordinated production.

Article 3

When the enterprises that enjoy the levying first and refunding later policy import the aforesaid key spare parts, the enterprises shall declare the imported goods to the Customs separately, and apply for the refund after the collection directly to the customs authorities at the ports of entry with the Confirmation Letter of Tax Refund to the Large Equipment Manufacturing Enterprise issued by the Ministry of Finance. The relevant specific operational procedures shall be handled pursuant to the relevant provisions currently in effect.

Article 4

The key spare parts imported from January 1, 2007 to the issuance date of this Announcement are permitted to go through "levying first and refunding later" formalities according to this Announcement.

This Announcement is hereby issued.

Circular on Certain Issues Concerning the Tax Treatment of Oil (Gas) Resource Exploration Enterprise Expense Deductions and for the Amortization and Depreciation of Relevant Fixed Assets Cai Shui.

No. 49 April 12, 2009.

To the financial departments (bureaus), state taxation bureaus, and local taxation bureaus of all provinces, autonomous regions, municipalities directly under the Central Government, and cities specifically designated in the state plan, and the financial bureau of Xinjiang Production & Construction Corps.

In accordance with Article 61 of the Implementing Regulations for the Enterprise Income Tax Law of the People's Republic of China (Order of the State Council No. 512, hereinafter referred to as the Implementing Regulations), the methods to be used for the amortization and depreciation of relevant fixed assets and the deduction of expenses incurred prior to the commencement of commercial production activities by oil and gas enterprises (hereinafter referred to as oil and gas enterprises) engaged in exploiting petroleum and natural gas mineral resources (including coal-bed gas, the same applies hereafter) are as follows:

I. Expenses and relevant fixed assets as referred to in these Circular mean expenses incurred and fixed assets formed as a result of expenses incurred prior to the commencement of commercial production activities by oil and gas enterprises in the acquisition of rights and interests in mining areas and in exploration and development.

Commercial production as referred to in this Circular means, in relation to any oil (gas) field (well), the stages of exploration, development, steady production and commercial sale of petroleum or gas.

II. Deduction of expenses incurred in acquiring rights and interests in mining areas.

1. Expenses incurred in acquiring rights and interests in mining areas refer to all expenses incurred by oil and gas enterprises in acquiring exploration rights, mining rights, and land use rights or sea use rights for a mining area, including royalties and relevant intermediary fees paid in acquiring rights or interests in any mining area and other reasonable expenses directly attributable to the acquisition of rights and interests in mining areas.
2. Expenses incurred by oil and gas enterprises prior to commencing commercial production may be deducted from income derived from the enterprise's other oil (gas) fields in the same period in which such expenses are incurred; or may be deducted by withdrawing the amount calculated according to the straight-line method over a period of three years from the month following commencement of commercial production in the corresponding oil (gas) field.
3. Where an oil and gas enterprise elects not to deduct expenses incurred in acquiring rights and interests in mining areas in the period in which such expenses are incurred and terminated operations due its failure to find a commercially viable oil (gas) structure, the expenses which have not yet been deducted shall be deducted as losses in the year in which operations are terminated.

III. Amortization of exploration expenses.

1. Exploration expenses refer to all expenses incurred in geological surveys, geophysical exploration, shaft exploration activities and other relevant activities of oil and gas enterprises undertaken to identify exploration areas and verify oil and gas reserves.
2. Exploration expenses (excluding exploration expenses incurred in respect of shafts that are anticipated to become assets) incurred by oil and gas enterprises prior to commencing commercial production may be deducted from income derived from the enterprise's other oil (gas) fields in the same period in which such expenses are incurred; or may be deducted by withdrawing the amount calculated according to the straight-line method over a period of three years from the month following commencement of commercial production in the corresponding oil (gas) field.
3. Where an oil and gas enterprise elects not to deduct exploration expenses in the period in which they are incurred and terminates operations due its failure to find a commercially viable oil (gas) structure, the expenses which

have not yet been deducted shall be deducted as losses in the year in which operations are terminated.

4. If a shaft is determined to be commercially viable and the assets formed as a result of the oil and gas enterprise's expenditure on exploration activities satisfy the conditions specified in Article 57 of the Implementing Regulations, such shaft exploration expenses shall be carried forward as the cost of developing such assets and depreciated in accordance with Article 4 of this Circular.

IV. Depreciation of development assets.

1. Development expenses refer to all expenses incurred in constructing or renovating shafts and facilities relevant to the acquisition of oil and gas in proven mining areas.
2. All development expenses incurred by an oil and gas enterprise prior to commercial productions hall, regardless of the purpose of such expenditure, be aggregated as the cost of developing such assets and deducted from the month following commencement of commercial production for the corresponding oil (gas) field using the straight-line depreciation method without retaining any residual value; the minimum depreciation period shall be 8 years.
3. Where an oil and gas enterprise terminate production in an oil (gas) field, outstanding depreciation charges for development assets shall be deducted as losses in the year in which production in the relevant oil (gas) field is terminated.

V. Oil and gas enterprises shall select the methods used for deduction, amortization or depreciation of relevant expenses or fixed assets and the years in which such deductions, amortization or depreciation is made or carried out in accordance with the provisions of this Circular; the methods and years shall not be changed once they have been determined.

VI. Expenses incurred by oil and gas enterprises in acquiring rights and interests in mining areas and in their exploration and development activities after commencing commercial production in an oil (gas) field shall be dealt with in accordance with the provisions of this Circular.

VII. This Circular shall come into effect on the date of its promulgation. Matters concerning the methods to be used for deducting expenses incurred in acquiring rights and interests in mining areas and exploration and development activities, and for depreciating or amortizing the fixed assets of oil and gas enterprises as of the date on which the Implementing Regulations come into effect prior to the promulgation of this Circular shall be handled in accordance with the provisions of this Circular.

The amortization or withdrawal of charges or depreciation for expenses incurred in acquiring rights and interests in mining areas or exploration and development activities, or for the fixed assets of oil and gas enterprises prior to the date on which the Implementing Regulations are implemented, shall not be adjusted. With regard to expenses that remain to be amortized and rights and interests in mining areas and relevant fixed assets whose use is to be continued, the residual or depreciated value that remains to be amortized or withdrawn shall be handled in accordance with the provisions of this Circular.

7.3 Announcements of the SAT for 2011

Announcement of the State Administration of Taxation on Issues Relating to the Adjustment of the Management Measures for the Preferential VAT Policy of Refund upon Collection Announcement of the State Administration of Taxation.

No. 60 November 14, 2011.

In order to speed up tax refunds, enhance efficiency in the utilization of tax paid by taxpayers and support the development of enterprises, the State Administration of Taxation has decided to adjust the management measures of assessment before refund taken for enterprises entitled to the preferential VAT policy of refund upon collection. Relevant issues are hereby announced as follows:

I. The management measures for the preferential VAT policy of refund upon collection shall be changed from assessment before refund to refund before assessment.

II. The competent tax authorities shall further strengthen the management of matters after the refund of VAT for enterprises entitled to the preferential VAT policy of refund upon collection and conduct periodic tax assessments according to the following indicators:

1. Formula for the calculation of variations in sales volume.
   (1) Month-on-month variation in the sale volume during the current period = (the sales volume of goods and labor services subject to the preferential VAT policy of refund upon collection during the current period-the sales volume of goods and labor services subject to the preferential VAT policy of refund upon collection during the previous period)/the sales volume of goods and labor services subject to the preferential VAT policy of refund upon collection during the previous period * 100%.
   (2) Month-on-month variation in the accumulated sales volume during the current period = (the accumulated sales volume of goods and labor services subject to the preferential VAT policy of refund upon collection during the current period-the accumulated sales volume of goods and labor services subject to the preferential VAT policy of refund upon collection during the previous period)/the accumulated sales volume of goods and labor services subject to the preferential VAT policy of refund upon collection during the previous period * 100%.

(3) Year-on-year variation in sales volume during the current period = (the sales volume of good sand labor services subject to the preferential VAT policy of refund upon collection during the current period-the sales volume of goods and labor services subject to the preferential VAT policy of refund upon collection during the previous year)/the sales volume of goods and labor services subject to the preferential VAT policy of refund upon collection during the previous year * 100%.

(4) Year-on-year variation in the accumulated sales volume during the current period = (the accumulated sales volume of goods and labor services subject to the preferential VAT policy of refund upon collection during the current period-the accumulated sales volume of goods and labor services subject to the preferential VAT policy of refund upon collection during the previous year)/the accumulated sales volume of goods and labor services subject to the preferential VAT policy of refund upon collection during the previous year * 100%.

2. Formula for the calculation of VAT burden ratio VAT burden ratio = tax payable for goods and labor services subject to the preferential VAT policy of refund upon collection during the current period/the sales volume of goods and labor services subject to the preferential VAT policy of refund upon collection during the current period * 100%.

III. All regions may, according to different projects subject to the preferential VAT policy of refund upon collection, design and improve the tax assessment indicators. If the competent tax authorities discover through tax assessments that any enterprise has an abnormal situation, they shall timely verify the reasons there for and deal with the matter in accordance with the relevant provisions.

IV. This Announcement shall come into effect on December 1, 2011. The Circular of the State Administration of Taxation on Issues relating to the Implementation of Assessment before Refund for the VAT Policy of Refund upon Collection (Guo Shui Han [2009] No. 432) shall be repealed simultaneously.
Announcement is hereby made.

Circular on Printing and Distributing the Pilot Proposals for the Collection of Value-added Tax in Lieu of Business Tax Cai Shui.

No. 110 November 16, 2011.

The finance departments (bureaus), offices of the state administration of taxation, local taxation bureaus of all provinces, autonomous regions, municipalities directly under the Central Government and cities specifically designated in the state plan and the finance bureau of Xinjiang Production and Construction Corps.

The Pilot Proposals for the Collection of Value-added Tax in Lieu of Business Tax has been approved by the State Council and is hereby issued to you for your compliance and implementation.

Pilot Proposals for the Collection of Value-added Tax in Lieu of Business Tax According to the spirit of the Fifth Plenary Session of the 17th Central Committee of the CPC, this Proposal is formulated in accordance with the tax reform objectives determined in the Outline for the Twelfth Five-Year Plan for National Economic and Social Development of the PRC, and the requirements of the 2011 Report on the Work of the Government.

I. Guiding Ideology and Basic Principles.

1. Guiding ideology.
We should establish a sound tax system conducive to scientific development, promote the adjustment of economic structure and support the development of the modern service industry.
2. Basic principles.
(1) Make an overall plan and implement the plan by steps. We should correctly deal with the relationship among reform, development and stability, make an overall plan for and take into full consideration the demand of economic and social development and, in light of the need to fully push forward the form and the current realities, make a plan in scientific manner and implement it steadily.
(2) Regulate the tax system and impose a reasonable tax burden. While ensuring that value-added tax ("VAT") is duly regulated, we should, according to the financial capacity and the characteristics of the development of different industries, reasonably set up the elements of the tax system, make the overall tax burden in the pilot reform industries not to be increased or to be slightly reduced, and basically eliminate the double taxation.
(3) Conduct comprehensive coordination and make a smooth transition. We should properly handle the connection of policies on VAT and business tax before and after the pilot program, coordinate the tax systems for pilot taxpayers and non-pilot taxpayers and establish a sound VAT management system adapting to the development of the tertiary industry and ensure that the pilot program is carried out in an orderly manner.

II. Main Contents of the Pilot Reform.

1. Scope and time of the pilot reform.
(1) Pilot regions. We should take into full consideration such factors as the development of the service industry, its financial capacity and the basic conditions for tax collection and first choose the regions which have an obvious economic radiation effect and play a strong role as a reform model to carry out the pilot program.
(2) Pilot industry. The pilot program shall be conducted in the production-oriented service industries such as the transportation industry and some modern service industries in the pilot regions and be gradually spread to other industries. When conditions permit, some industries may be selected to carry out the pilot program all over China.

(3) Pilot time. We should commence the pilot program on January 1, 2012, timely improve the program according to the circumstances and choose a right time to expand the scope of the pilot program.

2. Main tax system arrangements for the pilot reform.
   (1) Tax rates. On the base of the current standard VAT rate of 17% and low VAT rate of 13%, two low tax rates of 11 and 6% shall be added. The tax rate of 17% shall be applicable to those like lease of tangible personal property, the tax rate of 11% shall be applicable to the transportation industry and the construction industry, and the tax rate of 6% shall be applicable to other modern service industries.
   (2) Tax calculation method. The general VAT calculation method shall in principle apply to the transportation industry, the construction industry, the post and telecommunication industry, the modern service industry, the culture and sports industry, and the sale of real property and the transfer of intangible assets. The simplified VAT calculation method shall apply to the finance and insurance industries and the livelihood-oriented service industry.
   (3) Tax basis. In principle, the tax basis of a taxpayer shall be all income obtained from the taxable transactions concluded. As for those industries where there is a large amount of collection for payment transfer or, advance funds, the amount being collected and advanced may be deducted reasonably.
   (4) Import and export of service trade. The VAT shall be collected for the import of service trade in China and the zero-tax rate or tax-free system shall apply to the export of service trade.
3. Transitional policy arrangements during the period of the pilot reform.
   (1) Attribution of tax revenue. The current financial system shall remain basically unchanged during the period of the pilot reform and if the business tax revenue is originally attributed to the pilot regions, VAT which is collected instead shall still be attributed to the pilot regions and be turned over into the treasury respectively. Any decline in financial revenue as a result of the pilot reform shall be borne by the central finance and local finances respectively according to the current financial system.
   (2) Transition of preferential tax policies. The existing preferential business tax policies granted to the pilot industries by the State may be continued, but such preferential policies shall be abolished if the double taxation problem can be resolved through the reform. Proper transitional policies may be adopted, as the case maybe, during the period of the pilot program.
   (3) Coordination of cross-region tax categories. A pilot taxpayer shall take the location of its establishment as the place for payment of VAT and if he pays the same at another place, he is entitled to tax credit when the VAT is calculated and paid. Where a non-pilot taxpayer engages in business in the pilot regions, he shall continue to declare and pay

the business tax in accordance with the current relevant provisions on business tax.

(4) Connection of VAT credit policies. VAT invoices obtained by the existing VAT taxpayers through purchasing services from the pilot taxpayers may be credited against the input tax according to the existing provisions.

III. Organization and Implementation.

1. The Ministry of Finance and the State Administration of Taxation shall, according to this Program, formulate the specific implementation measures, relevant policies, provisions on budget management and the turning over of tax into the treasury and properly carry out the work of policy publicity and interpretation and, with the approval of the State Council, choose and determine the pilot regions and industries.
2. The offices of the State Administration of Taxation shall be responsible for the collection and administration of VAT collected in lieu of the business tax. The State Administration of Taxation shall be responsible for the formulation of the tax collection and administration measures for the pilot reform, expand the information system for the administration of VAT and the information system for tax collection and administration, design and uniformly print VAT invoices for the goods transportation industry and comprehensively and properly carry out the work of the relevant tax collection and administration preparation and implementation.

Announcement of the State Administration of Taxation on the Issues Concerning the Enjoyment of Taxpayers of the Policies of "Levy and Refund", "Refund after Collection" and "Exemption, Offset and Refund" of Value-added Tax Announcement of the State Administration of Taxation.

No. 69 December 1, 2011.

Issues concerning the enjoyment of taxpayers of the policies of "levy and refund", "refund after collection" and "exemption, offset and refund" of value-added tax are hereby set out as follows:

I. Where a taxpayer has VAT levy and refund, refund after collection items and export or other VAT taxable items, its VAT levy and refund and refund after collection items cannot be calculated into export VAT exemption, offset or refund items. The taxpayer shall calculate VAT levy and refund, refund after collection and export and other VAT taxable items respectively and apply for VAT levy and refund, refund after collection and exemption, offset or refund policies respectively.

II. Where it is unable to partition the input tax amount of VAT levy and refund item and refund after collection item, the following formula shall apply:

The part of input tax amount used for VAT levy and refund item and VAT refund after collection item unable to be partitioned = all input tax amount unable to be partitioned in the month * sales volumes of VAT levy and refund or refund after collection items/sum of all sales volume and turnover of the Month.

This Announcement shall come into effect on January 1, 2012. The Reply of the State Administration of Taxation on Issues concerning VAT on Airplane Maintenance Service (Guo Shui Han [2008] No. 842) and the Announcement of the State Administration of Taxation on VAT Treatment Methods for Aircraft Maintenance Business [2011] No. 5 shall be repealed simultaneously.

Announcement of the State Administration of Taxation, the Ministry of Finance and the General Administration of Customs on Launching the Pilot Program for Granting General Value-added Tax Taxpayer Status to Enterprises in Areas under Special Customs Supervision Announcement of the State Administration of Taxation, the Ministry of Finance and the General Administration of Customs [2016] No. 65 October 14, 2016.

In accordance with the Several Opinions of the State Council on Promoting the Stabilization and Recovery of Foreign Trade (Guo Fa [2016] No. 27), the State Administration of Taxation, the Ministry of Finance and the General Administration of Customs have selected parts of areas under special customs supervision to launch the pilot program for granting general value-added tax (VAT) taxpayer status to the enterprises therein. The related matters are hereby announced as below:

I. The pilot program for granting general VAT taxpayer status to enterprises has been launched in Kunshan Comprehensive Bonded Zone, Suzhou Industrial Park Comprehensive Bonded Zone, Shanghai Songjiang Export Processing Zone, Henan Zhengzhou Export Processing Zone, Zhengzhou Xinzheng Comprehensive Bonded Zone, Chongqing Xiyong Comprehensive Bonded Zone and Shenzhen Yantian Comprehensive Bonded Zone.
   Enterprises in the pilot zones above, which meet the provisions on registration administration for general VAT taxpayers, may voluntarily apply to competent tax authorities or customs to become pilot enterprises and handle the qualification registration of general VAT taxpayers with competent tax authorities in accordance with the law.
II. As of the date when the qualification of general VAT taxpayers comes into effect, the following tax policies shall apply to pilot enterprises.
   1. When importing self-use equipment (including machinery, building materials for infrastructure and office supplies), a pilot enterprise is temporarily exempted from import tariffs, import VAT and consumption tax (hereinafter referred to as the "import tax"). According to the customs supervision period for such imported self-use equipment, the import tax subject to temporary exemption shall be apportioned to each year, at the end of which the import tax subject to temporary exemption shall be divided according to the proportion of domestic or overseas sales. Tax policies for areas under special customs supervision where pilot enterprises are located shall apply to the proportion of overseas sales, while the supplemental tax shall be levied on the proportion of domestic sales by reference to tax policies for zones

outside the areas under special customs supervision (hereinafter referred to as "outside the areas").

2. In addition to the imported self-use equipment, bonded policies shall apply to purchased goods as below:
   (1) goods purchased overseas and entering pilot areas;
   (2) bonded goods purchased from areas under special customs supervision (except for pilot areas) or bonded places under customs supervision and entering pilot areas;
   (3) bonded goods purchased from non-pilot enterprises within pilot areas; and
   (4) bonded goods unprocessed and purchased from other pilot enterprises in pilot areas.
3. For the following goods on sale, VAT or consumption tax shall be declared to tax authorities for payment:
   (1) goods sold outside the territory of China;
   (2) goods sold to bonded zones or bonded places under supervision without tax rebates (except for bonded goods unprocessed); and
   (3) goods sold to other pilot enterprises within pilot areas (except for bonded goods unprocessed).
   Where bonded goods are included in the said goods sold by pilot enterprises, such enterprises shall, according to the status at the moment when bonded goods enter the areas under special customs supervision, declare to the Customs for payment of import tax and supplement the deferred tax interest according to provisions.
4. Bonded policies shall continuously apply to bonded goods unprocessed and sold to areas under special customs supervision or bonded places under customs supervision.
5. Export tax rebate (exemption) policies shall apply to the following goods on sale (except for bonded goods unprocessed) and tax authorities shall review and handle the export tax rebate (exemption) declared by pilot enterprises based on the electronic data on the customs declaration of exports corresponding to such goods, which is provided by the Customs.
   (1) goods leaving the territory for export;
   (2) goods sold to areas under special customs supervision (except for pilot areas and bonded zones) or bonded places under customs supervision (except for those without tax rebates); and (3) goods sold to non-pilot enterprises within pilot areas.
6. Unless otherwise specified by the Ministry of Finance, the General Administration of Customs and the State Administration of Taxation, the laws or regulations on tariffs, VAT and consumption tax outside the areas shall apply to pilot enterprises.

III. The current tax policies shall continuously apply to processing trade goods sold from places outside the areas to pilot enterprises, while other goods sold to pilot enterprises (including water, steam, electric power and fuel gas) shall no longer be governed by policies on export tax rebate but shall be subject to VAT and consumption tax according to the relevant provisions.

IV. Tax authorities and Customs shall strengthen the exchange of information on tax levying and supervision of goods. For goods to which policies on export tax rebate apply, the Customs shall transit electronic data on clearance information in customs export declaration forms.

V. This Announcement shall come into force as of November 1, 2016.

Circular on Budget Management Issues Concerning the Application of Tax Exemption, Offset and Refund on Zero VAT Rate Taxable Services in Regions of Pilot Collection of VAT in Lieu of Business Tax Cai Yu.

No. 65 May 15, 2012.

Shanghai Municipal Financial Bureau, Shanghai Municipal office of the State Administration of Taxation, Local Taxation Administration, Shanghai Head Office of the People's Republic of China, and Shanghai Financial Supervisor Office of the Ministry of Finance.

In accordance with the Pilot Proposals for the Collection of Value-added Tax in Lieu of Business Tax (Cai Shui [2011] No. 110) and the Administrative Measures for the Application of Tax Exemption, Offset and Refund on Zero VAT Rate Taxable Services in Regions of Pilot Collection of VAT in Lieu of Business Tax (Interim) (Public Announcement of STA [2012] No. 13), the notice is hereby given as follows with respect to budget management issues concerning some zero VAT rate trade in service in the pilot scheme of VAT in lieu of business tax:

I. Tax refunded in the tax exemption, offset and refund applied to zero VAT rate taxable services shall be handled by the competent tax authorities, and all tax refunded shall be paid by the Treasure.

II. As from 2012, Sub-Item 01 "Export Tax Refund in Collection of VAT in lieu of Business Tax" can added under Item 1010105 "Export Tax Refund in Collection of VAT in lieu of Business Tax" in the Categorized Items of Governmental Revenue and Expense. See the appendix for the specific items and notes.

III. The measures for allocating tax exempted and offset from the Treasure can be issued separately.

Announcement of the State Administration of Taxation on the Handling Procedures for Taxpayers to Apply for the Issue of Value-added Tax Invoices on Their Behalf Announcement of the State Administration of Taxation [2016].

No. 59 August 31, 2016.

The handling procedures for taxpayers to apply for the issue of value-added tax (VAT) invoices on their behalf (excluding the VAT invoices for real estate sold and other personal real estate leased by taxpayers which are issued by the local tax authorities on their behalf) are hereby announced as follows:

Article 1

Handling process.

1. Where local tax bureaus entrust local offices of the State Administration of Taxation (SAT) to collect taxes on their behalf, taxpayers shall handle the business in the following steps:

    (1) at the designated windows of the taxpayer service halls of the SAT offices:
        A. submit the Tax Return for Value-added Tax Invoice Issued on Behalf of Taxpayers (see Appendix);
        B. where a natural person applies for the issue of an invoice on its behalf, their identity card and a photocopy shall be submitted;
        For other taxpayers, a business license marked with a unified social credit code (or certificate of taxation registration or organization code certificate) and the identity card of the handling person and a photocopy are required.
    (2) declare and pay VAT and relevant taxes at the same window.
    (3) obtain the invoices at the same window.

2. In the taxpayer service halls under the collaboration and co-construction of offices of the SAT and local tax bureaus, taxpayers shall handle the business in the following steps:

    (1) at the designated windows for the SAT in the taxpayer service halls:
        A. submit the Tax Return for Value-added Tax Invoice Issued on Behalf of Taxpayers;
        B. where a natural person applies for the issue of an invoice on its behalf, their identity card and a photocopy shall be submitted;
        For other taxpayers, a business license marked with a unified social credit code (or certificate of taxation registration or organization code certificate) and the identity card of the handling person and a photocopy are required.
    (2) pay VAT at the same window.
    (3) declare and pay relevant taxes at the designated windows for local tax bureaus.
    (4) obtain the invoices by presenting the relevant proof of tax payment at the designated windows for the SAT.

Article 2

Based on this Announcement, the tax authorities of all provinces shall, combining local realities, develop a more refined, explicitly oriented and operable announcement on the handling procedures for taxpayers to apply for the issue of VAT invoices on their behalf, and effectively simplify and optimize the handling procedures.

Article 3

For the documents required for the issue of VAT invoices for real estate sold and other personal real estate leased by taxpayers on their behalf, Item 5 of Article 2 of the Circular of the State Administration of Taxation on Strengthening and Standardizing the Issues concerning the Issuing of Common Invoices by Tax Authorities (Guo Shui Han [2004] No. 1024) still apply.

This Announcement came into force as of November 15, 2016.

The Announcement is hereby given.

7.4 A Selection of Announcements of the SAT from 2014 to 2016

Announcement of the State Administration of Taxation on Promulgating the Administrative Measures for the Rebate of Value-added Tax and Consumption Tax concerning the Development of Hengqin and Pingtan Areas (for Trial Implementation).

No. 70 December 19, 2014.

In accordance with the Circular of the Ministry of Finance, the General Administration of Customs and the State Administration of Taxation on the Value-added Tax and Consumption Tax Policies for the Development of Hengqin and Pingtan Areas (Cai Shui [2014] No. 51), the State Administration of Taxation have formulated the Administrative Measures for the Rebate of Value-added Tax and Consumption Tax concerning the Development of Hengqin and Pingtan Areas (for Trial Implementation) (hereinafter referred to as the "Measures") upon the consent of the Ministry of Finance and the General Administration of Customs after discussion therewith. The Measures are hereby promulgated and take effect as of the date on which the relevant facilities subject to supervision are accepted and the abovementioned customs are officially put into operation.

It is hereby announced.

Administrative Measures for the Rebate of Value-added Tax and Consumption Tax concerning the Development of Hengqin and Pingtan Areas (for Trial Implementation).

Article 1

The Measures are formulated in accordance with the Circular of the Ministry of Finance, the General Administration of Customs and the State Administration of Taxation on the Value-added Tax and Consumption Tax Policies for the Development of Hengqin and Pingtan Areas (Cai Shui [2014] No. 51).

Article 2

The selling of goods (including water, steam, electric power and gas) subject to the value-added tax and consumption tax rebate policies from other areas in the People's

Republic of China (hereinafter referred to as "other areas") to Hengqin and Pingtan Areas (hereinafter referred to as "the area") shall be deemed as exportation, and the enterprises in the area purchasing the goods from other areas (hereinafter referred to as the "purchasers in the area") or utilities enterprises in the area shall be responsible for the declaration for value-added tax and consumption tax rebate to the competent national tax authorities.

Article 3

For the purpose of the Measures, purchasers in the area refer to the enterprises that transact the procedures of industrial and commercial registration, tax registration and customs registration in the area in accordance with the law and purchase goods from other areas; utilities enterprises in the area refer to the enterprises that transact the procedures of industrial and commercial registration and tax registration in the area in accordance with the law and purchase water, steam, electric power and gas from other areas.

Article 4

The purchasers and utilities enterprises in the area shall complete the application for export tax rebate (exemption) pursuant to the following provisions:

1. The purchasers in the area who fail to go through the filing and registration procedures for foreign trade operators shall complete the application within 30 days from the date on which the goods related to production are purchased from other areas for the first time, and they are not required to provide the Filing and Registration Form of Foreign Trade Operators or the Certificate of Approval of the People's Republic of China for Foreign Investment Enterprises.
2. The utilities enterprises in the area shall complete the application within 30 days from the date on which the water, steam, electric power and gas are purchased from other areas for the first time, and they are not required to provide the Registration Certificate of the Customs of the People's Republic of China for Customs Declaration of Imported and Exported Goods by Consignors and Consignees, or the Filing and Registration Form of Foreign Trade Operators or the Certificate of Approval of the People's Republic of China for Foreign Investment Enterprises.
3. Except for the above circumstances, the purchasers and utilities enterprises in the area shall complete the application for export tax rebate (exemption) pursuant to Article 3 of the Announcement of the State Administration of Taxation on Promulgating the Administrative Measures for Value-added Tax and Consumption Tax on Exported Goods and Services (Announcement of the State Administration of Taxation [2012] No. 24).

Article 5

The purchasers in the area shall, within each value-added tax declaration period from the next month following the day on which the goods subject to the procedure of declaration for export are purchased from other areas (subject to the day of export stated on the customs declaration of goods for export (specially for rebates)) to April 30 of the next year, provide the following materials to declare at the competent national tax authorities for tax rebates of value added tax and consumption tax on the goods purchased from other areas. The purchasers shall not be allowed to declare for tax rebates beyond the said declaration period.

1. Summary of Declaration for Tax Rebates for Enterprises in the Area (see Appendix I);
2. List and Declaration for Tax Rebates on Imports for Enterprises in the Area (see Appendix II), and fill "GHQYTS" in the column of "Business Type";
3. List and Declaration for Tax Rebates on Goods Entering the Area for Enterprises in the Area (see Appendix III), and fill "GHQYTS" in the column of "Business Type of Tax Rebate (Exemption)";
4. Official electronic data on declaration for tax rebate (exemption) of value added tax and consumption tax on the goods from other areas;
5. The following original certificates:
   (1) customs declaration of goods for export (specially for export tax rebates) obtained from selling enterprises in other areas;
   (2) schedule of imported goods (the copy shall be affixed with the seal of the Customs);
   (3) special invoice for value-added tax (deduction copy) and batch declaration form for imported goods with export tax rebates;
   (4) for taxable consumables, the special paid-in document or partition document for consumption tax;
   (5) other materials required by the competent national tax authorities.

Article 6

The utilities enterprises in the area purchasing the water, steam, electric power and gas related to production in the area from other areas shall, within each value-added tax declaration period from the next month following the day on which the special value-added tax invoice for water, steam, electric power and gas purchased from other areas is issued to April 30 of the next year, provide the following materials to declare at the competent national tax authorities for tax rebates.

The enterprises shall not be allowed to declare for tax rebates beyond the said declaration period.

1. Declaration for Tax Rebates on Imported Water, Electric Power and Gas (see Appendix IV), and fill "GJSDQ" in the column of business type;
2. Formal electronic data for declaration;
3. The following original certificates:
   (1) special invoice for value-added tax (deduction copy);
   (2) list of water, electric power and gas used (verified and sealed by the component industrial department of the local administrative committee at district level, see Appendix V).

Article 7

Before a formal declaration for tax rebates, the purchasers and utilities enterprises in the area shall make a pre-declaration at the competent national tax authorities and declare formally after that the competent national tax authorities confirm the correctness of the contents of declaration documents and corresponding electronic information of the administrative departments.

Before the expiry date for the declaration for tax rebates, if the enterprises fail to complete the pre-declaration as the declaration documents of tax rebate still have no corresponding electronic information of the administrative department, or the contents of the documents are inconsistent with the electronic information, it shall be handled in accordance with Article 4 of the Announcement of the State Administration of Taxation on Adjusting the Declaration Measures for Export Tax Rebate (Exemption) (Announcement of the State Administration of Taxation [2013] No. 61).

Article 8

A purchaser in the area shall set up a separate account for the goods (including water, steam, electric power and gas) declared for tax debates, to calculate the purchase amount and input tax.

Article 9

The declaration for the tax debates for goods (including water, steam, electric power and gas) purchased by the purchasers in the area from other areas are not subject to the management of registration documents.

Article 10

The competent national tax authorities will check the certificates, materials and relevant electronic information for tax rebate declaration provided by the purchasers in the area, and then go through the tax rebate formalities as required.

Article 11

If the competent national tax authorities find that the imported goods are used by the purchasers in the area for commercial real estate development projects, they will not process the tax rebates; if the tax debates have been processed, the rebated taxes shall be recovered.

Article 12

If the declaration for tax rebates by purchasers in the area is not covered by the Measures, it shall be handled according to the relevant provisions on deemed goods for export.

Article 13

The Measures will take effect as of the date on which the relevant facilities subject to supervision are accepted and the relevant customs are officially put into operation.

The goods (excluding water, steam, electric power and gas) purchased from other areas are subject to the day of export stated on the customs declaration of goods for export (specially for export tax rebates); the water, steam, electric power and gas purchased from other areas are subject to the day on which the special invoice for value-added tax is issued.

Announcement of the State Administration of Taxation on Issues Relating to the Issuance of Electronic Ordinary VAT Invoices Through the Electronic VAT Invoice System Announcement of the State Administration of Taxation.

No. 84 November 26, 2015.

To meet the requirements for economic and social development and promoting taxation modernization, the State Administration of Taxation has, on the basis of an upgraded VAT invoice system, developed an electronic ordinary VAT invoice system, and the system has undergone trial operation with steady performance. It is ready to be launched nationwide. To satisfy taxpayer needs for issuing electronic ordinary VAT invoices, an announcement on the relevant issues is hereby made as follows:

I. The invoice system is important to the development of electronic ordinary VAT invoices because it can lower taxpayers' operating costs, conserve social resources, facilitate the management and use of invoices by consumers, and contribute to a healthy and fair tax collection environment.

II. See Appendix 1 for the specimen of an electronic ordinary VAT invoice generated by the electronic VAT invoice system.

III. The invoice system can provide hard copies of electronic ordinary VAT invoices, which shall have the same legal effect and basic uses as paper invoices provided by the tax authorities and shall apply to the same basic provisions on the use of invoices.

IV. An electronic ordinary VAT invoice shall have a 12-digit serial number starting with zero with the following meanings: the second to fifth digits represent the code of provinces, autonomous regions or municipalities under the central government or cities under separate state planning; the sixth to seventh digits represent the year; the eighth to tenth digits represent the batch number; and the eleventh to twelfth digits represent the invoice type (11 represent electronic ordinary VAT invoice).

 Invoice numbers shall comprise eight digits and vary according to the year and batch number.

V. Except Beijing, Shanghai, Zhejiang and Shenzhen, VAT taxpayers in other localities using electronic invoices shall be connected to the related systems before December 31, 2015, begin operation of the invoice system from January 1, 2016, and stop using any other invoicing systems.

 See Appendix 2 for the technical schemes of the system.

VI. The tax authorities at all localities shall organize publicity programs for taxpayers and promote the use of electronic VAT invoices in sectors where invoices are frequently used, including e-commerce, telecommunications, courier and public utility sectors.

VII. This Announcement shall take effect as of December 1, 2015.
It is hereby announced.

Announcement of the State Administration of Taxation on Further Optimizing the Administration of Tax Rebates (Exemptions) on Exported Goods for Integrated Foreign Trade Service Enterprises Announcement of the State Administration of Taxation.

No. 61 September 19, 2016.

With a view to implementing the Several Opinions of the State Council on Promoting the Stabilization and Recovery of Foreign Trade (Guo Fa [2016] No. 27), accelerating the development of a management model for integrated foreign trade service enterprises ("ISEs"), promoting the ISE pilot program, and further optimizing the administration of tax rebates (exemptions) on exported goods for ISEs, the relevant matters are hereby announced as follows:

I. State tax authorities shall administer ISEs in a targeted manner following the principles of manageable risks, streamlining administration, delegating powers, strengthening regulation, improving services and facilitating compliance and tax services; and shall, pursuant to the criteria for classification specified in the Announcement of the State Administration of Taxation on Issuing the Revised Measures for the Targeted Administration of Enterprises Eligible for Export Tax Rebate (Exemption) (Announcement of the State Administration of Taxation [2016] No. 46), assess and adjust the category of ISEs eligible for export tax rebate (exemption) (the "tax rebate category"), effectively implement targeted administration and relevant service measures.

II. State tax authorities shall open green channels (special service areas) for Class I ISEs to give them priority on handling export tax rebate and build a key contact system to solve export tax rebate (exemption) issues for enterprises in a timely manner.

III. State tax authorities shall handle tax rebate (exemption) as follows based on the tax rebate category of ISEs:

1. For Class I ISEs which are deemed to meet the following requirements upon review, competent state tax authorities shall complete export tax rebate (exemption) formalities for such ISEs within five (5) working days from the date of accepting the application:
   (1) the electronic data submitted is consistent with the clearance information in the customs export declaration form and the information in the special VAT invoice;
   (2) the export tax rebate (exemption) amount is accurate;
   (3) no early warnings against risk identified by the State Administration of Taxation (the "SAT") and all the provincial offices of the SAT is involved; and
   (4) the taxation credit rating of the small- and medium-sized manufacturers such ISEs served as A or B.

2. For Class II ISEs which are deemed to meet the following requirements upon review, competent state tax authorities shall complete export tax rebate (exemption) formalities for such ISEs within ten (10) working days from the date of accepting the application:
   (1) the relevant provisions on export tax rebate (exemption) are met;
   (2) the electronic data submitted is consistent with the clearance information in the customs export declaration form and the information in the special VAT invoice; and
   (3) no doubt is found upon review or any doubts identified have been eliminated.
3. For Class III ISEs which are deemed to meet the following requirements upon review, competent state tax authorities shall complete export tax rebate (exemption) formalities for such ISEs within fifteen (15) working days from the day of accepting the application:
   (1) the relevant provisions on export tax rebate (exemption) are met;
   (2) the electronic data submitted is consistent with the clearance information in the customs export declaration form and the information in the special VAT invoice; and
   (3) no doubt is found upon review or any doubts identified have been eliminated.
4. For Class VI ISEs, competent state tax authorities shall check if the following requirements are met, and upon review and elimination of all doubts identified, complete export tax rebate (exemption) formalities within twenty (20) days from the date of accepting the application:
   (1) the hard copies of the documents and materials submitted match for and are logically consistent with the electronic data;
   (2) the electronic data submitted is consistent with the clearance information in the customs export declaration form and the information in the special VAT invoice; and
   (3) with respect to outsourced export goods for export tax rebate (exemption), state tax authorities shall, by issuing an official letter, review the invoices of a certain proportion of suppliers in a random manner.

IV. For ISEs involved in the ISE pilot program launched by the Ministry of Commerce, the General Administration of Customs, the SAT, the General Administration of Quality Supervision, Inspection and Quarantine and the State Administration of Foreign Exchange: CNBM International Corporation. Ningbo Shimaotong International Co. Ltd., Xiamen Justsun Supply Chain Co., Ltd., and Guangdong Huifu Holding Group Co. Ltd., if the provisions herein are met upon review, competent state tax authorities shall complete export tax rebate (exemption) formalities for such ISEs within five (5) working days.
In case of any of the following circumstances, competent state tax authorities shall conduct verification and take necessary actions, not being subject to the deadline of five (5) working days.

1. such pilot ISEs are filed against and investigated for being suspected of export tax rebate fraud;
2. such pilot ISEs defraud export tax rebate;
3. such pilot ISEs do not assist state tax authorities in administration of export tax rebate (exemption), and fail to collect, bind or retain vouchers and record-filing documents for export tax rebate (exemption) as required; or
4. other circumstances specified by the SAT.

V. Where an ISE exports goods with authorization from a small- and medium-sized enterprise and applies for issuance of the Certificate of Authorized Goods Export, such ISE shall indicate "WMZHFW" in the REMARK column of the Application Form for Certificate of Authorized Good Export. Competent state tax authorities shall, instead of issuing a hard copy of such Certificate, and may deliver the electronic copy to the competent state tax authority which has jurisdiction over the small- and medium-sized enterprise.
With respect to the export business where ISEs hold the Certificate of Authorized Goods Export, the authorizing enterprises shall apply for export tax rebate (exemption) subject to existing regulations, and no hard copy of Certificate of Authorized Goods Export is required.
VI. The Announcement comes into force as of October 1, 2016.

The Announcement is hereby given.

Announcement of the State Administration of Taxation on Issues concerning the Issue of Value-added Tax Invoices by Vehicle and Vessel Tax-withholding Insurance Institutions Announcement of the State Administration of Taxation.

No. 51 August 7, 2016.

Some matters concerning the issue of value-added tax invoices by vehicle and vessel tax-withholding insurance institutions are notified as follows:

Insurance institutions, as withholding agents of vehicle and vessel tax, shall provide detailed information on the vehicle and vessel tax withheld in the "Remarks" section of a value-added tax invoice issued by them, including the insurance policy number, tax payment period (month), amount of tax withheld, amount of late fee, and total amount. Such value-added tax invoices may serve as original vouchers for the accounting of vehicle and vessel taxes and late fees paid by taxpayers.

This Announcement shall take effect from May 1, 2016.

The Announcement is hereby given.

Announcement of the State Administration of Taxation on Matters relating to the Optimization and Improvement of Functions of VAT Invoice Selection and Confirmation Platforms and System Maintenance Announcement of the State Administration of Taxation.

No. 57 August 29, 2016.

To further optimize tax services, the matters relating to the optimization and improvement of functions of VAT invoice selection and confirmation platforms (original VAT invoice inquiry platforms) and system maintenance are hereby announced as follows:

I. A taxpayer may log on the VAT invoice selection and confirmation platform of his province to inquire, select or confirm the information of the VAT invoice for declaration of credits or export rebates.
II. Service providers of the VAT control system are responsible for maintaining the taxpayer-end system of the VAT invoice selection and confirmation platforms.
III. This Announcement shall come into force as of September 1, 2016. Article 1 of the Announcement of the State Administration of Taxation on Matters relating to the Optimization and Improvement of Functions of VAT Invoice Inquiry Platforms (Announcement of the State Administration of Taxation [2016] No. 32) is simultaneously repealed.

Announcement of the State Administration of Taxation on Issue concerning the VAT of Tap-Water Charges Collected by Property Management Services Announcement of the State Administration of Taxation.

No. 54 August 19, 2016.

The issues concerning the value added tax of tap-water charges collected by the property management services are hereby announced as follows:

The taxpayers providing property management services collect tap-water charges from the service recipient and use the tap-water charges after the deduction of external payment of tap-water charges as the sales volume, which is subject to a 3% VAT rate in accordance with the simple calculation method.
This announcement shall come into force as of the date of promulgation. No adjustments shall be made in connection with the matters that have occurred and have been handled after May 1, 2016.

The matters not yet dealt with will be handled in accordance with the provisions of this announcement.

7.5 Circulars of the MOF and the SAT for the Year of 2016

Circular of the State Administration of Taxation on Effectively Expanding the Pilot Reform for Replacing Business Tax with Value-added Tax ShuiZong Fa.

No. 32 March 8, 2016.

State and local tax bureaus of all provinces, autonomous regions, municipalities directly under the Central Government, and cities under separate state planning, The State Council proposed in the Report on the Work of the Government presented for deliberation at the Fourth Session of the 12th National People's Congress to launch pilot reform for replacing business tax with value-added tax nationwide ("Reform") as of May 1, 2016. In order to ensure the achievement of the objectives as scheduled, we put forward the following requirements for your implementation:

I. Staying fully mobilized and strengthening organizational support to ensure the working mechanism is in place.

1. Making proactive preparations.
   Prior to the formal approval of the Reform plan by the State Council, tax bureaus at various levels shall make proactive preparations at a proper pace and with proper strength, both internally and externally, take timely measures to make work arrangements, convey the essential points and requirements with respect to the Reform, motivate tax officers to proactively participate in the Reform with passion and energy, stay focused and avoid slacking off in the face of difficulties, and make concerted efforts to win the final battle of the Reform.
2. Strengthening organization and leadership.
   To continue to give play to the role of the leading groups for the Reform in overall planning and coordination, proactively report to the local governments, and strengthen communication and coordination with relevant departments. The leading groups of the tax authorities at various levels shall assume full responsibility and the leaders shall assume overall responsibility for the Reform.
   Special sessions shall be convened at key links of the Reform to analyze and solve prominent problems and contradictions arising in the previous stage, study and make plans for important work in the next stage in accordance with the general orientation of the Reform.
3. Improving the working mechanism.
   The tax authorities at various levels shall, in the preparation work for the Reform, enhance functional integration, improve the working methods and unify centralized management. Major leaders shall provide guidance for the Reform at the front line and decompose tasks in accordance with the Work Breakdown Structure for Tax Authorities of Provinces (Autonomous Regions, Municipalities) on Comprehensively Expanding the Reform for Replacing Business Tax with Value-added Tax (see the attachment) and work out unified timetables, working procedures, operating standards and quality-control norms. Efforts shall be made to set schedules in reversed order, formulate timetables and roadmaps, and with detailed division of responsibilities and duties, assign tasks and responsibilities to specific posts and individuals based on the Reform objectives, and ensure the Reform is orderly advanced and implemented.

II. Sparing no effort ensuring the measures are in place in key links.

4. Laying a solid data foundation for tax collection and management.
   The state and local tax departments shall transfer taxpayer data in an all-around way from the issue date hereof. The state tax departments shall

proactively receive, sort, collect and confirm data, and timely handle tax registration and registration for general taxpayers of value-added tax. The local tax departments shall work closely with the state tax departments in the management of invoices, quota and tax arrears during the transition period.

5. Strengthening technical support.
   To adjust and optimize the information infrastructure through coordinating existing equipment and CTAIS III equipment, and accelerate the development of auxiliary systems and plug-in software; to conduct online testing for information systems with regard to comprehensive tax collection and management, electronic tax declaration, new VAT invoice management system, and tax-treasury-bank horizontal network for electronic tax collection and put them into use in order of priority when conditions permit to ensure the information systems are available and function well as scheduled during the Reform.
6. Preparing tax control devices and invoices.
   To proactively coordinate and organize production and service providers of tax control devices, formulate task sheets and timetables for the release and installation of tax control devices and relevant training, and enhance supervision and administration; to estimate the quantity of tax control devices and invoices through in-depth surveys, field visits and reasonably locating of tax control devices, initialize and release the devices for installation to ensure that the tax control devices are in place and taxpayers involving in the Reform get invoices from them as scheduled.
7. Ensuring smooth tax declaration.
   For the first round of tax declaration, the local tax authorities shall select typical taxpayers based on the realities of business and use real business data for all-around system testing and verification in both a simulated environment and a production environment in advance, so that there is sufficient time for handling possible issues. Timely notice or alert shall be issued on the websites of the tax authorities, by telephone or by means of short messages to remind taxpayers of their tax declaration obligations. A variety of tax declaration methods shall be provided to alleviate the pressure of tax service halls and ensure timely and orderly declaration of tax by taxpayers.
8. Properly allocating tax service resources.
   To reasonably allocate human resources in tax service halls, strictly implement the bureau chief-headed key staff on-duty system, and moderately adjust or increase the number of service windows; to set up special consultation/guide desks for technical service providers to dispatch personnel to offer guidance and assistance for taxpayers; to make rational use of service space and set up temporary tax service halls by renting or vacating space in order to facilitate taxpayers handling one-off procedures in advance, such as tax registration, tax type verification, general taxpayer registration, application for a new value-added tax invoice management system,

and maintenance of bank-tax agreements. Green channels for the Reform may be set up in eligible tax service halls to provide special services and create a favorable tax environment for taxpayers.

Sufficient and reasonable tax collection and service arrangements shall be made particularly for tax matters relating to second-hand housing transactions to ensure all transactions are not affected.

9. Attaching importance to training and publicity.
   To provide multistep internal and external training, including training for the "12366" tax service hotline operators, and free training for taxpayers; to strictly observe the codes of media conduct, make publicity plans and release information in a uniform way to correctly guide public opinions, convey the positive meanings of the Reform, promote social recognition of the Reform, help taxpayers adapt themselves to, obey and benefit from the new tax system, and create a favorable public opinion climate for the smooth progress of the Reform.
10. Making reasonable contingency plans.
   The tax authorities at various levels shall sort out possible contingencies, item by item, for the purposes of free, safe and steady operations, and establish and improve their contingency plans for dealing with system crashes, mass rallies and tax-related claims and for maintaining order.
   Contingency teams shall be established at various levels, and relevant departments and personnel shall be organized to gain familiarity with the contents of the contingency plans in order to properly respond to and deal with various possible situations.

III. Attaching importance to effective operation and supervision throughout the process to ensure the requirements are effectively implemented.

11. Strengthening coordination and cooperation.
   To expand the Reform in an all-around way is an overall test for the mobilization ability, organization and leadership in the tax administration system. The tax authorities at various levels must work closely with each other, with the focus on cooperation between departments. The state and local tax departments shall communicate with each other as early as possible from the perspective of politics and overall situation, clarify responsibilities, and make concerted efforts to accomplish their respective tasks on time and ensure the progress of the Reform as scheduled.
12. Enhancing supervision and accountability.
   The tax authorities at various levels shall incorporate the Reform work to the supervision and performance appraisal system. Entities and individuals failing to perform their duties in the course of the Reform or delaying the progress of the Reform at a critical point of time as a result of dereliction of duty shall be punished in strict accordance with the accountability system.

13. Deepening effect analysis.
    To continuously track the operations of pilot projects, make solid efforts to collect data, and profoundly evaluate the effects of the Reform, timely identify and solve problems, and timely report important issues to higher-level tax authorities; to enhance tax payment appraisal, tax source monitoring, tax auditing and law enforcement supervision to prevent tax risks.
14. Strengthening monitoring of public opinions.
    Tax authorities at various levels shall establish a sound system for monitoring, disposing and reporting public opinions, keep track of the development of public opinions, timely respond to taxpayers' concerns, seriously handle taxpayers' claims, avoid the spread of negative public opinions, and nip issues in the bud at the earliest time possible, in order to ensure the smooth progress of the entire Reform.

Circular of the State Administration of Taxation on Entrusting Local Tax Authorities with the Collection and Invoicing of Value-added Taxes in Lieu of Business Taxes ShuiZong Han.

No. 145 March 31, 2016.

State and local tax authorities of all provinces, autonomous regions, municipalities directly under the Central Government, and cities specifically designated in the state plan.

In order to ensure the smooth transition of the relevant work of the state and local tax authorities after the business tax to value-added tax (VAT) reform and to facilitate the handling of taxes by taxpayers, and in accordance with the requirements of the PRC Law on the Administration of Tax Collection, the Circular of the Ministry of Finance and the State Administration of Taxation on the Comprehensive Promotion of the Pilot Program for the Collection of Value-added Tax in Lieu of Business Tax (Cai Shui [2016] No. 36), and the Circular of the State Administration of Taxation on Enhancing Tax Collection through Mutual Entrustment between State and Local Tax Authorities (ShuiZong Fa [2015] No. 155), relevant issues concerning the collection and invoicing of VAT with respect to sales of immovable property by taxpayers and letting of immovable property by other individuals after the business tax to VAT reform are notified as follows:

I. Arrangement for Division of Duties.
   VAT is administered and collected by the state tax authorities in China. To facilitate taxpayers after the business tax to VAT reform, it is tentatively decided that the acceptance of tax declarations, assessment of taxable prices, collection of taxes, filing of tax benefits and VAT invoicing with respect to sales of immovable property by taxpayers and letting of immovable property by other individuals shall be handled by the local tax authorities, who are also responsible for tax payment into and withdrawal from the treasury, use of tax vouchers of the local tax authority, revenue reconciliation, accounting, data collection and reporting, without the need of signing tax collection entrustment agreements with the state tax authorities.

Where taxpayers selling immovable property or other individuals letting immovable property apply for issuance of tax invoices, the collecting local tax authorities shall issue special VAT invoices or general VAT invoices ("VAT invoices"). Government departments with the necessary conditions for secure VAT invoice management and network connectivity for VAT collection and invoicing under the effective supervision of the local tax authorities may be empowered by the local tax authorities at the county (district) level or above to collect VAT and issue VAT invoices if deemed by the latter through risk assessment that risks are controllable.

The state tax authorities shall complete training on the VAT invoicing operation and related policies for the local tax authorities at the same level on or before April 25, 2016.

II. Invoicing Procedure.

The local tax authorities shall issue VAT invoices for taxpayers pursuant to the relevant regulations on the collection and administration of VAT on the sales of immovable property by taxpayers and the letting of immovable property by other individuals based on the VAT invoicing procedure of the state tax authority, and the local tax authorities shall cease the use of the original business tax invoices.

(I) Registration of invoicing departments.

The information of invoicing departments of the local tax authorities shall be registered and maintained in the China Taxation Administration Information System (CTAIS) or the Golden Taxation System (3rd Edition) based on the existing VAT invoicing model of the state tax authority. The code of the invoicing department of a local tax authority shall consist of 15 digits, including "D" at the 11th digit and other digits coded in accordance with the requirements of the Circular of the State Administration of Taxation on the Supply of Anti-forgery Value-added Tax Control and Special Invoice System Equipment and Application Software (Guo Shui Fa [2004] No. 139).

(II) Issuance of special-purpose tax control equipment.

The VAT invoice management system shall be updated simultaneously with the registration of information of invoicing departments of the local tax authorities. The state tax authorities shall provide special-purpose tax control equipment embedded with digital tax certificate for invoicing departments of the local tax authorities at the same level in accordance with the existing procedure for issuing VAT invoicing equipment.

(III) Supply of invoices.

The state tax authorities shall provide the local tax authorities at the same level with six-copy special VAT invoices and five-copy general VAT invoices.

(IV) Issuance of invoices.

Small-sized VAT taxpayers selling immovable property and other individuals letting immovable property to those other than other individuals may, after paying VAT, apply to the local tax authorities for issuance of special VAT invoices. Small-sized taxpayers selling immovable property and other individuals letting immovable property that cannot issue general VAT invoices on their own may apply to the local tax authorities for issuance of general VAT invoices. The invoicing departments of the local tax authorities shall issue VAT invoices using the updated VAT invoice management system, which will automatically print the words "Authorized Issuance" on the invoices.

The invoicing departments of the local tax authorities shall issue unified six-copy special VAT invoices and five-copy general VAT invoices for taxpayers. The fourth copy shall be kept by invoice issuers for the purpose of supplementary entry of electronic invoice data; the fifth copy shall be kept by tax collectors for the purpose of regular verification of VAT invoices with VAT amounts; and other copies shall be kept by taxpayers.

Invoice issuers shall fill in a VAT invoice as follows:

1. Fill in the "Tax Rate" column with the VAT rate. For tax-free items or the letting of immovable property by other individuals taxed at a reduced rate of 1.5% or margin tax items, the column will be automatically filled with "***";
2. Fill in the "Seller's Name" column with the name of the invoicing local tax authority;
3. Fill in the "Seller's Taxpayer ID Number" column with the code of the invoicing local tax authority;
4. Fill in the "Seller's Bank & Account Number" column with the code and number of the tax payment receipt (for general VAT invoices for tax-free items, leave the column blank);
5. Fill in the "Remarks" column with the name and ID number (or organizational code) of the taxpayer who sells or lets immovable property, and the detailed address of the immovable property;
6. For margin tax invoices, input the amount of tax-inclusive sales (or amount of estimated tax-inclusive sales) and the amount of deductions via the margin tax invoicing function of the system, the system will automatically calculate the taxable price and the amount of tax, and automatically print the words "Margin Tax" in the "Remarks" column;
7. For sales of immovable property by taxpayers, fill in the column of "Name of Goods or Taxable Service" with the name of immovable property and the house ownership certificate number, and fill in the "Unit" column with the unit of area;
8. For taxes on certified taxable prices, fill in the "Amount" column with the tax-exclusive taxable price, the "Remarks" column with "on the basis of the certified taxable price, the actual tax-inclusive transaction price of RMBXXX".

   Fill in other items in accordance with the relevant VAT invoice filling requirements.

The invoicing departments of the local tax authorities shall affix the special seal of the local tax authority for invoices onto the "Remarks" column of VAT invoices.

(V) Transmission of invoicing data.
The invoicing departments of the local tax authorities shall transmit invoicing data through the network to the updated VAT invoice management system on a real-time or regular basis.

(VI) Reissuance of invoices.
Where an invoicing department of the local tax authority applies for reissuance of VAT invoices, the state tax authority shall verify and cancel the used invoices through the system and reissue invoices after the invoiced tax data are filed.

III. Invoice Management.

(I) Safe management of special invoices.
The local tax authorities shall intensify security and take effective measures to ensure the security of VAT invoices in accordance with the existing provisions of the state tax authority on the management of VAT invoices.

(II) Daily information check.
The local tax authorities shall enhance internal management and check the invoicing data from the invoice issuers with the tax data from the tax collectors on a weekly basis and solve any problem in accordance with relevant provisions in a timely manner.

(III) Follow-up information check.
The State Administration of Taxation will, based on relevant work schedule, check the tax data with the invoicing data taken from the local tax authorities, and guard against risks such as issuance of special VAT invoices without the collection of taxes, and issuance of invoices with insufficient collection of taxes.

IV. Upgrading of the Information System.
For provinces where the Golden Taxation System (3rd Edition) is not available on or before April 25,2016, the local tax authorities shall timely upgrade the information system in accordance with the requirements of the State Administration of Taxation, coordinate the tax collection and administration resources, and standardize the processes for the acceptance of tax declarations and collection of taxes. For provinces where the Golden Taxation System (3rd Edition) is available, the Department of Collection and Technology Development of the State Administration of Taxation will be responsible for the unified commissioning of the information system.

V. Supply and Maintenance of the Special-purpose Tax Control Equipment.
The local tax authorities of all provinces shall report the number of special-purpose tax control equipment needed for the issuance of VAT invoices to the state tax authorities of their respective provinces on or before April 5, 2016, and

the state tax authorities shall report the number of special-purpose tax control equipment needed to be initialized to the Department of Goods and Labor Tax of the State Administration of Taxation via a secure file transfer protocol (FTP) on or before April 8. The state tax authorities of all provinces shall provide special-purpose tax control equipment for the local tax authorities on or before April 20. The state tax authorities shall be responsible for coordinating VAT control system service providers for the installation and maintenance of the VAT invoice system for the local tax authorities.
The collection and invoicing of VAT entrusted to the local tax authorities by the state tax authorities is an important move for state and local tax authorities to perform official duties, promote interdepartmental cooperation and enhance cohesion. The state and local tax authorities of various localities shall effectively fulfill their duties and enhance coordination and cooperation to form synergy; increase publicity and education on relevant policies for taxpayers; provide excellent services and convenience for taxpayers to facilitate their tax declaration and payment; and formulate contingency plans, keep a close watch on the feedback from taxpayers and public opinions and ensure the smooth transition of the tax policy.

Circular of the State Council on Issuing the Transitional Proposals for Adjusting the Division of Value-added Tax Revenue of the Central Government and Local Governments after Comprehensively Promoting the Pilot Collection of Value-added Tax in Lieu of Business Tax Guo Fa.

No. 26 April 29, 2016.

The people's governments of all provinces, autonomous regions and municipalities directly under the Central Government, and all ministries and commissions of the State Council and all institutions directly under the State Council.

The Transitional Proposals for Adjusting the Division of Value-added Tax Revenue of the Central Government and Local Governments after Comprehensively Promoting the Pilot Collection of Value-added Tax in Lieu of Business Tax are hereby issued to you for your earnest implementation.

Transitional Proposals for Adjusting the Division of Value-added Tax Revenue of the Central Government and Local Governments after Comprehensively Promoting the Pilot Collection of Value-added Tax in Lieu of Business Tax The pilot collection of value-added tax ("VAT") in lieu of business tax ("BT") will be comprehensively promoted as of May 1, 2016. Since it is required at the Third Plenary Session of the 18th National Congress of the Communist Party of China to "maintain the overall stability of the existing financial resource structure of the Central Government and local governments and further make clear the income division between the Central Government and local governments in combination with the tax reform and based on tax attributes", the State Council has decided to formulate the transitional proposals for adjusting the division of VAT revenue of the Central Government and local governments after comprehensively promoting the pilot collection of VAT in lieu of BT considering that the tax reform is not entirely completed and there is a long way to promote the reform of the division of administrative power and expenditure liabilities of the Central Government and local governments.

I. Basic Principles.

1. Maintain the existing financial resource structure. Both the existing financial resources of local governments (so as not to affect their smooth operation), and the current 50/50 sharing of the Central Government and local governments as a whole shall be maintained.
2. Focus on stimulating the enthusiasm of local governments. Appropriate increase in the proportion at which local governments share VAT according to the locality of tax payment is conducive to the mobilization of economic development and expansion of financial resources by local governments to ease current downward pressure.
3. Take into account the interests of the eastern, central and western regions. The revenue turned over to the Central Government will be returned to local governments by means of tax refund based on the relevant numbers in 2014 to ensure that the existing financial resources of local governments remain unchanged. After adjustment, the income increment will be distributed to the central and western regions on a priority basis to focus on intensifying support for the underdeveloped areas and to promote the equalization of basic public services.
   Meanwhile, in speeding up the reforms of the construction of local tax system and the promotion of the division of administrative power and expenditure responsibilities of the Central Government and local governments, the transitional proposals and the following fiscal and taxation system reform shall be well aligned.

II. Main Content.

1. The base for refund by the Central Government and turning in by local governments shall be assessed based on the relevant numbers in 2014.
2. The VAT paid by enterprises in all industries shall be included in the scope of sharing between the Central Government and local governments.
3. The Central Government will share 50% of VAT.
4. Local governments will share 50% of VAT based on the locality of tax payment.
5. The revenue turned over to the Central Government will be returned to local governments by means of tax refund to ensure that the existing financial resources of local governments remain unchanged.
6. The revenue increment collected by the Central Government will be distributed to local governments via balanced transfer and payment and be mainly used to enhance the support for the central and western regions of China.

III. Implementing Time and Transition Period.
These Proposals will be simultaneously carried out with the comprehensive pilot collection of VAT in lieu of BT as of May 1, 2016. The transition period is tentatively determined to be two to three years; after the transition period expires, the State Council will study whether to make appropriate adjustments according to the progress in the reforms of the division of administrative power and expenditure responsibilities of the Central Government and local governments, local tax system construction and other aspects.

Circular of the State Administration of Taxation on Promoting the Overall Analysis of the Pilot Program of Value-added Tax in Lieu of Business Tax to Improve Taxation Services ShuiZong Fa.

No. 95 June 20, 2016.

The offices of the State Administration of Taxation and local taxation bureaus of all provinces, autonomous regions, municipalities directly under the Central Government, and cities specially designated in the state plan.

The pilot program of value-added tax replacing business tax is going into an overall analysis stage.

In order to better advance all works under the pilot program and ensure tax reduction rather than increase in all pilot sectors, the tax authorities at different levels shall step up efforts to do the analysis of the pilot program well by bearing in mind targeted analysis and services, striving for perfection, and adopting a rigorous, earnest and meticulous attitude. To that end, the works on promoting the overall analysis of the pilot program and improve taxation services are hereby notified as follows:

I. Promoting the overall analysis of the pilot program.

(I) In-depth analysis of the implementation of the pilot program: We shall use big data on taxation to make an overall analysis of the number of registered entities and trends of the construction, real estate, finance and consumer services sectors (the "Four Pilot Sectors") since the pilot program is extended to such sectors; make a systematic analysis of the operation of taxpayers in respect of invoicing, tax return declaration and policy application; analyze the work of the tax authorities and identify relevant problems in invoice supply, agency invoicing, tax return declaration acceptance, taxpayer services and system availability, so as to lay a solid foundation for targeted improvement in the works of the tax authorities and better services for taxpayers.

(II) Detailed analysis of the tax burden of pilot sectors: We shall employ the approach of integrating point and sphere to comprehensively track and faithfully reflect the changes in the tax burden of the four pilot sectors and subsectors thereof on the basis of clear understanding of the basic principles of sector tax burden analysis. With respect to enterprises and sectors showing abnormal tax burden changes, we shall analyze the causes from the perspectives of characteristics of the tax system, policy changes, tax levy and administration, operation and management and investment cycle, so as to solve the problems on the taxpayers' side.

(III) In-depth analysis of the effect of the pilot program: We shall strengthen the analysis of changes in tax revenue amount and mix since the implementation of the pilot program to detect the tax changes in the four pilot sectors, "3 + 7" pilot sectors (transport, postal and telecommunication +seven modern service sectors) and original VAT taxpayers; on the basis of informative data and real cases, analyze and reflect the effects of the pilot program in promoting the transformation and upgrading of economic structure, optimizing division of labor, increasing investment and boosting employment in a multi-dimensional, multi-tier and multi-angle manner and objectively evaluate the achievements of the pilot program. The SAT offices and local taxation bureaus at different levels shall jointly build teams under working arrangements to assess the effects of the pilot program, in order to conduct a comprehensive and effective analysis.

II. Proactively using the analysis results to serve for taxpayers.

(IV) Improving invoice supply services: We shall formulate a contingency plan to cope with the dramatically increasing demand for VAT invoices in July and ensure adequate supply of various invoices at windows and self-service terminals; increase the efficiency of invoice supply and agency invoicing services and reduce the work load at taxpayer service halls by setting up more windows, installing more self-service terminals, providing online pre-application services, employing the QR code-based data collection technology, optimizing the functions of the information systems and streamlining work procedures.

(V) Extending the tax return period in July: The State Administration of Taxation arrived at a decision of extending the tax return period in July until July 20 to adapt to the actual situation that both monthly and quarterly taxpayers are required to file tax returns. Local SAT offices shall prepare well in advance for processing dramatically increased tax return declarations, improve services, expand service access, as well as adopt effective measures to decentralize tax return declarations such as online declaration, declaration through appointment or special windows, and review of tax return materials in advance, thus ensuring a smooth tax return period.

(VI) Refining the guidance for completing tax return forms: We shall comb through and classify the questions on completing tax return forms and provide targeted guidance to make taxpayers be fully familiar with the meaning of the items in tax return forms, especially the data coverage of relevant items in and the logical relation between the Input Tax Deduction Statement for the Current Period and the Tax Burden Calculation and Comparison Statement under the Reform of Replacing Business

Tax with Value Added Tax, enabling taxpayers to correctly complete the tax return forms.

(VII) Optimizing the functions of the online tax return declaration system: We shall further optimize the functions of the online tax return declaration system to provide taxpayers the experience of user-friendly interface and easy operation; add the function of necessary online logic check of tax return data to remind taxpayers of incorrect or illegal inputs, so as to reduce errors and improve the quality and efficiency of tax return declarations.

(VIII) Strengthening introductory policy training: We shall, based on the analysis results, provide more targeted, introductory and repetitive training for taxpayers involved in the pilot program, enabling such taxpayers to better understand the VAT system and relevant policies, and further standardize internal management, improve financial and accounting systems, optimize operation, make more scientific decisions and enjoy the fruits of the tax system reform.

(IX) Conducting tax burden comparison among peer taxpayers: We shall conduct a detailed analysis of the tax burden gap between taxpayers in the same sector and help above-average taxpayers identify underlying causes and make comparison, enabling such taxpayers to reduce tax burden in an appropriate way by improving operation and management and implementing the input tax deduction policy.

(X) Reminding taxpayers of tax risks: The competent tax authorities shall voluntarily remind taxpayers of their incorrect, non-compliant and non-fulfilled operations identified in the analysis in respect of invoicing, tax return declaration and policy application and help them make correction to prevent possible tax risks.

(XI) Optimizing the taxpayer communication mechanism: We shall strengthen the communication with taxpayers and industrial associations by way of forum, site visit and opinion solicitation, solicit opinions from a wide range of taxpayers, put taxpayers' demand in high priority and voluntarily reply to questions raised by taxpayers so as to heighten their satisfaction for the services of the pilot program.

(XII) Encouraging the sharing of service resources: Local SAT offices and taxation bureaus shall enhance the integration of taxpayer service resources and leverage counterparts' taxpayer service halls to provide services; accelerate the progress of form-free services in 6 business categories (e.g. invoicing, tax return declaration and certificate issuance) involving 24 types of forms. Local tax bureaus at different levels shall actively gain support from local governments in employing information technology to strengthen the business and technological integration with the real estate transaction administrative authorities, so as to simplify the tax and certificate-related procedures for second-hand property transactions, reduce repetitive entry of the information of taxpayers and improve service efficiency.

(XIII) Promoting the cooperation between local SAT offices and local taxation bureaus: We shall encourage implementing the Cooperation Codes for Offices of the State Administration of Taxation and Local Taxation Bureaus (Version 3.0) which expand cooperative items from 44 to 51, improve cooperation programs, establish detailed implementation standards, and make such services be available to taxpayers of both local SAT offices and local taxation bureaus at the joint taxpayer service halls as registration of additional tax information, tax return declaration, invoice management, acceptance of application for tax incentives and tax certificate issuance, allowing taxpayers to enjoy more convenient services.

(XIV) Strengthening the supervision of service providers and the safeguard of the rights and interests of taxpayers: We shall fully respect taxpayers' opinions and permit them to select qualified VAT control system service providers at their discretion. SAT offices at different levels shall strengthen the supervision over service providers and impose penalties against violations such as non-quality service, illegal tie-in sales of equipment or software and arbitrary charges; expand access to 12366 hotline and other channels for taxpayer filing complaints, rigorously implement the Administrative Measures for Tax Service Complaints and effectively safeguard the legitimate rights and interests of taxpayers.

III. Actively using the analysis results to serve for economic development.

(XV) Actively serving for a favorable business environment: We shall further advance the effective implementation of the policies of replacing business tax with VAT on the basis of the analysis of the pilot program and give rein to the role of the reform in standardizing taxation economic order so as to create a more fair taxation environment and a better business market for taxpayers.

(XVI) Serving for forging new growth drivers for the economy: We shall mine the inner correlation between the analysis data of the pilot program and the operation of the economy, thoroughly analyze the changes in economic tax sources as a result of the pilot program, grasp the characteristics of economic structural changes and make proposals on economic growth, transformation and upgrading of economic structure and new growth drivers for the economy.

(XVII) Actively servicing for strengthening and improving social governance: We shall leverage the big data advantages derived from the analysis of the pilot program to properly respond to social concerns, promote the sharing of tax information, expand the application of such big data in strengthening social governance and public services and thus improve social governance.

IV. Actively using the analysis results to serve for taxation service improvement
(XVIII) Promoting targeted adjustments and improvements in policies: We shall

further open up feedback channels and optimize the mechanism for solving policy problems identified in the analysis.
With respect to the policies requiring improvement and adjustment, the tax authorities shall work with the fiscal authorities to conduct an in-depth investigation and research and solicit public opinions to provide the decision-making basis for the fiscal and tax authorities at the higher level.

(XIX) Carrying out targeted taxation administration improvement: We shall encourage the implementation of the Norms for National Tax Levy and Administration (Version 1.2) to suit the new requirements since the comprehensive implementation of the pilot program; conduct a detailed research into administrative issues identified in the analysis and take targeted measures; spare no efforts to promptly make remedies and rectification of the problems relating to operation and implementation and arrange for adjusting and improving the management systems and information systems with problems identified; establish and optimize the experience sharing mechanisms to learn from others and support each other in administration.

(XX) Strengthening targeted supervision and evaluation: We shall enhance targeted supervision and evaluation against major problems and weaknesses identified in the analysis and promptly make improvement; issue a notice of criticism to or hold to account those who fail to rectify problems or bolster weaknesses; constantly improve the services of the pilot program through rigorous supervision and evaluation.

7.6 Circulars on Specific Business Segments Published in 2016

Circular of the Ministry of Finance and the State Administration of Taxation on Further Specifying the Policies on Financial Industry under the Comprehensive Promotion of the Pilot Collection of Value-added Tax in Lieu of Business Tax Cai Shui.

No. 46 April 29, 2016.

Finance departments (bureaus), offices of the State Administration of Taxation and local tax bureaus of all provinces, autonomous regions, municipalities directly under the Central Government and cities specifically designated in the state plan, and the Finance Bureau of Xinjiang Production and Construction Corps, Upon research, the policies on financial industry during the implementation of the pilot collection of value-added tax ("VAT") in lieu of business tax ("BT") are notified in a supplementary manner as follows:

I. The interest income obtained by a financial institution from carrying out the following business belongs to that from inter-bank financial transactions mentioned in Paragraph 23 of Article 1 of the Provisions on Transitional Policies for the Pilot Program of the Collection of Value-added Tax in Lieu of Business Tax (Cai Shui [2016] No. 36, the "Provisions"):

1. Pledge-style purchase of financial instruments under resale agreement.
   Pledge-style purchase of financial instruments under resale agreement refers to a kind of short-term financing business carried out by both parties to a transaction with bonds and other financial instruments as the pledge of rights.
2. Holding of policy-based financial bonds.
   Policy-based financial bonds refer to the bonds issued by development and policy-based financial institutions.

II. According to Paragraph 21 of Article 1 of the Provisions, personal insurance with a term of one year or more and the return of principal and interest and exempted from VAT includes other annuity insurance, which refers to the annuity insurance other than pension annuity insurance.

III. The incomes from providing financial services obtained by rural credit cooperatives, rural banks, rural fund mutual-aid cooperatives, loan companies solely initiated and invested by banking institutions, and rural cooperative banks and rural commercial banks whose corporate bodies are located in regions at or below the county level (including county-level city, district and banner) maybe subject to VAT calculated and paid under the simple tax calculation method at a rate of 3%.

Rural banks refer to the banking financial institutions that are established in rural areas upon approval by the China Banking Regulatory Commission in accordance with the relevant laws and regulations and with the investment from domestic and overseas financial institutions, domestic non-financial institutions as legal persons and domestic natural persons, mainly for providing financial services for the development of local farmers, agriculture and rural economy.

Rural fund mutual-aid cooperatives refer to the community mutual-aid banking financial institutions incorporated upon approval by banking regulatory authorities and in the form of voluntary buying of shares thereof by farmers in countries (towns) and administrative villages and rural small enterprises, for providing deposit, loan, settlement and other services for members thereof.

Loan companies solely initiated and invested by banking institutions refer to the non-banking financial institutions that are established in rural areas, upon approval by the China Banking Regulatory Commission in accordance with the relevant laws and regulations, by domestic commercial banks or rural cooperative banks, especially for providing loan services for the development of county farmers, agriculture and rural economy.

The county (including county-level city, district and banner) does not include urban areas governed by municipalities directly under the Central Government and prefecture-level cities.

IV. For Agricultural Bank of China's sub-branches in counties (also called "business departments at the county level") that are under branches of provinces,

autonomous regions, municipalities directly under the Central Government and cities specifically designated in the state plan and under the branch of the Xinjiang Production and Construction Corps and included in the pilot reform of the "financial business department of agriculture, rural areas and farmers", their interest incomes from providing loans for peasant households, rural enterprises and other rural organizations (see the Appendix for the list of specific loans) may be subject to VAT calculated and paid under the simple tax calculation method at a rate of 3%.
Loans for peasant households refer to the loans granted by financial institutions to peasant households, excluding the petty loans for peasant households that are exempted from VAT as specified in Paragraph 19 of Article 1 of the Provisions. Peasant households refer to those mentioned in Paragraph 19 of Article 1 of the Provisions.
Loans for rural enterprises and other rural organizations refer to the loans granted by financial institutions to enterprises and organizations registered in rural areas.

V. This Circular shall take effect as of May 1, 2016.

Appendix: List of Agriculture-Related Loans Entitled to the Preferential VAT Policies.

1. Agricultural loans to legal persons
2. Forestry loans to legal persons
3. Animal husbandry loans to legal persons
4. Fisheries loans to legal persons
5. Loans for agriculture, forestry, animal husbandry and fishery service industries to legal persons
6. Other agriculture-related loans to legal persons (except agriculture-related loans to legal persons in respect of coal, tobacco, mining, real estate, urban infrastructure construction and other types)
7. Loans for small irrigation and water conservancy facilities
8. Improvement of large irrigation areas
9. Improvement of low or medium-yield farmland
10. Construction of flood and drought control and disaster mitigation systems
11. Loans for agricultural product processing
12. Loans for manufacture of agricultural means of production
13. Loans for circulation of agricultural materials
14. Loans for circulation of agricultural and sideline products
15. Loans for export of agricultural products
16. Loans for agricultural science and technology
17. Development of comprehensive agricultural production capacity
18. Construction of irrigation and water conservancy facilities
19. Construction of circulation facilities for agricultural products
20. Construction of other agricultural production infrastructure
21. Safe drinking water projects in rural areas
22. Construction of rural highways

23. Construction of rural energy
24. Construction of rural methane
25. Construction of other rural life infrastructure
26. Construction of rural educational facilities
27. Construction of rural sanitary facilities
28. Construction of rural cultural and sport facilities
29. Construction of forestry and ecological environment
30. Agricultural loans to individuals
31. Forestry loans to individuals
32. Animal husbandry loans to individuals
33. Fisheries loans to individuals
34. Loans for agriculture, forestry, animal husbandry and fishery service industries to individuals
35. Loans for other production and operation to peasant households
36. Educational loans to peasant households
37. Healthcare loans to peasant households
38. Housing loans to peasant households
39. Other consumption loans to peasant households.

Circular on Restoring the Export Rebate Rate for Highly Processed Corn Products Cai Shui.

No. 92 August 19, 2016.

Finance departments (bureaus) and offices of the State Administration of Taxation of all provinces, autonomous regions, municipalities directly under the Central Government and cities specifically designated in the state plan, and the Finance Bureau of Xinjiang Production and Construction Corps, Upon approval by the State Council, the export rebate rate of value-added tax for highly processed corn products such as corn starch and alcohol will be restored to be 13% as of September 1, 2016.

See the Appendix for the list of highly processed corn products. The export rebate rate applicable to the goods listed in this Circular shall be determined according to the export date marked on the export goods declaration form.

Appendix: List of Highly Processed Corn Products No. Product Code Product Name Rebate Rate (%) after the Adjustment 1 11081200 Corn starch 132 21039010 Monosodium glutamate 133 22071000 Unmodified ethyl alcohol with the concentration not less than 80% 13 4 23031000 Residue generated during the production of corn starch and similar articles 135 29054200 Pentaerythritol 136 29054300 Mannitol 137 29054400 Sorbitol 138 29181100 Lactic acid and lactate 139 29181600 Gluconic acid and gluconate 1310 29224110 Lysine 13.

Circular on Increasing the Export Tax Rebate Rates for Electromechanical Products, Refined Oils and Other Products Cai Shui.

No. 113 November 4, 2016.

The finance departments (bureaus) and offices of the state administration of taxation of all provinces, autonomous regions, municipalities directly under the Central

Government, cities specifically designated in the state plan, and the finance bureau of the Xinjiang Production and Construction Corps:

It is approved by the State Council to increase the export tax rebate rates for electromechanical products, refined oils and other products. The relevant matters are hereby notified as follows:

I. The export tax rebate rates for cameras, video cameras, internal combustion engines, gasoline, aviation fuel, diesel and other products have been increased to 17%. A list of products subject to the increase of export tax rebate rate is attached.
II. This Circular shall enter into force as of November 1, 2016. The export tax rebate rate applicable to the goods listed in this Circular is defined by the export date indicated on the declaration form for exported goods.

7.7 Circulars on VAT Rates for 2018

Circular of the Ministry of Finance and the State Administration of Taxation on Adjusting Value-added Tax Rates.

Cai Shui [2018] No. 32.

April 4, 2018.

Finance departments (bureaus), local SAT offices and local tax bureaus of all provinces, autonomous regions, municipalities directly under the Central Government, and cities separately listed in the State plan, and the Finance Bureau of Xinjiang Production and Construction Corps.

For the purpose of improving the value-added tax system, adjustments to relevant policies on VAT rates are notified as below:

I. Where a taxpayer engages in a taxable sales activity for the value-added tax (VAT) purpose or imports goods, the previous applicable 17 and 11% tax rates are adjusted to be 16 and 10% respectively.
II. The original 11% deduction rate, applicable to agricultural products bought by a taxpayer, will be lowered to 10%.
III. For agricultural products bought by a taxpayer for the production or sales purposes or for processing goods on a commission basis subject to 16% tax rate, the input VAT shall be calculated at the 12% deduction rate.
IV. Exported goods, originally subject to 17% tax rate and 17% export rebate rate, will be subject to a lower export rebate rate, a decrease to 16%, while exported goods and cross-border taxable activities, subject to 11% tax rate and 11% export rebate rate, will be subject to 10% export rebate rate.
V. For goods specified in Article IV exported by, and cross-border taxable activities specified in Article IV sold by a foreign trade enterprise before July 31, 2018, where VAT has been levied at the former rate, applicable before the adjustment, on such goods or activities when they are purchased, the export

rebate rate that applies before the adjustment shall still apply; however, if VAT is levied at the adjusted rate on such goods or activities when they are purchased, the adjusted export rebate rate shall apply. For goods specified in Article IV exported by, and cross-border taxable activities specified in Article IV sold by a manufacturer before July 31, 2018, the export rebate rate that applies before the adjustment shall still apply.
The time to implement the adjusted rebate rates for exported goods and the time when goods were exported, shall be determined based on the date of export set out on the export goods declaration, while the time to implement the adjusted rebate rates for cross-border taxable activities and the time when cross-border taxable activities were undertaken, shall be determined based on the date when the export invoice is issued.

VI. This Circular shall come into force as of May 1, 2018. Where there is any discrepancy between relevant former provisions and the VAT rates, deduction rates and export rebate rates specified in this Circular, this Circular shall prevail.

VII. All regions shall attach great importance to the adjustment of the VAT rates, be fully prepared in all aspects before the implementation of such adjustments, and work effectively on the monitoring, analysis, publicity and interpretations along the way when such adjustments are implemented, to ensure the effort to adjust VAT rates will proceed in a stable and orderly manner. In case of any issues, please timely report to the Ministry of Finance and the State Administration of Taxation.

7.8 Circulars on VAT Rates for 2019

Circular of the Ministry of Finance and the State Administration of Taxation on Implementing the Policy on Inclusive Tax Reliefs for Small and Micro Enterprises.

Cai Shui [2019] No.13.

January 17, 2019.

Finance departments (bureaus) of all provinces, autonomous regions, municipalities directly under the Central Government and cities specifically designated in the state plan, the Finance Bureau of Xinjiang Production and Construction Corps, and offices of the State Administration of Taxation in all provinces, autonomous regions, municipalities directly under the Central Government and cities specifically designated in the state plan.

In order to implement the decisions and arrangements of the CPC Central Committee and the State Council and further support the development of small and micro enterprises, the matters relating to the implementation of the policy on inclusive tax reliefs for small and micro enterprises are hereby notified as follows:

I. A small-scale value-added tax (VAT) payer whose monthly sales volume is no more than CNY 100,000 shall be exempted from VAT.

II. For small low-profit enterprises, the portion of less than CNY 1 million, and the portion of more than CNY 1 million but less than CNY 3 million, of the annual taxable income, will be included in the actual taxable income at 25% and 50% respectively, based on which the enterprise income tax payable will be calculated at the reduced tax rate of 20%.

The aforesaid small low-profit enterprise refers to an enterprise engaged in the industry not restricted or prohibited by the State and meeting three conditions, namely its annual taxable income is not more than CNY 3 million, the number of its employees is not more than 300, and its total assets are not more than CNY 50 million.

The number of employees consists of the number of staff members who have established labor relationships with the enterprise and the number of workers dispatched to the enterprise. The number of employees and the total assets shall be determined based on the quarterly average number of a single year. Specifically, the calculation formulas are given below:

$$\text{Quarterly average number} = (\text{number at the beginning of a quarter} + \text{number at the end of the quarter}/2$$

$$\text{Quarterly average number of a single year} = (\text{sum of four quarterly average numbers in a single year})/4$$

In the event that an enterprise commences its business or terminates its business activities in the middle of a year, the aforesaid indicators shall be determined with the actual business period as a tax year.

III. People's governments of provinces, autonomous regions, and municipalities directly under the Central Government may, in light of the actual local conditions and the needs of macro-control, determine that the resource tax, urban maintenance and construction tax, property tax, urban land use tax, stamp tax (excluding stock trading stamp tax), cultivated land occupation tax, education surcharge and local education surcharge imposed on small-scale VAT payers may be reduced within a tax rate range of 50%.

IV. Small-scale VAT payers who have enjoyed the resource tax, urban maintenance and construction tax, property tax, urban land use tax, stamp tax, cultivated land occupation tax, education surcharge, local education surcharge and other preferential policies may still enjoy the preferential policies stipulated in Article 3 hereof.

V. In the conditions for a technology-oriented start-up as stipulated in Item 1 of Article 2 of the Circular of the Ministry of Finance and the State Administration of Taxation on the Tax Policies for Venture Capital Enterprises and Individual Angel Investors (Cai Shui [2018] No. 55), "it employed up to 200 practitioners" is adjusted to "it employed up to 300 practitioners", and "neither its total assets nor annual sales revenues surpass CNY 30 million" is adjusted to "neither its total assets nor annual sales revenues surpass CNY 50 million".

For investments which are made between January 1, 2019 and December 31, 2021, last for two years and meet the provisions of the Circular and other conditions as stipulated in the Document (Cai Shui [2018] No. 55), the tax policies as stipulated in the Document (Cai Shui [2018] No. 55) may apply. For investments which are made within two years before January 1, 2019, last for two years as of January 1, 2019 and meet the provisions of the Circular and other conditions as stipulated in the Document (Cai Shui [2018] No. 55), the tax policies as stipulated in the Document (Cai Shui [2018] No. 55) may apply.

VI. The Circular shall be implemented from January 1, 2019 to December 31, 2021. The Circular of the Ministry of Finance and the State Administration of Taxation on Extending the Value-added Tax Policies for Small and Micro-sized Enterprises (Cai Shui [2017] No. 76) and the Circular of the Ministry of Finance and the State Administration of Taxation on Further Expanding the Coverage of the Preferential Income Tax Policy for Small Low-profit Enterprises (Cai Shui [2018] No. 77) shall be repealed simultaneously.

VII. Finance and taxation departments at all levels shall earnestly improve their political stance, thoroughly implement the decisions and arrangements of the CPC Central Committee and the State Council on the tax and fee reduction, fully understand the importance of, earnestly assume the primary responsibility for the implementation of and take as a major task, the inclusive tax reliefs for small and micro enterprises, strengthen organization and leadership, make careful planning and deployments, and implement the policy in full. They shall devote greater efforts and find innovative ways to strengthen publicity and guidance, optimize tax services, and facilitate the handling of tax affairs to ensure that taxpayers and contributors may enjoy the benefits of the policy on tax and fee reduction. They shall closely track the implementation of the policy, strengthen investigation and research, and provide timely feedback to the Ministry of Finance and the State Administration of Taxation on the outstanding issues and suggestions reflected in the implementation of the policy.

Announcement of the State Administration of Taxation on Issues concerning Tax Collection and Administration under the Value-added Tax Exemption Policy for Small-scale Taxpayers.

Announcement of the State Administration of Taxation [2019] No. 4.

January 19, 2019.

According to the Circular of the Ministry of Finance and the State Administration of Taxation on Implementing the Policy on Inclusive Tax Reliefs for Small and Micro Enterprises (Cai Shui [2019] No. 13), issues concerning tax collection and administration under the value-added tax exemption policy for small-scale taxpayers with monthly sales amounting to CNY 100,000 or below are hereby announced as follows:

I. A small-scale taxpayer that carries out sales acts subject to value-added tax (VAT) with total monthly sales amounting to CNY 100,000 or below (or quarterly sales amounting to CNY 300,000 or below if one quarter is a tax period, hereinafter the same) shall be exempted from VAT.
If a small-scale taxpayer carries out sales acts subject to VAT with total monthly sales amounting to more than CNY 100,000 which, after deducting the sales from selling real estate incurred in the current period, are less than CNY 100,000, its sales from selling goods, labor services, services and intangible assets shall be exempted from VAT.

II. For a small-scale taxpayer subject to VAT on the difference, the sales after deduction shall be used to determine whether it is entitled to the VAT exemption policy stipulated in the Announcement.
The relevant columns of "tax-free sales" in the Value-added Tax Return (Applicable to Small-scale Taxpayers) shall be filled in with the sales after deduction.

III. A small-scale taxpayer who pays tax on a periodic basis may choose to take one month or one quarter as a tax period which, once chosen, may not be changed for one fiscal year.

IV. If any of the other individuals referred to in Article 9 of the Implementing Rules for the Interim Value-added Tax Regulations of the People's Republic of China leases out his/her immovable property by collecting rental on a lump sum basis, his/her rental income may be apportioned evenly over the corresponding lease period; if the monthly rental income after apportionment is CNY 100,000 or below, he/she shall be exempted from VAT.

V. If a general taxpayer obtains cumulative sales of CNY 5 million or below for the 12 consecutive months (if one month is a tax period) or for the four consecutive quarters (if one quarter is a tax period) prior to the re-registration date, it may choose to be re-registered as a small-scale taxpayer prior to December 31, 2019.
Other matters relating to the re-registration of a general taxpayer as a small-scale taxpayer shall be subject to the relevant provisions of the Announcement of the State Administration of Taxation on Several Value-added Tax Issues related to the Harmonization of the Criteria for Small-scale Taxpayers (Announcement of the State Administration of Taxation [2018] No. 18) and the Announcement of the State Administration of Taxation on Export Tax Refund (Exemption) Issues related to the Harmonization of the Criteria for Small-scale Taxpayers (Announcement of the State Administration of Taxation [2018] No. 20).

VI. If a small-scale taxpayer that is required to make advance payment of VAT according to the existing provisions realizes monthly sales of CNY 100,000 or below in the place of advance payment, it need not make advance payment of VAT in the current period. If it has made advance payment of VAT before the issuance of the Announcement, it may apply to the competent tax authority of the place of advance payment for return of such advance payment.

VII. Whether entities and individual businesses within the scope of small-scale taxpayers shall make advance payment of VAT for their sales of immovable property shall be determined according to their tax period, Article 6 of the Announcement and other existing policies and provisions; other individuals shall continue to be exempted from VAT for their sales of immovable property in accordance with the existing provisions.

VIII. If a small-scale taxpayer with monthly sales of CNY 100,000 or below has paid tax in the current period due to the issuance of special VAT invoices, it may apply to the competent tax authority for a refund of such paid tax after all copies of the special VAT invoices are recovered or special red invoices are issued as required.

IX. If a small-scale taxpayer obtains sales of CNY 100,000 or below in January 2019 (or CNY 300,000 or below in the first quarter of 2019 if a quarter is a tax period) but has paid tax in the current period due to agent issuance of plain invoices, it may apply to the competent tax authority for a refund of such paid tax when handling its tax declaration.

X. A small-scale taxpayer with monthly sales of CNY 100,000 or below shall issue plain VAT invoices, unified invoices for the sale of motor vehicles, and electronic plain VAT invoices by use of the VAT invoice management system. For a small-scale taxpayer that has used the VAT invoice management system, if its monthly sales amount to CNY 100,000 or below, it may continue to use the existing tax control equipment to issue invoices; if it has issued special VAT invoices itself, it may continue to issue special VAT invoices itself and calculate and pay VAT based on the sales amount for which special VAT invoices have been issued.

XI. The Announcement shall come into force as of January 1, 2019. Item 2 of Article 3 and Item 4 of Article 6 of the Announcement of the State Administration of Taxation on Matters relating to Tax Levying and Administration concerning the Comprehensive Promotion of the Pilot Collection of Value-added Tax in lieu of Business Tax (Announcement of the State Administration of Taxation [2016] No. 23), Article 3 of the Announcement of the State Administration of Taxation on Specifying Several Issues concerning Tax Collection and Administration under the Pilot Program of Collection of Value-added Tax in Lieu of Business Tax (Announcement of the State Administration of Taxation [2016] No. 26), Article 2 of the Announcement of the State Administration of Taxation on Several Issues concerning the Tax Collection Administration under the Pilot Program of the Collection of Value-added Tax in Lieu of Business Tax (Announcement of the State Administration of Taxation [2016] No. 53) and the Announcement of the State Administration of Taxation on Issues concerning Exempting Small and Micro-sized Enterprises from Value-added Tax (Announcement of the State Administration of Taxation [2017] No. 52) shall be simultaneously repealed.

The Announcement is hereby given.

Announcement of the State Taxation Administration on Adjusting Matters Concerning the Declaration of Value-added Tax Returns.

Announcement of the State Taxation Administration [2019] No. 15.

March 21, 2019.

To implement the decisions and arrangements of the CPC Central Committee and the State Council on tax and fee cuts, further optimize tax services and ease the burden on taxpayers, the adjustments to matters concerning the declaration of value-added tax returns are hereby announced as follows:

I. In accordance with the decisions of the State Council on deepening the value-added tax reform, the Value-added Tax Return (Applicable to General Taxpayers), Schedule (I) to the Value-added Tax Return, Schedule (II) to the Value-added Tax Return, Schedule (III) to the Value-added Tax Return and Schedule (IV) to the Value-added Tax Return have been revised and re-promulgated.

II. As of the tax period for March 2019, the ending balance in Column 6 "Input VAT to Be Credited for Immovable Property at the End of the Current Period" in Schedule (V) to the Value-added Tax Return in Appendix 1 to the Announcement of the State Taxation Administration on Matters relating to the Declaration of Value-added Tax Returns after the Comprehensive Promotion of the Pilot Program of the Collection of Value-added Tax in Lieu of Business Tax (Announcement of the State Taxation Administration [2016] No. 13) may be carried over and filled out in Column 8b "Other" in Schedule (II) to the Value-added Tax Return upon the implementation hereof.

III. After this Announcement comes into effect, for declaration of taxable items previously subject to the original 16% or 10% VAT rate, taxpayers shall fill out the relevant columns of the adjusted form respectively according to the correspondence of items between the adjusted form and the old form.

IV. See Appendix 1 attached hereto for the revised Value-added Tax Return (Applicable to General Taxpayers) and its annexed schedules; see Appendix 2 attached hereto for the instructions on completing the relevant forms.

V. This Announcement shall become effective as of May 1, 2019. Schedule (V) to the Value-added Tax Return in Appendix 1 to the Announcement of the State Taxation Administration on Matters relating to the Declaration of Value-added Tax Returns after the Comprehensive Promotion of the Pilot Program of the Collection of Value-added Tax in Lieu of Business Tax (Announcement of the State Taxation Administration [2016] No. 13), the Announcement of the State Taxation Administration on Adjusting Certain Matters relating to the Declaration of Value-added Tax by Pilot Taxpayers Subject to the Collection of Value-added Tax in Lieu of Business Tax (Announcement of the State Taxation Administration [2016] No. 30) and the Announcement of the State Taxation Administration on Adjusting the Matters relating to the Declaration of Value-added Tax Returns (Announcement of the State Taxation Administration

[2017] No. 19) and the Announcement of the State Administration of Taxation on Adjusting Matters Concerning the Declaration of Value-added Tax Returns (Announcement of the State Taxation Administration [2018] No. 17) shall be repealed simultaneously.

This Announcement is hereby given.

7.9 Circular on Seeking Public Comments on the Law of the People's Republic of China on Value-added Tax (Draft for Comment)

Circular on Seeking Public Comments on the Law of the People's Republic of China on Value-added Tax (Draft for Comment).

November 27, 2019.

In order to improve tax laws and systems, enhance the public participation in legislation, extensively cohere social consensuses and promote scientific, democratic and public legislation, we have drafted the Law of the People's Republic of China on Value-added Tax (Draft for Comment), on which public comments are hereby sought. The public may make comments through the following channels and methods, prior to December 26, 2019.

1. Offer opinions by logging into the "Information Management System for Soliciting Opinions on Financial Laws and Regulations" (http://lisms.mof.gov.cn/lisms) on the homepage of the Ministry of Finance of the People's Republic of China (http://www.mof.gov.cn); or, the opinion collection system on the homepage of the State Taxation Administration (http://www.chinatax.gov.cn).
2. Offer opinions by sending correspondence to the address: the Law and Treaty Department of the Ministry of Finance, No. 3 Nansan Lane, Sanlihe, Xicheng District, Beijing Municipality, 100820, or, the Goods and Service Tax Department of the State Taxation Administration, No. 5 Yangfangdian West Road, Haidian District, Beijing Municipality, 100038, with the words "Soliciting Opinions on the Law on Value-added Tax" indicated on the envelope.

Law of the People's Republic of China on Value-added Tax (Draft for Comment)

Chapter I General Provisions

Article 1

In the case of transactions with value-added tax payable ("taxable transactions") as well as the import of goods within the territory of the People's Republic of China ("within the territory"), the value-added tax shall be paid in accordance with the Law.

Article 2

In the case of any taxable transaction, the value-added tax shall be calculated and paid as per the general tax calculation method, except where the State Council stipulates the application of a simplified tax calculation method.With respect to the import of goods, the value-added tax shall be calculated and paid as per the gross taxable price and applicable tax rate provided hereunder.

Article 3

Under the general tax calculation method, the taxable amount is calculated by the balance of output tax after deducting input tax.Under the simplified tax calculation method, the taxable amount is calculated by the taxable transaction sales value (the "sales value") and tax rate, with input tax not deducted.

Article 4

As the value-added tax is the tax excluded in the price, the taxable price of the taxable transactions excludes the value-added tax amount.

Chapter II Taxpayers and Parties Who Have the Obligation of Withholding Tax

Article 5

Entities and individuals that conduct the taxable transactions within the territory and with a sales value reaching the threshold for levying value-added tax, as well as consignees of imported goods are taxpayers of value-added tax.

The threshold for levying value-added tax is the quarterly sales value of CNY 300,000.

Entities and individuals with a sales value not reaching the threshold for levying value-added tax are not taxpayers specified hereunder, but they may voluntarily opt to pay value-added tax in accordance with the Law.

Article 6

For the purpose of the Law, entities refer to enterprises, administrative units, public institutions, military units, social organizations and other organizations.

For the purpose of the Law, individuals refer to individual businesses and natural persons.

Article 7

Concerning the taxable transactions within the territory conducted by entities and individuals outside the People's Republic of China ("outside the territory"), purchasers are parties who have the obligation of withholding tax.

If the State Council has any other provisions, such provisions shall prevail.

Chapter III Taxable Transactions

Article 8

Taxable transactions refer to sales of goods, services, intangible assets, real estate and financial commodities.

The sales of goods, real estate and financial commodities refer to the paid transfer of ownership of goods, real estate and financial commodities.

The sales of services refer to the paid provision of services.

The sales of intangible assets refer to the paid transfer of ownership or use right of intangible assets.

Article 9

Taxable transactions within the territory as set out in Article 1 hereof refer to:

1. as for the sales of goods, the starting place of carriage or location of the goods is within the territory;
2. as for the sales of services and intangible assets (except the use right of natural resources), sellers are domestic entities and individuals, or services and intangible assets are consumed within the territory;
3. as for the sales of real estate and the transfer of use rights of natural resources, the location of real estate and natural resources is within the territory; and
4. as for the sales of financial commodities, sellers are domestic entities and individuals, or financial commodities.

Article 10

The import of goods means that the starting place of carriage of goods is outside the territory, and the destination is within the territory.

Article 11

The following circumstances shall be deemed as taxable transactions, and value-added tax shall be paid pursuant to the Law:

1. entities and individual businesses use goods which are self-produced or entrusted to be processed for collective welfare or individual consumption;
2. entities and individual businesses freely donate goods, except for use for public welfare;
3. entities and individuals freely donate intangible assets, real estate or financial commodities, except for the use for public welfare; and
4. any other circumstance stipulated by the competent departments for finance and taxation under the State Council.

Article 12

The following items are deemed as non-taxable transactions, and no value-added tax will be levied:

1. services provided by an employee with salary or wage paid for an employment unit or employer;
2. administrative and institutional fees and government funds collected by administrative institutions;
3. compensation obtained due to collection and expropriation;
4. income from deposit interests; and
5. any other circumstance stipulated by the competent departments for finance and taxation under the State Council.

Chapter IV Tax Rates and Levying Rate

Article 13

Value-added tax rates:

1. Taxpayers that sell goods, processing, repair, replacement or tangible personal property leasing services or import goods and do not fall within the scope as specified in Item 2, Item 4 or Item 5 of this Article shall be subject to a 13% tax rate.
2. Taxpayers that sell transport services, postal services, basic telecommunication services, construction services, or real property leasing services, sell real property, transfer land use rights, or sell or import the goods listed below and do not fall within the scope as specified in Item 4 or Item 5 of this Article shall be subject to a 9% tax rate:

   (1) agricultural products, edible vegetable oil, and common salt;
   (2) tap water, heat supply, air-conditioning, hot water, gas, liquefied petroleum gas, natural gas, dimethyl ether, methane and civil-use coal products;
   (3) books, newspapers, magazines, audio-visual products, and electronic publications; and
   (4) feeds, chemical fertilizers, pesticides, agricultural machinery and mulching films.

3. Taxpayers that sell services, intangible assets or financial commodities and do not fall within the scope as specified in Item 1, Item 2 and Item 5 of this Article shall be subject to a 6% tax rate.
4. Taxpayers who export goods are subject to a zero tax rate, unless otherwise specified by the State Council.
5. Domestic entities and individuals that sell services or intangible assets under the scope specified by the State Council across borders are subject to a zero tax rate.

Article 14

The levying rate of the value-added tax is 3%.

Chapter V Taxable Amount

Article 15

Sales value refers to the consideration obtained by a taxpayer due to a taxable transaction, including all monetary or non-monetary economic benefits and excluding the output tax calculated as per the general tax calculation method and the taxable amount calculated as per the simplified tax calculation method.

Where the State Council provides that the sales value may be calculated by difference, such provisions shall prevail.

Article 16

Where any transaction is deemed as a taxable transaction and the sales value is in a non-monetary form, the sales value shall be determined as per the fair market value.

Article 17

Sales value shall be calculated in Renminbi. Taxpayers who sell goods in currencies other than Renminbi shall convert their sales value into Renminbi.

Article 18

Where the sales value of a taxpayer is significantly lower or higher and there is no reasonable commercial purpose, the tax authority will be entitled to verify its sales value by a reasonable method.

Article 19

The output tax refers to the value-added tax calculated by multiplying the sales value by the tax rate provided hereunder for a taxable transaction of a taxpayer. The formula for the calculation of the output tax is as follows:

$$\text{Output Tax} = \text{Sales Value} \times \text{Tax Rate}$$

Article 20

The input tax refers to the value-added tax paid or undertaken by a taxpayer for the goods, services, intangible assets, real estate and financial commodities purchased by it and relating to the taxable transaction.

Article 21

The taxable amount calculated as per the general tax calculation method refers to the balance of output tax offsetting input tax in the current period. The formula for the calculation of the taxable amount is as follows:

$$\begin{aligned}\text{Taxable Amount} &= \text{Output Tax in the Current Period}\\ &\quad - \text{Input Tax in the Current Period}\end{aligned}$$

where the input tax in the current period is more than the output tax in the current period, the balance may be carried forward to the next period for continuous deduction; or, be returned. Specific methods will be formulated by the competent departments for finance and taxation under the State Council.

The input tax shall be deducted by virtue of legitimate and effective vouchers.

Article 22

The following input tax shall not be deducted from output tax:

1. input tax corresponding to goods, services, intangible assets, real property and financial commodities purchased for items subject to the simplified tax calculation method, items exempted from value-added tax, or for collective welfare or personal consumption. In particular, the involved fixed assets, intangible assets and real estate only refer to those specially used for the aforesaid items;
2. input tax corresponding to items damaged or lost in abnormal circumstances;
3. input tax corresponding to catering services, daily services for residents and entertainment services purchased and directly used for consumption;
4. input tax corresponding to loan services purchased; and
5. other input taxes stipulated by the State Council.

Article 23

The taxable amount calculated as per the simplified tax calculation method refers to the value-added tax calculated as per the sales value and levying rate in the current period, with no input tax deducted. The formula for the calculation of the taxable amount is as follows:

$$\text{Taxable Amount} = \text{Sales Value in the Current Period} \times \text{Levying Rate}$$

Article 24

Taxpayers who import goods shall calculate their taxable amount by multiplying the gross taxable price by the tax rates provided hereunder. The formulae for the gross taxable price and the taxable amount are as follows:

$$\begin{aligned}\text{Gross Taxable Price} &= \text{Price after Customs Duty} + \text{Customs Duty}\\ &\quad + \text{Consumption Tax}\\ \text{Taxable Amount} &= \text{Gross Taxable Price} \times \text{Tax Rate}\end{aligned}$$

The price after customs duty excludes the consideration related to service trade.

Article 25

Where a taxpayer can select the simplified tax calculation method as per provisions of the State Council, once the said method is selected, it shall not be changed within 36 months.

Article 26

Taxpayers who conduct taxable transactions subject to different tax rates or levying rates shall separately calculate the sales value based on the applicable tax rates or levying rates. Where the sales values are not calculated separately, the higher tax rate applies.

Article 27

Where one taxable transaction of a taxpayer involves two or more tax rates or levying rates, the primary tax rate or levying rate applies.

Article 28

Where the party who has the obligation of withholding tax withholds tax as per Article 7 hereof, the said party shall calculate the tax to be withheld by multiplying the sales value by the tax rate. The formula for the calculation of the tax to be withheld is as follows:

$$\text{Tax To Be Withheld} = \text{Sales Value} \times \text{Tax Rate}$$

Chapter VI Tax Preferences

Article 29

The items listed below shall be exempted from value-added tax:

1. agricultural products produced and sold by agricultural producers themselves;
2. prophylactic drugs and devices;
3. antique books;
4. imported instruments and equipment to be directly used in scientific research, scientific experiments and teaching;
5. materials and equipment imported by foreign governments and international organizations for gratis aid;
6. products exclusively for the disabled directly imported by organizations for the disabled;
7. sales of goods used by sellers themselves;
8. nursing services provided by nurseries, kindergartens, homes for the aged and welfare institutions for the handicapped, matchmaking and funeral services;
9. services provided by individuals with disabilities;
10. medical services provided by hospitals, clinics and other medical institutions;
11. education services provided by schools and other education institutions, and services provided by students under a work-study program;
12. agricultural mechanical plough, irrigation and drainage, insect control, plant protection, agriculture and animal husbandry insurance as well as relevant technical training business, and the hybridization and disease prevention and treatment of poultry, livestock and aquatic animals;

13. ticket proceeds from cultural activities organized by memorials, museums, cultural centers, administrative institutions for heritage conservation units, arty galleries, exhibition centers, painting and calligraphy academies and libraries, and those from cultural and religious activities organized by religious venues; and
14. insurance products provided by domestic insurance agencies for exported goods.

Article 30

In addition to the provisions hereof, as per demands of national economic and social development or in the case of great influence of emergencies and other reasons on the business activities of taxpayers, the State Council may formulate special preferential policies of value-added tax, and report them to the Standing Committee of the Sixth National People's Congress for record-filing.

Article 31

Taxpayers who are concurrently trading in items exempted from value-added tax and with value-added tax deductible shall separately calculate the sales value of such items so that sales values not separately calculated shall not be exempted or deductible.

Article 32

Where a taxpayer conducts a taxable transaction subject to provisions on exemption from or deduction of value-added tax, the taxpayer may waive the exemption or deduction, and pay the value-added tax pursuant to the Law.

Where a taxpayer is subject to two or more exempted or deductible items, the taxpayer may waive the exemption or deduction by different exempted and deductible items.

Tax will not be exempted from or deducted for exempted or deductible items waived within 36 months.

Chapter VII Tax Payment Time and Places

Article 33

The time when value-added tax liability occurs (the "tax point") shall be determined as below:

1. In the case of any taxable transaction, the tax point shall be the date on which the full payment is made or the receipt of the payment is delivered. Should the invoice be issued in advance, the tax point shall be the date on which the invoice is issued;
2. Where it is deemed that a taxable transaction occurs, the tax point shall be the date on which the taxable transaction finishes; and
3. For imported goods, the tax point shall be the date on which the goods enter the customs area.

The tax point for withholding value-added tax shall be the date on which value-added tax liability on taxpayers occurs.

Article 34

Localities accepting value-added tax payments shall be determined as below:

1. A taxpayer with a fixed production and business place shall file tax returns with the competent tax authority at the location of the party's office or domicile; Headquarters and local offices located in different counties (cities) shall separately file tax returns with the competent local tax authorities in their localities. Upon approval of the competent departments for finance and taxation under the State Council or the authorized departments for finance and taxation, headquarters may file tax returns with the competent tax authorities within their localities for themselves and their local offices;
2. A taxpayer without a fixed production and business place shall file tax returns with the competent tax authority where the taxable transaction occurs; if the taxpayer fails to file tax returns, the competent tax authority at the location of the party's office or domicile supplementarily levies the tax;
3. A natural person, who provides building services, sells or leases real estate or transfers the use right of natural resources, shall file tax returns with the competent tax authority at the place of occurrence of building services or at the location of the real estate or natural resources;
4. A taxpayer of imported goods shall file tax returns with the Customs at the place of customs declaration; and
5. The party who has the obligation of withholding tax shall file tax returns for the withheld tax with the competent tax authority at the location of the party's office or domicile.

Article 35

The value-added tax period shall be ten days, 15 days, one month, one quarter or half a year. The specific tax period of a taxpayer shall be determined by the competent taxation authority based on the taxable amount. The provision on the half-a-year tax period does not apply to taxpayers calculating the tax as per the general tax calculation method. A natural person who is unable to pay value-added tax on a periodical basis may pay tax after every single transaction.

Taxpayers whose tax periods are on a monthly, quarterly or half-a-year basis shall file tax returns within 15 days after the end of the tax period. Taxpayers whose tax periods are on the tenth or 15th day of each month shall pre-pay tax within five days after the end of the tax period, and, between the first and 15th days of the following month, file tax returns and settle the balance of the taxable amount for the previous month.

The periods for tax calculation and filing of tax returns for parties who have the obligation of withholding tax shall be fixed in line with the previous two paragraphs.

Taxpayers who import goods shall pay tax within 15 days after the Customs sends out the Customs Import Value-added Tax Payment Notice.

Chapter VIII Collection and Administration

Article 36

Value-added tax shall be levied by tax authorities. The tax authorities entrust the Customs to levy value-added tax on imported goods by proxy.

The Customs shall share the information on the value-added tax levied by proxy and the tax declaration for exported goods with tax authorities.

The calculation and levying methods of value-added tax on articles carried or posted by individuals to China will be formulated by the State Council.

Article 37

A taxpayer shall faithfully file value-added tax returns with the competent tax authority, and submit the value-added tax returns and relevant tax payment materials.

Where a taxpayer exporting goods, services or intangible assets is subject to zero tax rate, the taxpayer shall declare a tax refund (exemption) to the competent tax authority. The practical rules shall be drafted by the competent department for taxation under the State Council.

The party who has the obligation to withhold tax shall faithfully submit the withholding and payment report form as well as other relevant materials required by the tax authority according to the actual needs.

Article 38

Two or more taxpayers meeting the stipulated conditions may be consolidated for tax payment. The practical rules shall be drafted by the competent departments for finance and taxation under the State Council.

Article 39

In the case of a taxable transaction, a taxpayer shall faithfully issue an invoice.

Article 40

A taxpayer shall use invoices as per provisions. Where any taxpayer fails to use an invoice as per provisions, punishments will be imposed as per the relevant laws and administrative regulations. If the circumstances are serious and a crime is constituted, the taxpayer shall be investigated for criminal liability according to laws.

Article 41

A taxpayer shall issue value-added tax invoices by tax-control facilities.

Article 42

A tax authority shall be entitled to conduct tax inspections in terms of the use of invoices, tax declaration, tax exemption and deduction and so on of taxpayers.

Article 43

A taxpayer shall pay the value-added tax as per provisions, with specific measures to the formulated by the State Council.

Article 44

The relevant departments of the State shall coordinate with tax authorities regarding value-added tax management activities according to laws, administrative regulations and respective duties. Tax authorities, banks, the Customs, foreign exchange administrations, market supervision departments and so on shall establish a value-added tax information sharing and work coordination mechanism, and strengthen the value-added tax levying and administration.

Chapter IX Supplementary Provisions

Article 45

Where it is truly necessary to renew the tax policies released before the publication of the Law, the renewal may last at the latest till the end of five years following the effectiveness of the Law, as stipulated by the State Council.

Article 46

The State Council will formulate the implementing regulations in accordance with the Law.

Article 47

The Law shall come into force as of XX, 20XX. The Decision of the Standing Committee of the National People's Congress concerning the Application of Interim Regulations on Such Taxes as Value-added Tax, Consumption Tax and Business Tax to Enterprises with Foreign Investment and Foreign Enterprises (Order of the President of the People's Republic of China No. 18) and the Interim Value-added Tax Regulations of the People's Republic of China (Order of the State Council of the People's Republic of China No. 691) shall be abolished simultaneously.

Chapter 8
Other Relevant VAT Provisions

8.1 Collection of Circulars and Other Regulations from 1993 to 1997

Value Added Tax (VAT) Law.

Interim Regulations of the People's Republic of China on Value-added Tax.

No. 134 of the State Council, December 13, 1993.

Article 1

All units and individuals engaged in the sales of goods, provision of processing, repairs and replacement services, and the importation of goods within the territory of the People's Republic of China are taxpayers of Value-added Tax (hereinafter referred to as 'taxpayers'), and shall pay VAT in accordance with these Regulations.

Article 2

VAT rates:

(1) For taxpayers selling or importing goods, other than those stipulated in subparagraphs (2) and (3) of this Article, the tax rate shall be 17%.
(2) For taxpayers selling or importing the following goods, the tax rate shall be 13%.

   i. Food grains, edible vegetable oils;
   ii. Tap water, heating, air conditioning, hot water, coal gas, liquefied petroleum gas, natural gas, methane gas, coal/charcoal products for household use;
   iii. Books, newspapers, magazines;
   iv. Feeds, chemical fertilizers, agricultural chemicals, agricultural machinery and covering plastic film for farming;
   v. Other goods as regulated by the State Council.

L. Riccardi and G. Riccardi, *China VAT*,
https://doi.org/10.1007/978-981-15-5967-9_8

(3) For taxpayers exporting goods, the tax rate shall be 0%, except as otherwise stipulated by the State Council.
(4) For taxpayers providing processing, repairs and replacement services (hereinafter referred to as 'taxable services'), the tax rate shall be 17%.
Any adjustments to the tax rates shall be determined by the State Council.

Article 3

For taxpayers dealing in goods or providing taxable services with different tax rates, the sales amounts for goods or taxable services with different tax rates shall be accounted for separately. If the sales amounts have not been accounted for separately, the higher tax rate shall apply.

Article 4

Except as stipulated in Article 13 of these Regulations, for taxpayers engaged in the sales of goods or the provision of taxable services (hereinafter referred to as 'selling goods or taxable services'), the tax payable shall be the balance of output tax for the period after deducting the input tax for the period. The formula for computing the tax payable is as follows:

$$\text{Tax payable} = \text{Output tax payable for the period} - \text{Input tax for the period}$$

If the output tax for the period is less than and insufficient to offset against the input tax for the period, the excess input tax can be carried forward for set-off in the following periods.

Article 5

For taxpayers selling goods or taxable services, the output tax shall be the VAT payable calculated based on the sales amounts and the tax rates prescribed in Article 2 of these Regulations and collected from the purchasers.

The formula for computing the output tax is as follows:

$$\text{Output tax} = \text{Sales amount} * \text{Tax rate}$$

Article 6

The sales amount shall be the total consideration and all other charges receivable from the purchasers by the taxpayer selling goods or taxable services, but excluding the output tax collectible.

The sales amount shall be computed in Renminbi. The sales amount of the taxpayer settled in foreign currencies shall be converted into Renminbi according to exchange rate prevailing in the foreign exchange market.

Article 7

Where the price used by the taxpayer in selling goods or taxable services is obviously low and without proper justification, the sales amount shall be determined by the competent tax authorities.

Article 8

For taxpayers who purchase goods or receive taxable services (hereinafter referred to as 'purchasing goods or taxable services'), VAT paid or borne shall be the input tax.

The amount of input tax that can be credited against the output tax, other than the situations specified in Paragraph 3 of this Article, shall be restricted to the amount of VAT payable as indicated on the following VAT credit document:

(1) VAT indicated in the special VAT invoices obtained from the sellers;
(2) VAT indicated on the tax payment receipts obtained from the customs office.

The creditable input tax for the purchasing of tax-exempt agricultural products is calculated based on a deemed deduction rate at 10% on the actual purchasing price. The formula for calculating the input tax is as follows:

$$\text{Input tax} = \text{Purchasing price} \ast \text{Deduction rate}$$

Article 9

Where taxpayers purchasing goods or taxable services have not obtained and kept the VAT credit document in accordance with the regulations, or the VAT payable and other relevant items in accordance with the regulations are not indicated on the VAT credit document, no input tax shall be credited against the output tax.

Article 10

Input tax on the following items shall not be credited against the output tax:

(1) Fixed assets purchased;
(2) Goods purchased or taxable services used for non-taxable items;
(3) Goods purchased or taxable services used for tax exempt items;
(4) Goods purchased or taxable services used for group welfare or personal consumption;
(5) Abnormal losses of Goods purchased;
(6) Goods purchased or taxable services consumed in the production of work-in progress or finished goods which suffer abnormal losses.

Article 11

Small-scale taxpayers engaged in selling goods or taxable services shall use a simplified method for calculating the tax payable.

The criteria for small-scale taxpayers shall be regulated by the Ministry of Finance.

Article 12

The rate leviable on the small-scale taxpayers selling goods or taxable services shall be 6%.

Any adjustment to the leviable rate shall be determined by the State Council.

Article 13

For small-scale taxpayers selling goods or taxable services, the tax payable shall be calculated based on the sales amount and the leviable rate prescribed in Article 12 of these Regulations. No input tax shall be creditable.

The formula for calculating the tax payable is as follows:

$$\text{Tax payable} = \text{Sales amount} * \text{leviable rate}$$

The sales amount shall be determined in accordance with the stipulations of Article 6 and Article 7 of these Regulations.

Article 14

Small-scale taxpayers with sound accounting who can provide accurate taxation information may, upon the approval of the competent tax authorities, not be treated as small-scale taxpayers. The tax payable shall be computed pursuant to the relevant stipulations of these Regulations.

Article 15

For taxpayers importing goods, tax payable shall be computed based on the composite assessable price and the tax rates prescribed in Article 2 of these Regulations. No tax will be credited. The formulas for computing the composite assessable price and the tax payable are as follows:

$$\begin{aligned}\text{Composite assessable price} &= \text{Customs dutiable value} \\ &\quad + \text{Customs Duty} + \text{Consumption Tax} \\ \text{Tax payable} &= \text{Composite assessable price} * \text{Tax rate}\end{aligned}$$

Article 16

The following items shall be exempt from VAT:

(1) Self-produced agricultural products sold by agricultural producers;
(2) Contraceptive medicines and devices;
(3) Antique books;
(4) Importation of instruments and equipment directly used in scientific research, experiment and education;
(5) Importation of materials and equipment from foreign governments and international organizations as assistance free of charge;

(6) Equipment and machinery required to be imported under contract processing, contract assembly and compensation trade;
(7) Articles imported directly by organizations for the disabled for special use by the disabled;
(8) Sale of goods which have been used by the sellers.

Except as stipulated in the above paragraph, the VAT exemption and reduction items shall be regulated by the State Council. Local Governments or departments shall not regulate any tax exemption or reduction items.

Article 17

For taxpayers engaged in tax exempt or tax reduced items, the sales amounts for tax exempt or tax reduced items shall be accounted for separately. If the sales amounts have not been separately accounted for, no exemption or reduction is allowed.

Article 18

For taxpayers whose sales amounts have not reached the VAT minimum threshold stipulated by the Ministry of Finance, the VAT shall be exempt.

Article 19

The time at which a liability to VAT arises is as follows:

(1) For sales of goods or taxable services, it is the date on which the sales sum is received or the documented evidence of right to collect the sales sum is obtained.
(2) For importation of goods, it is the date of import declaration.

Article 20

VAT shall be collected by the tax authorities. VAT on the importation of goods shall be collected by the customs office on behalf of the tax authorities.

VAT on self-used articles brought or mailed into China by individuals shall be levied together with Customs Duty. The detailed measures shall be formulated by the Tariff Policy Committee of the State Council together with the relevant departments.

Article 21

Taxpayers selling goods or taxable services shall issue special VAT invoices to the purchasers. Sales amounts and output tax shall be separately indicated in the special VAT invoices.

Under one of the following situations, the invoice to be issued shall be an ordinary invoice rather than the special VAT invoice:

(1) Sale of goods or taxable services to consumers;
(2) Sale of VAT exempt goods;
(3) Sale of goods or taxable services by small-scale taxpayers.

Article 22

The place for the payment of VAT is as follows:

(1) Businesses with a fixed establishment shall report and pay tax with the local competent tax authorities where the establishment is located. If the head office and branch are not situated in the same county (or city), they shall report and pay tax separately with their respective local competent tax authorities. The head office may, upon the approval of the State Administration of Taxation or its authorised tax authorities, report and pay tax on a consolidated basis with the local competent tax authorities where the head office is located.
(2) Businesses with a fixed establishment selling goods in a different county (or city) shall apply for the issuance of an outbound business activities tax administration certificate from the local competent tax authorities where the establishment is located and shall report and pay tax with the local competent tax authorities where the establishment is located. Businesses selling goods and taxable services in a different county (or city) without the outbound business activities tax administration certificate issued by the local competent tax authorities where the establishment is located, shall report and pay tax with the local competent tax authorities where the sales activities take place. The local competent tax authorities where the establishment is located shall collect the overdue tax which has not been reported and paid to the local competent tax authorities where the sales activities take place.
(3) Businesses without a fixed base selling goods or taxable services shall report and pay tax with the local competent tax authorities where the sales activities take place.
(4) For importation of goods, the importer or his agent shall report and pay tax to the customs office where the imports are declared.

Article 23

The VAT assessable period shall be one day, three days, five days, ten days, fifteen days or one month.

The actual assessable period of the taxpayer shall be determined by the competent tax authorities according to the magnitude of the tax payable of the taxpayer; tax that cannot be assessed in regular periods may be assessed on a transaction-by-transaction basis.

Taxpayers that adopt one month as an assessable period shall report and pay tax within ten days following the end of the period. If an assessable period of one day, three days, five days, ten days or fifteen days is adopted, the tax shall be prepaid within five days following the end of the period and a monthly return shall be filed with any balance of tax due settled within ten days from the first day of the following month.

Article 24

Taxpayers importing goods shall pay tax within seven days after the issuance of the tax payment certificates by the customs office.

Article 25

Taxpayers exporting goods with the applicable 0% tax rate shall, upon completion of export procedures with the customs office, apply for the tax refund on those export goods to the tax authorities on a monthly basis based on such relevant documents as the export declaration document. The detailed measures shall be formulated by the State Administration of Taxation.

Where the return of goods or the withdrawal of the customs declaration occurs after the completion of the tax refund on the export goods, the taxpayer shall repay the tax refunded according to the laws.

Article 26

The collection and administration of VAT shall be conducted in accordance with the relevant provisions of the Law of the People's Republic of China on Administration of Tax Collection and relevant provisions of these Regulations.

Article 27

The collection of VAT from enterprises with foreign investment and foreign enterprises shall be conducted in accordance with the resolutions of the Standing Committee of the National People's Congress.

Article 28

The Ministry of Finance shall be responsible for the interpretation of these Regulations and for the formulation of the rules for the implementation of these Regulations.

Article 29

These Regulations shall enter into force as of January 1, 1994. The Regulations (Draft) of the People's Republic of China on Value-added Tax and the Regulations (Draft) of the People's Republic of China on Product Tax promulgated by the State Council on September 18, 1984 shall be repealed simultaneously.

Rules for the Implementation of the Provisional Regulations on Value Added Tax of the People's Republic of China.

No. 38 of the Ministry of Finance on Dec. 25, 1993.

Article 1

These Rules are formulated in accordance with Article 28 of the "Provisional Regulations on Value Added Tax of the People's Republic of China" (hereinafter referred to as "the Regulations").

Article 2

"Goods" mentioned in Article 1 of the Regulations refer to tangible movable objects including electricity, heat and gas.

"Processing" mentioned in Article 1 of the Regulations refers to the business of processing in compliance with the requirements of the consignor on contracts with the raw material and other main materials provided by the consignor for processing charges in return.

"Repairs and Replacements" mentioned in Article 1 of the Regulations refer to the business of making repairs and/or replacing parts with parts provided on goods damaged or having lost functions for the purpose of restoring the functions thereof.

Article 3

"Sales of goods" mentioned in Article 1 of the Regulations refers to the paid transfer of the proprietary right of goods.

"Providing services of processing, repairs and replacements" mentioned in Article 1 of the Regulations refers to paid services of processing, repairs and replacements. However, this excludes like services provided by the employees for the employing units or individual operators.

"Paid" in these Rules covers remunerations in currency, in kind and other economic interests obtained from the buyer.

Article 4

The activities of an institution or individual operator cited below shall be deemed as sales of goods:

1. Consigning goods to a consignee to be marketed;
2. Marketing goods on consignment;
3. A taxpayer having two or more institutions under unified accounting taking goods from one institution to other(s) for sale, unless the said institutions are located in the same county (city);
4. Using goods made on his own or on consignment in non-taxable items;
5. Making investment in another institution or individual operator with goods made on his own or on consignment or goods purchased;
6. Distributing goods made by the operator, on consignment or purchased to shareholders or investors;
7. Using goods made on his own or on consignment for collective welfare or individual consumption; and
8. Giving goods made on his own or on consignment as presents to others.

Article 5

A marketing activity involving both goods and non-taxable labour service shall be deemed mixed marketing activity. The mixed marketing activities of an enterprise, public institution or individual operator engaged in manufacturing, wholesale or retail business shall be deemed as being engaged in marketing goods and liable to value added tax (VAT); the mixed marketing activities of other institutions and individuals shall be deemed selling non-taxable labour service which is free from VAT.

The tax collecting departments under the State Administration of Taxation shall determine whether a taxpayer's marketing activity is a mixed marketing activity or not.

"Non-taxable labour service" mentioned in paragraph one of this Article refers to the labour services included in the scope of taxable items in the industries of transport and communications, construction, banking and insurance, postal and telecommunications, cultural and sports undertakings, entertainment and service trades liable to business tax.

"An enterprise, public institution or individual operator engaged in manufacturing, wholesale or retail business" mentioned in paragraph of this Article includes an enterprise, public institution or individual operator engaged in the production, wholesale or retail business of goods as the main line and also in providing non-taxable labour service as a side-line.

Article 6

A taxpayer engaged in non-taxable labour services as a side-line shall compute the volumes of goods and taxable service and non-taxable labour service separately. Without separate computations or without accurate computations, the non-taxable labour service shall be included into those liable for VAT.

It shall be up to the tax collecting department of the State Administration of Taxation to determine whether the non-taxable service should be included into those liable for VAT.

Article 7

"Goods marketed within the territory of the People's Republic of China" mentioned in Article 1 of the Regulations refer to goods originating in or located in China.

"Taxable service provided within the territory of China" mentioned in Article 1 of the Regulations refers to the sold service that takes place in China.

Article 8

"Institutions" mentioned in Article 1 of the Regulations refer to state-owned enterprises, collective enterprises, private enterprises, joint stock enterprises, other enterprises, administrative undertakings, other public institutions, military institutions, social organizations and other institutions.

"Individuals" mentioned in Article 1 of the Regulations refer to individual business operators and other individuals.

Article 9

When an enterprise is leased or contracted to another person, the lessee or contractor shall be the taxpayer.

Article 10

For a taxpayer engaged in marketing goods and taxable services at different tax rates and in providing non-taxable services subject to VAT, the non-taxable services shall be levied VAT at the higher rate thereof.

Article 11

When a taxpayer other than a small-scale taxpayer (hereinafter referred to as "general taxpayer") refunds VAT to the buyer on account of the sold goods having returned for the full amount of the price or at a discount, the VAT shall be deducted from the current sales tax on the goods thus returned; and the VAT retrieved on account of the purchased goods having returned for the full amount of the price or at a discount shall be deducted from the current tax paid on the goods.

Article 12

"The other charges in addition to the price of the goods" mentioned in Article 6 of the Regulations refer to commissions, subsidies, funds, capital contributions, returned profits, awards, fines for defaults (interests for delayed payment), packaging charges, rents on packaging material, storage charges, quality surcharges, charges on loading/unloading, collection trusted, payments on behalf of others and all other charges paid in addition to the price of goods. But the following are excluded:

1. The tax on the sales of goods collected from the buyer.
2. The consumption tax on the consumer goods used in the processing of goods on consignment collected or paid on behalf of others.
3. Freight charges paid in advance which meet the following conditions:

   (1) The freight charge invoice is issued by the consignee to the buyer,
   (2) The freight charge invoice is forwarded by the taxpayer to the buyer.

All charges paid in addition to the price of the goods shall be added to the sales amount for computation of taxation, regardless of the accounting system.

Article 13

As for the mixed marketing activities and side-line non-taxable labour services which are liable to VAT in accordance with Article 5 and Article 6 of these Rules, the amount of sales thereof may be the aggregate of the sales of the goods and the sales of the non-taxable services or the aggregate of the sales of the goods or taxable services and the sales of non-taxable services.

Article 14

When a general taxpayer chooses the method of fixing the price sales for the goods for sale by adding up sales amount and tax on the sales, the following formula shall apply:

$$\text{Sales amount} = \text{sales amount including tax}/(1 + \text{tax rate})$$

Article 15

When a taxpayer settles his sales amount in a foreign currency, the sales amount shall be converted into RMB either at the Chinese official exchange rate of the day of settlement or of the first day of the current month (the average rate in principle) in accordance with the provisions of Article 6 of the Regulations. The taxpayer shall announce his decision on which rate to choose in advance, and once decided, there shall be no further change in a year.

Article 16

When a taxpayer's goods are sold or services taxable provided at a conspicuously low price without a proper reason as cited in Article 7 of the Regulations or when a taxpayer's activity without indication of the sales amount is deemed as sales of goods as provided in Article 4 of these Rules, the amount of sales shall be determined in order as follows:

1. At the average price of the goods of the same category sold in the same month;
2. At the average price of the goods of the same category sold in a recent period of time;
3. At the taxable value of the goods. The formula for computing the taxable value is:

$$\text{The taxable value} = \text{costs} \times (1 + \text{ratio of profit to cost})$$

With regard to goods subject to consumption tax, the consumption tax shall be added to the taxable value thereof.

The "cost" in the formula above refers to the actual production cost of the goods produced by the taxpayer for sale, or if the goods for sale is purchased from another party, the actual cost shall be the cost of the purchase. The ratio of profit to cost shall be determined by the State Administration of Taxation.

Article 17

The "purchase price" mentioned in (3) of Article 8 of the Regulations covers the price of the goods a taxpayer pays to an agricultural producer for the purchase as well as the tax on special farm products paid in advance for the purchaser in accordance with the government regulations.

The "price of goods" mentioned previously refers to the price indicated on the deed of purchase approved to be used by the tax authorities.

Article 18

With regard to mixed marketing activities and side-line non-taxable services liable for VAT in accordance with the provisions of Article 5 and Article 6 of these Rules, the amount of tax on the non-taxable services involved in the mixed marketing activities and the goods bought for use in the side-line non-taxable services shall be permitted to be deducted from the volume of tax on the sales, provided it complies with the provisions of Article 8 of the Regulations.

Article 19

The "fixed assets" mentioned in Article 10 of the Regulations refer t.

1. The machines, other equipment, tools of transportation and other equipment, tools and articles involved in production and/or business operation that have been in use for more than one year,
2. Major equipment valued at more than 2000 Yuan apiece and in use for more than two years but not involved in production or operation.

Article 20

The "non-taxable items" mentioned in Article 10 of the Regulations refer to the provision of non-taxable services, transfer of intangible assets, sales of fixed assets and fixed assets under construction.

The rebuilding, renovating, expanding, repairing and decorating of a building by a taxpayer shall all be deemed fixed asset under construction, regardless of the way of settlement under whichever accounting system.

Article 21

The "abnormal losses" mentioned in Article 10 of the Regulations refer to losses other than the proper losses in production and business operation, including:

1. Losses inflicted by natural adversities,
2. Losses resulting from theft or rotting or deterioration of the goods owing to poor management,
3. Other abnormal losses.

Article 22

As for the purchased goods or the taxable services whereupon the VAT has been deducted under one of the circumstances cited in 2–6 of Article 10 of the Regulations, the amount of tax on the purchased goods or the purchases of the taxable services shall be deducted from the amount of tax on the purchases of the current period. If the amount of tax on purchases cannot be ascertained, deduction shall be made on the deductible volume of the tax in the actual current cost.

Article 23

When a taxpayer runs as a side-line operation an item entitled to tax exemption or a non-taxable item (excluding fixed asset under construction) and it is impossible to delineate the amount of tax on the purchases not allowed for tax deduction, such amount of tax shall be computed by the following formula:

$$\text{Tax amount not to be deducted} = \text{total amount of tax on income of current month} \times (\text{aggregate of volume of sales of current month of tax} - \text{free item and turnover of non} - \text{taxable item}) \div \text{aggregate of total sales and business turnover of the month.}$$

Article 24

The norms for a "small-scale taxpayer" as mentioned in Article 11 of the Regulations are as follows:

1. The sales amount liable to annual VAT is below one million yuan for a taxpayer who produces goods or the providing taxable services or who produces goods or providing taxable services as the main line and also operates wholesale or retail business as a side-line;
2. The sales volume liable to annual VAT is below 1.8 million yuan for a taxpayer who operates wholesale or retail business.

An individual with annual volume of sales exceeding that of the taxable volume of a small-scale taxpayer, a non-enterprise institution, and an enterprise having taxable activities irregularly shall be deemed a small-scale taxpayer for paying tax.

Article 25

The sales amount of a small-scale taxpayer shall not include its tax amount.

When a small-scale taxpayer adopts the same pricing method for both his sales of goods or taxable services and tax amount, the sales volume shall be computed by the following formula:

$$\text{The sales volume} = \text{taxable volume of sales} \div (1 + \text{tax rate})$$

Article 26

When a small-scale taxpayer refunds the buyer in full value or at a discount for returns of goods from the buyer, the refund shall be deducted from the current proceeds of the sales whereby the refunding occurs.

Article 27

"Sound accounting settlement" mentioned in Article 14 of the Regulations refers to the accurate settlements of the taxable sales, taxable purchases and tax amount computed in line with the accounting system and the requirements of the tax authorities.

Article 28

An individual business operator in compliance with the conditions prescribed by Article 14 of the Regulations and with the approval of the tax bureau directly under the State Administration of Taxation may be deemed as a general taxpayer.

Article 29

A small-scale taxpayer who has been designated as a general taxpayer shall not resume the title of a small-scale taxpayer.

Article 30

When a general taxpayer is in one of the following states, the tax amount shall be computed at the VAT rate on the sales amount and no deduction shall be made for tax on purchases and no special VAT invoices shall be used:

1. The accounting is unsound or no accurate taxation information is provided;
2. No procedure for designation of the title of a general taxpayer has been performed, although it meets the requirements for a general taxpayer.

Article 31

The scope of the part of tax-exempt items cited in Article 16 of the Regulations is defined as follows:

1. "Agriculture" in 1 of paragraph one refers to farming, aquaculture, forestry, animal husbandry, and aquatic products industry. "Farmers" include institutions and individuals engaged in agricultural production.
2. "Old books" in 3 of paragraph one refers antique books and second-hand books purchased from society.
3. "Articles" in 8 of paragraph one refers to yachts, motorcycles, and other motor vehicles liable for consumption tax, and other articles

"Articles used by the owner" refer to the other articles used by the owner cited in Article 8 of these Rules.

Article 32

The starting point of VAT provided in Article 18 of the Regulations shall be applicable only to individual business operators. The range of the starting point of VAT is as follows:

1. The starting point of VAT on sales of goods is 600–2000 Yuan;
2. The starting point of VAT on taxable services is 200–800 Yuan;
3. The starting point of VAT on the sales volume of each transaction (or of each day) is 50–80 Yuan.

The "sales volume" mentioned above refers to that of a small-scale taxpayer as provided in clause 1, Article 25 of these Rules.

The tax bureaus directly under the State Administration of Taxation shall define the starting point of VAT within the prescribed range in the light of the local reality and report to the State Administration of Taxation for the record.

Article 33

The time at which VAT payable shall arise for sales of goods or taxable services as provided in 1 of Article 19 of the Regulations shall be determined in the light of the specific settlements of sales, specifically:

1. As for direct payment for sales of goods, it shall be the same day when the payment for the sales or the bill collectable for payment for the sales arrives, no matter whether the goods have been dispatched;
2. As for the sales payment entrusted for collection or authorized a bank to collect, on the day of the dispatch of the goods when the procedure of authorization for collection is completed;
3. As for sales of goods in the form of sales on credit or by instalment payment, on the day prescribed in the contract;
4. As for sales of goods in the form of advance payment, on the day the goods are dispatched;
5. As for goods marketed by other taxpayers as agents, on the day the consignee's report arrives;
6. As for sales of taxable services, on the day when the service is provided, and payment received or the bill collectable for the sales arrives;
7. As for activities cited in 3–8 of Article 4 of these Rules, which are deemed as sales of goods, on the day goods are dispatched.

Article 34

As for taxable services sold in China by foreign institutions or individuals without sites of business operation, the tax payable thereof shall be withheld by the agent, and if there is no agent, the buyer shall act as the withholder.

Article 35

As for itinerant businesspersons selling goods or taxable services in other counties (cities) without filing tax returns to the local authorities, the tax authorities of the location or residence thereof shall collect the VAT.

Article 36

"Tax authorities," mentioned in Article 20 of the Regulations refer to the State Administration of Taxation and its bureaus in charge of tax collecting.

"Tax authorities and tax collecting departments" mentioned in the Regulations and these Rules all refer to the State Administration of Taxation and its subsidiaries at or higher than the level of a sub-bureau.

Article 37

The terms "above" and "below" used in these Rules include the starting point.

Article 38

Interpretation of these Rules rests with the Ministry of Finance or the State Administration of Taxation.

Article 39

These Rules shall come into effect as from the day of promulgation. The "Rules for the Implementation of the Regulations of the People's Republic of China on VAT (DRAFT)" and the "Rules for the Implementation of the Regulations (Draft) of the People's Republic of China on Product Tax" promulgated by the Ministry of Finance on September 28, 1984, shall be abrogated therefrom.

Provisional Regulations on Value Added Tax of the People's Republic of China.

2007-10-27.

(Promulgated on the Order of the State Council [1993] No. 134 On Dec. 13, 1993).

Article 1

An institution or individual engaged in marketing goods and/or providing processing, repair and/or replacements services within the territory of the People's Republic of China shall be a payer of value added tax (hereinafter referred to as "taxpayer") and shall pay value added tax (VAT) in accordance with these Regulations.

Article 2

Rates of VAT

1. The rate of VAT on goods marketed or imported by a taxpayer shall be 17%, except for those provided in 2 and 3 of this article.
2. The rate of VAT on the following goods marketed or imported by a taxpayer shall be 13%:
   (1) Cereals, edible vegetable oils;
   (2) Running water, central heating, air conditioning, hot water, gas, LPG, natural gas, methane gas, coal/charcoal products for household use;
   (3) Books, newspapers, magazines;
   (4) Feed, chemical fertilizer, chemical pesticides, agricultural machinery, and farm-use plastic sheets;
   (5) And other goods stipulated by the State Council.
3. The rate of VAT shall be zero on goods exported by a taxpayer, unless otherwise stipulated by the State Council.
4. The rate of VAT shall be 17% on the processing, repair and/or replacements services (hereinafter referred to as taxable labour service) provided by a taxpayer and any readjustment thereof shall be determined by the State Council.

Article 3

For a taxpayer dealing in goods or providing taxable services taxable at different rates, the volumes of the sales of goods and taxable labour service at different tax rates shall be computed separately. The volumes of sales not computed separately for different rates of VAT shall be subject to the highest rate.

Article 4

The tax payable on goods marketed or taxable services provided by a taxpayer (hereinafter referred to as goods marketed or taxable services) shall be the amount of the current amount of tax on sales minus the current amount of tax on purchases, except for those provided under Article 13 of these Regulations. The formula shall be:

$$\text{Tax payable} = \text{amount of tax on sales} - \text{amount of tax on purchases}$$

In the event the amount of tax on sales is less than the current amount of tax on purchases and insufficient to offset the amount of tax on purchases, the balance shall be carried over to the next term to be further deducted.

Article 5

The amount of VAT assessed on the basis of the sales volume of goods and/or taxable services at the rate prescribed in Article 2 of these Regulations and collected from the buyer by the taxpayer shall be the amount of tax on sales. The formula shall be:

$$\text{Amount of tax on sales} = \text{sales volume} \times \text{VAT rate}$$

Article 6

The sales volume shall be the total payment for the price of the goods sold and other charges in addition to the price of the goods collected from the buyer by the taxpayer selling goods or providing services taxable, but excluding the amount of tax on sales.

The sales volume shall be computed in RMB. The taxpayer shall convert the payment settled in a foreign currency into RMB for computation at the current exchange rate.

Article 7

Should the goods sold or services taxable provided by a taxpayer be at a conspicuously low price and without a proper reason, the tax authorities shall determine the sales volume thereof.

Article 8

The amount of VAT payable on goods or services taxable bought by the taxpayer (hereinafter referred to as goods and taxable services bought) paid or borne by the taxpayer shall be the amount of tax on purchases.

The amount of tax on purchases permitted to be deducted from the amount of tax on sales, in addition to those as provided by Article 3 of these Regulations, shall be limited to the amount of VAT payable indicated in the following tax credit vouchers:

1. The amount of VAT payable indicated on the special VAT invoices obtained from the seller;
2. The amount of VAT payable indicated on customs duties payment vouchers obtained from the customs house.

The amount of tax on purchases of tax-free agricultural products permitted to be deducted shall be computed on the basis of the purchase price and a 10% tax credit. The tax amount shall be computed by the following formula:

$$\text{Tax amount on purchases} = \text{payment for the purchase} \times \text{tax credit rate}$$

Article 9

In case a taxpayer in purchasing goods or services taxable has not obtained or kept the voucher for VAT deduction or the VAT deduction document has not indicated the amount of VAT and the relevant matters in accordance with the regulations, the amount of tax on purchases shall not be deducted from the amount of tax on sales.

Article 10

The amount of tax on purchases of the following items shall not be deducted from the amount of tax on sales:

1. Fixed asset purchased;
2. Purchased goods or taxable services to be used in items not taxable;
3. Purchased goods or taxable services to be used in tax-free items;
4. Purchased goods or taxable services to be used for collective welfare or for personal consumption;
5. Purchased goods or taxable services abnormally damaged or lost;
6. Purchased goods or taxable services abnormally damaged and consumed in the course of making products or semi-finished products.

Article 11

A simplified system of computation of tax payable shall be applied to small-scale taxpayers engaged in selling goods or taxable services.

The norm for the scale of such taxpayers shall be determined by the Ministry of Finance.

Article 12

The VAT rate for small taxpayers engaged in selling goods or taxable services shall be 6%.

Any readjustment thereof shall be determined by the State Council.

Article 13

The amount of tax payable on the goods or taxable services which a small-scale taxpayer sells and is computed in accordance with the volume of sales and at the tax rate provided by Article 12 of these Regulations shall not be deducted by the amount of tax on purchases. The amount of tax payable shall be computed by the following formula:

$$\text{The amount of tax payable} = \text{amount of sales} \times \text{tax rate}$$

The amount of sales shall be determined with reference to the provisions of Article 6 and Article 7 of these Regulations.

Article 14

A small-scale taxpayer using a sound accounting assessment system and capable of producing documents indicating his accurate performance of tax obligations may not be deemed as a small-scale taxpayer with the approval of the relevant tax authorities and the amount of tax payable thereof may be computed in accordance with the relevant provisions of these Regulations.

Article 15

The tax payable on goods imported by a taxpayer shall be computed on the basis of the composite assessable price and the tax rate provided in Article 2 of these Regulations that shall allow no deduction by the amount of tax on purchases. Formulae for the composite assessable price and tax amount payable are as follows:

$$\text{Composite assessable price} = \text{customs dutiable value} + \text{customs duty} + \text{consumption tax}$$

$$\text{Tax amount payable} = \text{composite assessable price} \times \text{tax rate.}$$

Article 16

The following items are free from VAT:

1. Agricultural products sold by farmers themselves;
2. Contraceptive medicine and tools;
3. Old books;
4. Imported instruments and meters to be used directly in scientific research and experiments and/or teaching;
5. Imported goods and equipment granted gratis by foreign governments or international organizations;
6. Equipment needed for processing with supplies provided, assembling with parts provided and other compensation trade;
7. Goods imported by organizations of the handicapped and to be used only for the handicapped;

8. Used articles sold by the user(s).

Except for the above-listed, any item for VAT exemption or reduction shall be determined by the State Council. No locality or department shall determine any item for VAT exemption or reduction.

Article 17

A taxpayer dealing also in items entitled to tax exemption or reduction shall be subject to separate computation of the sales volumes of those items entitled thereto; and no tax exemption or reduction shall be granted to those items without separate computation of the sales volumes thereof.

Article 18

When a taxpayer's sales volume is below the starting point of VAT, it is free from VAT.

Article 19

The time at which VAT payable shall arise:

1. For sales of goods or taxable services, on the day the payment for the sales is collected or the bill payable for the sales is collected.
2. For imported goods, the day the import declared at the customs house.

Article 20

VAT in general shall be collected by tax authorities and VAT on imports shall be collected by the customs house in behalf of the tax authorities.

VAT on imported goods for personal use carried on by the user or mailed in shall be collected together with the customs duties. A detailed procedure thereof shall be formulated by the Tax Rules Committee of the State Council together with the relevant departments.

Article 21

A taxpayer selling goods or taxable services shall issue to the buyer special VAT invoices and indicate thereon the sales volume and the tax amount payable on the sales.

A general invoice instead of a special VAT invoice shall be issued whereupon an invoice is need in one of the circumstances cited below:

1. Selling goods or taxable services to a consumer;
2. Selling tax-free goods;
3. When a small-scale taxpayer sells goods or taxable service.

Article 22

Locations for paying VAT:

1. An owner of a fixed business operation shall file tax returns to the local tax authorities. When the head office and subsidiaries are located at different counties (cities), they shall file tax returns to their respective local tax authorities for tax payment; or with the approval of the State Administration of Taxation or the tax bureaus authorized thereby, the head office may file tax returns for the head office and subsidiaries to the local authorities of the head office for tax payment.
2. When the owner of a fixed business operation sells goods at another county (city), it shall apply to the tax authorities of its residence for a certificate confirming the tax administration over its out port business operation and file tax returns to the tax authorities of its residence. Without a certificate for sales operation issued by the tax authorities of its residence, the owner of the business shall file tax returns to the tax authorities of the locality of its out port business for tax payment; and if the taxpayer fails to do so, the tax authorities of its residence shall levy the tax in arrears.
3. Owners of mobile business operations shall file tax returns to the tax authorities of the localities of the sales for tax payment.
4. For imported goods, the importer or its agent shall file tax returns to the customs house where import declaration is made.

Article 23

The prescribed time limit for paying VAT shall be one day, three days, five days, ten days, 15 days or one month. The prescribed time limit to tax payment for a taxpayer shall be defined by the tax authorities in the light of the tax amount, and in case tax cannot be paid within the time limit, the taxpayer may pay tax on each transaction.

When a taxpayer's time allowance for tax payment is one month, he shall file tax returns within ten days after expiration of the time limit; if the term is one day, three days, five days, ten days or 15 days, the taxpayer shall make an advance payment within five days after the expiration of the term and file tax returns and clear the tax payable of the previous month within ten days beginning on the first day of the succeeding month.

Article 24

A taxpayer shall pay VAT on imported goods within seven days beginning the next day of the issuance of the tax-paying certificate by the customs house.

Article 25

If the goods a taxpayer exports enjoys zero VAT, the taxpayer shall complete the export procedure with the customs house and with the export declaration document apply to the tax authorities for reimbursement of the tax paid thereon at the end of each month. The concrete procedure thereof shall be formulated by the State Administration of Taxation.

If the exported goods are returned or withdrawn from the customs house after the VAT thereupon has been reimbursed, the taxpayer shall pay back the reimbursed tax to the tax authorities in accordance with the law.

Article 26

The collection and administration of VAT shall follow the relevant provisions of the Law of the People's Republic of China on the Administration of Tax Collection and these Regulations.

Article 27

VAT shall be levied from enterprises with foreign investment and foreign enterprises in accordance with the relevant resolutions of the Standing Committee of the National People's Congress.

Article 28

The Ministry of Finance shall be responsible for the interpretation of these Regulations and formulate the Rules for the implementation thereof.

Article 29

These Regulations shall go into effect as from January 1, 1994. The "Regulations of the People's Republic of China on Value Added Tax" (Draft) and the "Regulations of the People's Republic of China on Product Tax" (Draft) promulgated by the State Council on September 18, 1984 shall be abrogated therefrom.

8.2 Measures of State Administration of Taxation in 2002

Commissioner of State Administration of Taxation.

Measures for the Administration of the Collection of Value-added Taxes of Refined Oil Retail Gas Stations.

April 2, 2002.

Article 1

In order to improve the administration of the collection of value-added taxes ("VAT") of refined oil retail gas stations and to plug loopholes in tax administration, these Measures are formulated in accordance with the Law of People's Republic of China on the Administration of Tax Collection, the Provisional Regulations of the People's Republic of China Concerning Value-added Tax and other taxation policies and regulations.

Article 2

These Measures shall apply to individual or institutional businesses with fixed operating facilities, duly registered with the industry and commerce administration authority and the tax authority, which are approved by the State Economic and Trade Commission to engage in the refined oil retail business through automatic gas supply equipment (hereinafter referred to as the "Gas Station").

Article 3

The Gas Station as referred to under Article 1 hereof shall be identified without exception as the standard VAT taxpayer pursuant to the Circular of State Administration of Taxation Requiring Gas Stations to be Treated As General VAT Taxpayers (Guoshui Han [2001] No. 822) and shall be subject to the tax collection administration in accordance with the Provisional Regulations of the People's Republic of China Concerning Value-added Tax.

Article 4

If the Gas Station without independent accounting status that is operating under the central distribution arrangement is located in the same county or city as its head office, the head office shall pay the VAT on consolidation basis. Where the branch and the head office are located in different counties or cities within the same province, the provincial tax authority shall determine whether the VAT shall be paid on consolidation basis. State Administration of Taxation shall make such determination if the branch and the head office are located across different provinces.

In case that any cross-county or cross-city transfer of refined oil is carried out by a refined oil retail business with the unified accounting system and the consolidated VAT taxpayer status as approved by the relevant tax authority, no VAT shall be levied on such transfer.

Article 5

All refined oil sales amount of a gas station shall be subject to VAT despite its settlement means (for example, cash, check, bill of exchange, gas coupon (or register), gas supply card). In respect to the refined oil distributed by a gas station, separate accounts must be kept according to the types of the refined oil, and the taxable sales amount shall be accurately calculated. No gas station may issue a VAT special invoice to the customer purchasing refined oil with the gas coupon or gas supply card.

Article 6

The taxable sales amount of a gas station shall include the taxable sales amount of the refined oil of the current month and that of the other taxable sales of goods and labour. The taxable sales amount of the refined oil shall be calculated pursuant to the following formula:

$$
\begin{aligned}
&\text{The Taxable Sales Amount of the Refined Oil}\\
&= (\text{The Monthly Total Sale Volume of the Refined Oil}\\
&\quad - \text{the Volume of Refined Oil Deductible})\\
&\quad \times \text{Unit Price of the Refined Oil.}
\end{aligned}
$$

Article 7

All gas stations must establish a recording system as required by the Gas Station Daily Refined Oil Sales Bench Sheet (Appendix 1, hereinafter referred to as the "Bench Sheet"). Gas stations shall, in accordance with the daily bench sheet, by day or by shift prepare the complete and detailed records for the refined oil sales per day or per shift as well as the Consolidated Table for Gas Station Monthly Refined Oil Sales (Appendix 2). The Bench Sheet shall be bound up in a volume on a monthly basis and reserved for a certain period of time in accordance with the requirement for reservation of original accounting records and books for the audit and inspection by the competent tax authority.

Article 8

Gas stations shall submit to the competent tax authority the following materials in addition to the declaration material as required under the measures for filing tax returns by standard VAT taxpayers:

1. Gas Station Reined Oil Sales Detail in the Month of (Appendix 3) or the Refined Oil Sales IC Card;
2. Consolidated Table for Gas Station Monthly Refined Oil Sales;
3. Detailed Purchase, Sales and Inventory of Refined Oil (Appendix 4).

Article 9

If the refined oil supplied by a gas station through its gas supply equipment fits into any of the following cases, such supply is deductible from the monthly refined oil sales volume:

1. Self-use refined oil for the vehicles owned by the gas station as confirmed by the competent tax authority;
2. Refined oil purchased by another entity, which is stored at the gas station's refined oil storage facility;
   If the gas station is engaged in the business mentioned in 2 hereof, it must put on file with the competent tax authority the storage agreement and the copies of the refined oil purchase invoice of the consignor.
3. Warehousing turnover refined oil;
   The gas station shall report any warehousing turnover business handled to the competent tax authority in advance and the tax authority shall designate its personnel for on-site inspection and supervision.
4. Gas station's refined oil used for test purposes (i.e. the can-returning refined oil).

The gas station shall report to the competent tax authority of the volume of such deductible refined oil at the end of each month in accordance with the Consolidated Table for Gas Station Monthly Refined Oil Sales.

Article 10

The local tax authority supervising manufacturers or wholesalers of refined oil shall, on a monthly basis, provide the local tax authority administering refined oil purchasing enterprises with information concerning the refined oil sales by such manufacturers or wholesalers through the Golden Tax Project network (a national taxation computer network).

Article 11

If the gas station fails to maintain proper accounting practice but has installed tax-control gas supply equipment, the VAT shall be collected according to the taxable sales amount calculated based on the data recorded by such tax-control gas supply equipment. The competent tax authority shall require the gas station that fails to fully install the tax-control gas supply equipment (including failure to install) or whose tax-control gas supply equipment does not function properly, to strictly implement the Bench Sheet system and to file the Refined Oil Purchase, Sales and Inventory Detail on a monthly basis. The competent tax authority shall make an inventory of the refined oil of such gas station on a monthly basis, and perform a check and inspection periodically to the gas station jointly with other relevant enforcement agencies.

The competent tax authority shall include all the gas stations without proper accounting practice in those subject to the VAT payment evaluation. Based on the refined oil purchase information from enterprises as well as the level of tax burden of the local enterprises in the same industry and other information obtained through the Golden Tax Project network, the competent tax authority shall conduct a VAT payment evaluation on such gas stations in accordance with Circular of State Administration of Taxation Concerning Strengthening the VAT Payment Evaluation of the Commercial and Trading Enterprises (Guoshuifa [2001] No. 140). The case of any discrepancy identified must be transferred to the inspection department and a tax inspection shall be immediately initiated.

The competent tax authority may appraise and fix the VAT of the gas station without proper accounting practice according to the information available about the actual operating performance of it.

The tax authority shall provide the gas station without proper accounting practice with the special invoices subject to the limitation in value and in volume as stipulated under the special invoice administrative regulations as well as based on the actual operating performance of such gas station.

Article 12

The taxpayer that sells refined oil through issuing gas supply cards and gas coupons (hereinafter referred to as the "Pre-selling Entity") shall properly record such payment as advance payment in its bookkeeping practice and such advance payment is not subject to the VAT.

The pre-selling entity may issue a general invoice to the customer of the gas supply card or gas coupon. If the customer requests for the VAT special invoice to be issued, the VAT special invoice may be issued to the customer based on the actual refined oil consumption by the customer as reflected by such gas supply card or gas coupon. The entity that sells refined oil through acceptance of the gas supply card or gas coupon shall issue a VAT special invoice to the pre-selling entity based on the actual payment settled between such entity and the pre-selling entity.

Article 13

The competent tax authority shall collect the refined oil sales data through the inspection card from gas stations within its jurisdiction once in a quarter and shall verify the data collected against the VAT Returns, the Gas Station Daily Refined Oil Sales Bench Sheet, the Consolidated Table for Gas Station Monthly Refined Oil Sales and other materials. The tax authority shall also conduct a comprehensive tax inspection over the determination of the volume deductible, the purchase, sales and storage of the refined oil and other matters.

Article 14

These Measures shall enter into effect as of May 1, 2002.

Ministry of Finance State Administration of Taxation.

Circular of the Ministry of Finance and State Administration of Taxation on Relevant Issues concerning Consumption Taxes in the Import.

No 33/2006.

The General Administration of Customs, for the purpose of meeting the requirements for social and economic development and perfecting the consumption tax system, adjustments are made to the tax items, tax rates and the relevant consumption tax policies upon the approval of the State Council. In light of the Circular of Ministry of Finance and State Administration of Taxation on Adjusting and Perfecting Consumption Tax Policies (Cai Shui [2006] No. 33), a notice on relevant issues concerning the collection of consumption taxes in the import link is hereby circulated as follows:

I. Consumption taxes shall be collected on such new taxable items as golf balls and golf equipment, luxury watches, yachts, disposable wooden chopsticks, solid wood flooring, naphtha, solvent oil, lubrication oil, fuel oil, aviation kerosene, and so on. Consumption taxes on skin care and hair care products shall be cancelled. And the consumption tax rates on cars, motorcars, automobile tyres and white spirits shall be adjusted. The tax rates on naphtha, solvent oil, lubrication oil, and fuel oil shall be 30% of the amount of consumption taxes payable at interim; consumption tax on aviation kerosene shall not be collected at interim; and consumption tax on radial tyres shall be exempted.
II. Up to 14 categories of commodities are subject to import link consumption tax after the adjustment, and see the Attachment for the specific tax items and tax rates.
III. The relevant provisions of the Circular of the Ministry of Finance, the General Administration of Customs, and the State Administration of Taxation on Printing and Distributing the Provisions on Issues of Tax Policy concerning

Collection of Taxes on Imported Goods by the Customs in the Import Link (Cai Guan Shui [2004] No. 7) shall be observed when handling issues concerning the policy on the import link consumption tax.

IV. The present Notice shall come into force as of the day of April 1, 2006. In case that any former provision conflict with this Notice, the present Notice shall prevail. Attachment: Table of Tax Items and Tax Rates for Taxable Commodities Subject to Import Link Consumption Taxes.

Ministry of Finance State Administration of Taxation March 30, 2006.

State Administration of Taxation.

Supplementary Circular of the State Administration of Taxation to the Relevant Issues Concerning the Tax-exemption Policies for the Export of Products Containing Gold.

January 20, 2006.

GuoShui Fa [2006] No. 10.

The state taxation bureaus of all provinces, autonomous regions, municipalities directly under the Central Government, and cities specifically designated in the state plan:

Considering the problems in the implementation of the Notice of the State Administration of Taxation about the Tax Policies on the Export of Products Containing Gold (No. 125 [2005] of the State Administration of Taxation), a supplementary notice is given as follows:

I. From May 1, 2005, for the export goods (See the concrete list in the Annex) of which the customs commodity codes are 3824909090, 7115901090, 7114200090, 71110000 and 28439000 but which don't contain gold or platinum, the tax refund (exemption) policies for export shall continue to apply. For the aforesaid goods already exported prior to the issuance of this Notice, if the time limit for export tax refund declaration has expired, the tax organs of all places shall accept the tax rebate declarations of the export enterprises in gear. During the course of examining and approving the tax refund for export, none of the tax organs may complete the tax refund formalities unless it, upon strict examination, is sure that the above-mentioned goods do not contain any gold or platinum. For other goods which are inside the above-mentioned customs commodity codes but which do not contain gold or platinum, the State Administration of Taxation of all provinces and cities shall first conduct a strict examination, then put forward handling opinions and finally submit formal documents to the State Administration of Taxation for approval.

II. With regard to the export products containing gold (including gold and platinum) other than those inside the commodity codes as listed in the document No. 125, for instance, "91131000" "valuable metal watchband" the platinum watchband, shall be enforced the value-added tax exemption policy according to the regulations in the document No. 125. Article 6 of the Notice of the Ministry of Finance and State Administration of Taxation about the Tax Policies on Platinum and Its

Products (No. 86 [2003] of the Ministry of Finance), which provides that "the tax refund for export does not apply to the input value-added tax on the part of the raw material of platinum of the export platinum products, the tax refund only applies to the processing fee in the processing link of platinum products on the basis of the prescribed tax rebate rate", shall not be implemented as of May 1, 2005.

III. The products containing gold or platinum, which are exported in the form of processing with imported materials, shall be exempt from the value-added tax according to the document No. 125.

Annex: Statistic Form of Products Not Containing Gold (Platinum) (Omitted).

State Administration of Taxation.

January 20, 2006.

Supplementary Notice of the State Administration of Taxation on the relevant Transfer Issues concerning Inspection Information of Value-added Tax Special Invoices of Export Goods of Export Enterprises.

No. 093 of October 9, 2005.

The bureaus of state taxation of all provinces, autonomous regions, municipalities directly under the Central Government and the cities specifically designated in the state plan.

After the distribution of the Notice of the State Administration of Taxation on the relevant Transfer Issues concerning Inspection Information of Value-added Tax Special Invoices of Export Goods of Foreign Trade Enterprises. (No. 859 [2005] of the State Administration of Taxation), some local authorities reported that, because the audit and assistance in investigation information of value-added tax invoices which are offered by all local information technology departments and shall be audited before May, 2005 failed to be input to the Examination System for Tax Refund for Exports, verifications and comparisons by computer can't be conducted. Therefore, we hereby make the following supplementary notice upon research:

I. According to Article 2 of Document No. 859 [2005] of the State Administration of Taxation, where the tax refund departments of bureaus of state taxation at all levels have received the audit and assistance in investigation information of value-added tax invoices which are offered by information technology department and shall be audited before May, 2005, they may take the way of checking, by hand, against the data declared by export enterprises. Those verified as correct shall, after being dealt with by manual selecting in the Examination System for Tax Refund, be gone through relevant formalities for tax refund in accordance with existing export tax refund provisions.

II. The tax refund departments and information technology departments of bureaus of state taxation shall properly settle the transitional and linking work of transferring the information mentioned above, clarify functions and liabilities with each other, ensure the security and accuracy of information transfer. If the information obtained by information technology departments is reflected in the carriers of paper when offered to the tax refund departments, both parties shall sign on it for confirmation. If the information is offered directly in the form of electronic data, both parties shall handle properly the work of confirmation and backup of information

Circular of the Ministry of Finance and the State Administration of Taxation on Some Policies concerning Value-added Tax.

No. 165/2005.

The public finance departments (bureaus), bureau of state taxes and those of local taxes of all provinces, autonomous regions, municipalities directly under the Central Government, and cities specifically designated in the state plan, the Financial Bureau of Xinjiang Production and Construction Corps.

Upon deliberation, some problems concerning the value-added tax are hereby clarified as follows:

I. With regard to the determination of the time when the value-added tax obligation arises from the selling of self-produced goods, as well as the provision of labour services subject to value-added tax and construction labour services, the Circular of State Administration of Taxation on Some Issues Concerning the Turnover Taxes Imposed on the Taxpayers Who Sell Self-produced Goods, Provide Labour Services Subject to Value-added Tax and Simultaneously Provide Construction Labour Services (GuoShui Fa [2002] No. 117) provides that the time when the obligation arises for a taxpayer to pay value-added tax for selling self-produced goods and providing labour services subject to value-added tax and construction labour services simultaneously shall be determined in accordance with the Article 33 of the Detailed Rules for the Implementation of the Interim Regulations of the People's Republic of China on Value-added Tax.

II. The determination of the time when tax obligation arises in the case of an enterprise' selling of goods on the commission basis and without a checklist of such goods.

   (1) Where a taxpayer sells goods on a commission basis, if it receives the full payment or a partial payment for goods before receiving the checklist of such goods, the time when tax obligation arises shall be the day when it receives the full payment or a partial payment for the goods.
   (2) Where a taxpayer fails to receive any payment for the goods and the checklist within 180 days after the consignment of the goods sold on a commission basis, the sale shall be deemed as completed and the taxpayer shall pay the value-added tax. The time when tax obligation arises shall be the day when the 180th day after the consignment of the goods sold on a commissioned basis expires.

III. Some issues concerning the offset of the amount of input tax of some particular goods to which value-added tax rates are applied differently in the import link and the domestic link or in different areas within China.
Where value-added tax rates are applied differently to some particular goods (such as primary agricultural products and mineral products) in the import link and the domestic link or in different areas within China, a taxpayer shall offset the input tax against the value-added tax in the amount as specified on the special value-added tax invoice and the certificate of the customs for payment of import duties.
Where competent tax authorities find that there are different value-added tax rates applicable to the same goods in the import link and the domestic link or in different areas within China, they shall report the relevant information, level by level, to the common tax authority at the next higher level, which shall give a definite reply.

IV. With regard to the calculation and division of input tax which may not be offset against the value-added tax.
If the taxpayer concurrently engaging in any tax exemption item or non-taxable item (excluding fixed assets under construction) is unable to precisely divide the amount of input tax may not be offset, the amount shall be computed according to the following formula:

$$
\begin{aligned}
&\text{Amount of input tax may not be offset} = (\text{Total amount of input tax of the} \\
&\quad \text{current month} - \text{Amount of input tax of the current month that can be} \\
&\quad \text{precisely divided into taxable items and non} - \text{taxable items)} \\
&\quad \times (\text{Gross sales of the tax} - \text{exempt items and the turnover of non} \\
&\quad - \text{taxable items of the current month} \\
&\quad \div \text{Aggregate amount of the gross sales and turnover} \\
&\qquad \text{of the current month)} \\
&\quad + \text{Amount of input tax of the current month that can be precisely divided} \\
&\quad \text{into tax} - \text{exempt items and non} - \text{taxable items.}
\end{aligned}
$$

V. With regard to the change of a general taxpayer of value-added tax (hereinafter referred to as the general taxpayer) into a small-scale taxpayer.
Once a taxpayer is formally determined as a general taxpayer, it may not be changed back into a small-scale taxpayer. The change of a general taxpayer within the tutorship period into a small-scale taxpayer shall still be handled according to the relevant provisions of the Urgent Circular of the State Administration of Taxation on Strengthening the Administration of VAT Collection on Newly Established Trading and Commercial Enterprises (No. 37 [2004] of the State Administration of Taxation).

VI. With regard to the inventory and the to-be-offset tax amount when a general taxpayer is cancelled.

Where a general taxpayer is changed into a small-scale taxpayer because it is cancelled or disqualified from being a general taxpayer during the tutorship period, its inventory shall not be treated as transfer-out of input and the to-be-offset tax amount shall not be refunded.

VII. With regard to the offset upon transport invoices.

(1) Where a general taxpayer buys or sells any goods (excluding fixed assets outside the Northeast of China) by railway transport and obtains the transport invoice issued by the railway department, if the name of the consigner or consignee indicated on the railway transport invoice is not the same as the name of the taxpayer, but the name of the taxpayer is given in the column of the consigner or the column of remarks of the railway transport invoice (it shall be invalidate if handwritten), the transport invoice may be regarded as a voucher for offset or deduction of the input tax and it is allowed to compute the amount of input tax to be offset.

(2) The transport freight paid by a VAT general taxpayer in its production or business operations may not be used to calculate the input tax.

(3) The international goods transport agency invoice and international goods transport invoice that a VAT general taxpayer obtains may not be used to calculate the input tax.

(4) The transport invoice that a VAT general taxpayer obtains for all the goods it has purchased in an accumulative way is allowed to be used to calculate the input tax if it is accompanied by a transport checklist issued by the transporting enterprise which bears the special seal for finance or for issuing invoices.

(5) The transport invoice that a VAT general taxpayer obtains but which is insufficiently filled out may not be used to calculate the input tax, with the exception of the transport invoice issued in an accumulative way and accompanied by a transport checklist.

VIII. Whether to levy value-added tax on one-time fees collected by taxpayers engaging in public utilities

Where one-time fees collected by a VAT taxpayer engaging in heating, electric power, gas, water supply, and other public utilities is directly related to the sales volume of goods, such fees shall be subject to value-added tax; if they are not directly related to the sales volume of goods, it shall not be subject to value-added tax.

IX. Whether to levy value-added tax on the fees collected by taxpayers on behalf of administrative departments

Where a fee collected by taxpayers on behalf of the relevant administrative department meets all of the following requirements and if it is not an extra? Price fee, it is not subject to value-added tax.

(1) It is approved by the State Council, the relevant department of the State Council, or the government at the provincial level;

(2) Special voucher has been issued for the administrative charge upon approval of the public finance department;
(3) Such fee is entirely turned over to the state treasury; or if not turned over to the state treasury, it shall be subject to government supervision and be used for the special purpose as approved.

X. With regard to the taxation issue relating to the insurance premiums, vehicle purchase tax and license plate fees collected on a commissioned basis Insurance premiums collected by a VAT taxpayer at the time of selling goods against the buyer for buying insurances for the goods on behalf of the buyer, and the vehicle purchase taxes and vehicle license plate fees collected and withheld by a VAT taxpayer engaged in the sale of vehicles against and on behalf of the buyer, shall not be treated as ex-price fees and thus shall not be subject to value-added tax.

XI. With regard to the issue of levying value-added tax on computer software products

(1) The built-in software does not fall within the scope of the software products that may enjoy the preferential value-added tax policies as provided in the Circular of the Ministry of Finance and the State Administration of Taxation Concerning Some Taxation Policies for Encouraging the Development of the Software Industry and the Integrated Circuit Industry (Cai Shui [2000] No. 25);
(2) The income derived from the software installation fees, maintenance fees, and training fees which are collected upon the sale of the software product involved shall be subject to value-added tax according to the relevant provisions on mixed selling and may enjoy the preferential value-added tax policy of "refund immediately upon payment";
However, the maintenance fees, technical service fees, and training fees charged by instalments or each time when the service is provided after the software product has already been delivered for use shall not be subject to value-added tax.
(3) For the income derived by a VAT taxpayer for the development of a software products upon the entrustment of anyone else, if of the software product belongs to the client, it shall subject to value-added tax; if the copyright belongs to both the developer and the client shall not be subject to value-added tax.

XII. With regard to the taxation issue concerning printing enterprises entrusted by publishing enterprises to print newspapers, books and periodicals by buying paper themselves.
Where a printing enterprise buys paper by itself to print books, newspapers and magazines which have a code number (CN) or an ISBN upon the entrustment of a publisher, such prices it charges for such printing shall be treated as sale of goods and be subject to value-added tax.

XIII. Income from membership fees.

The membership fees charged from value-added tax taxpayers shall not be subject to value-added tax.

Ministry of Finance.

State Administration of Taxation.

November 28, 2005.

8.3 Circulars from 2000 to 2005

Circular of the State Administration of Taxation Concerning the Relevant Issues on Strengthening the Administration of Special VAT Invoices.

No. 150, September 12, 2005.

The state taxation bureaus of all provinces, autonomous regions, municipalities directly under the Central Government and cities specifically designated in the state plan:

It is recently reported by some regions that it is prevalent that some general VAT taxpayers (hereinafter referred to as the general taxpayers) issue special VAT invoices to the general taxpayers as the third party for tax frauds where no special VAT invoice (hereinafter referred to as the special invoices) needs to be issued in the dealings with small-scale taxpayers. With a view to guarding against falsification of special invoices and stopping the frauds of the deduction of value-added tax and export tax refund by false special invoices, you are hereby notified of the relevant issues as follows:

I. The taxation authorities shall intensify the administration on small-scale taxpayers. A comprehensive check of small-scale taxpayers shall be conducted, and any taxpayer whose annual sales amount exceeds the standard of small-scale taxpayers shall be regarded as a general taxpayer by the taxation authority according to the relevant provisions. Where a taxpayer meets the conditions of general taxpayers but fails to apply for going through the formalities for the confirmation of general taxpayers, his taxable amount shall be calculated at the VAT rate on the basis of the sales amount, the input taxes may not be deducted and no special invoice may be used therefor. Where a taxpayer who has exceeded the standard of small-scale taxpayers is not confirmed as a general taxpayer according to law, the handling person or person responsible for examination and approval shall be investigated for legal liabilities.

II. The taxation authorities shall do a good job in the confirmation work of a general taxpayer. The qualification confirmation of a general taxpayer shall be subject to strict examination and approval in accordance with the relevant existing provisions, and any taxpayer that meets the conditions for confirmation of a general taxpayer shall be urged to apply for the qualification confirmation of a general taxpayer. Whenever a taxpayer files an application for the qualification confirmation of a general taxpayer with the taxation authority, the competent taxation authority shall timely carry out the examination and approval of the case, make an appointment for interviews and conduct on-spot verification. If the conditions for confirmation are met, the competent taxation authority shall timely confirm it, and may not delay it under any excuse, nor may it refuse to make confirmation without any justifiable reason.

III. The taxation authorities shall intensify the administration on special invoices of general taxpayers.

1. It is necessary to intensify the administration on the use of special VAT invoices by general taxpayers and require the taxpayers to issue special invoices in strict compliance with the Provisions on the Use of Special VAT Invoices and other relevant provisions.
2. The general taxpayer, whose tax declaration is abnormal, shall be subject to key examination to find whether or not the names of goods indicated in the acquired special invoices or lists of the sold goods accord with the scope of its business or the raw materials consumed in the course of production, and to find whether or not the actual dealer is the issuer of the special invoices in light of the taxpayer's relevant materials, such as the purchase-and-sale contract and the settlement voucher issued by the bank.
   Anyone who violates the Provisions on the Use of Special VAT Invoices shall be punished in accordance with relevant provisions; and anyone that is suspected of issuing invoices for any third party or defrauding the input tax deduction or export tax refund shall be transferred to the auditing department for auditing.

IV. When a taxation authority carries out the authentication of special invoices, it shall seriously examine the content of special invoices, and detain and transfer to the auditing department for auditing those invoices with wrong cryptograph, inconsistent authentication (excluding the inconsistent authentication of taxpayers' identification numbers or the inconsistent authentication of invoices' codes) or repeated authentication.

V. The taxation authorities shall intensify the work relating to the tax payment evaluation, and shall lay emphases on the tax payment evaluation of those general taxpayers that deduct VAT input taxes by paying for goods in cash, purchasing goods on credit or entrusting any other entity or individual to pay for goods, and shall conduct on-the-spot verification when necessary. Where it finds that any taxpayer purchases any goods that is inconsistent with its actual business, or that the taxpayer fails to pay for the goods for a long time, or entrusts any other person to make large payment without any justifiable reason, or has not concluded a purchase-and-sale contract (excluding the sporadic purchases or sales) for the purchase and sale of goods or the provision of taxable services, the taxpayer shall be transferred to the auditing department for auditing.

Please carry them out accordingly.

The State Administration of Taxation.

September 12, 2005.

8.4 Notices of the SAT and Circulars from 2005 and 2006

Notice of the Ministry of Finance and the State Administration of Taxation on Some Issues concerning Land Value-added Taxes.

No. 21 of March 2, 2006.

The public finance departments or bureaus and local taxation bureaus of all provinces, autonomous regions, municipalities directly under the Central Government and cities specifically designed in the state plan, and the finance bureau of Xinjiang Production and Construction Corps.

In pursuance of the spirit as embodied in the Interim Regulations of the People's Republic of China on Land Value-added Taxes (hereinafter referred to as the Regulations) and the detailed rules for the implementation thereof as well as relevant provisions, we hereby clarify the relevant issues concerning land value-added taxes as follows:

I. As for issues concerning the tax collection and exemption in the sale of residential houses of ordinary standard as built by taxpayers as well as in the transfer of ordinary residential houses by individual residents.
The "residential houses of ordinary standard" as mentioned in Article 8 of the Regulations and the "ordinary residential houses" as mentioned in Article 3 of the Notice of the Ministry of Finance and the State Administration of Taxation on Adjusting the Tax Policies for the Real Estate Market (Cai Shui Zi [1999] No. 210) shall be recognized all according to the standards for the "small or medium-sized ordinary residential houses at moderate and low prices" as formulated and publicized to the general public by the people's governments of each province, autonomous region or municipality directly under the Central Government in accordance with the Notice of the General Office of the State Council transmitting the Opinions on Doing a Good Job in Stabilizing the Real Estate Price of the Ministry of Construction and Other Departments (Guo Ban Fa [2005] No. 26). Where any taxpayer builds ordinary residential houses as well as other commercial houses, the amount of land added values shall be verified respectively.
As for ordinary standard residential houses, for which, before the day when this document is publicized, an application for tax exemption has been filed to the tax authority at the locality of the real estate and has been given the treatment of exemption from land value-added taxes upon examination in accordance with the standards for ordinary standard residential houses as determined by

the people's governments of a province, autonomous region or municipality directly under the Central Government, adjustment shall be retroactively made to the exempted land value-added taxes.

II. As for Issues concerning the Calculation under the Item of Deduction in the Transfer of Old Houses.

Where any taxpayer transfers any old house or building, if he fails to obtain the assessed price but is able to provide the house purchase invoice, the amount under the item of deduction as provided for in items (1) and (3) of Article 6 of the Regulations may, upon the recognition of the local tax authority, be calculated in light of an increased interest rate of 5% on an annual basis of the amount held on it for a term spanning from the year of purchase to the year of transfer. As for the deed tax by a taxpayer when purchasing a house, if the relevant deed tax payment certificate can be presented, it may be deducted as "tax relating to the transfer of real estate" and shall not be included into the base corresponding to the interest rate of 5%.

As to the transfer of any old house or building, in the case of no relevant assessed price or house purchase invoice, the local tax authority may conduct tax collection upon verification in accordance with the provisions of Article 35 of the Law of the People's Republic of China on Tax Collection and Administration (hereinafter referred to as the Tax Collection and Administration Law).

III. As for issues concerning the advance collection of land value-added taxes as well as the settlement thereof.

All regions shall further improve the measures on the advance collection of land value-added taxes, and decide the advance collection rate in a scientific and reasonable manner and adjust it at a proper time in light of the value addition level of the real estate as well as the market development condition within the respective regions and on the basis of the different house categories such as ordinary houses, non-ordinary houses and commercial houses. After a project is completed, the relevant settlement shall be made in a timely manner, with any overpayment refunded or any underpayment supplemented.

In case any tax fails to be paid in advance during the advance collection term, the late fees shall be collected additionally as of the day next to the expiration of the prescribed advance collection term in accordance with the relevant provisions of the Tax Collection and Administration Law as well as the detailed rules for its implementation.

As for any real estate project that has been finished and has gone through the check and acceptance, where the building area of the real estate as transferred makes up 85% or more of the saleable building area, the tax authority may require the relevant taxpayer to conduct settlement of land value-added taxes on the transferred real estate in light of the matching principles regarding the proportion between the income as generated from the transfer of real estate and the amount under the item of deduction. The specific settlement methods shall be provided for by the local tax authority of a province, autonomous region, municipality directly under the Central Government and city specifically designed in the state plan.

IV. As for issues concerning the tax collection and exemption for the real estate as transferred by a taxpayer himself due to the relocation as required for the implementation of urban planning and state construction.
In Paragraph 4 of Article 11 of the Detailed Rules for Implementing the Interim Regulations of the People's Republic of China on Land Value-added Taxes, it prescribes that the relocation due to "the implementation of urban planning" refers to the relocation since that the reconstruction of an old city or enterprise pollution or disturbing the residents (producing so excessive waste gases, waste water, waste residues and noises, that the life of urban residents is affected to a certain degree) and thus the government or the relevant administrative departments of the government decides and thereafter carries out the relocation in light of the urban planning that has been examined and approved; the "relocation as required by state construction" refers to a situation under which relocation is required for the purpose of implementing any construction project that has been approved by the State Council, a provincial people's government, or the relevant ministry or commission of the State Council.

V. As for Issues concerning the tax collection and exemption for the investment or joint management with real estate.
As for any investment or association by using land (real estate) as payment for the purchase of shares, where an enterprise involved in the investment or joint management engages in the real estate development or where any other real estate development enterprise makes investment or conducts joint management with the commercial houses built by itself, it shall not be subject to Article 1 of the Notice of the Ministry of Finance and the State Administration of Taxation on the Provisions on Some Specific Issues regarding Land Value-added Taxes (Cai Shui Zi [1995] No. 048) on the interim exemption of land value-added taxes.

VI. The present Notice shall go into effect as of March 2, 2006.

Notice of the State Administration of Taxation on the Issues relating to the Valued-added Tax of Its Common Taxpayer in Forward Business.

No. 1060, November 9, 2005.

To the bureaus of state taxation of all provinces, autonomous regions and city specifically designated in the state plan.

In order to reasonably solve problems relating to the collection of tax payments and issuing of special invoice in forward business premium, notice of policies relating to the valued-added tax of its common taxpayer in forward business is hereby given as follows:

I. Where the common taxpayer of value-added tax, no matter premium or discount, sells goods through forward business in commodity exchange, the taxpayer hereof may, in accordance with the quantity of goods noted expressively in standard warrant (its form is shown in Appendix 1) and the settlement price of delivery, issue special invoice for value-added-tax.

II. Where premium occurs in forward business when the warrant registrant register the goods, the registrant shall, when the warrant is cancelled (i.e. withdrawing goods from forward circulation), issue special VAT invoice to the canceler for the fund of the premium part and withdraw VAT on sales, and the canceler shall calculate creditable input tax by means of the obtained special invoice.
In case that discount occurs, the registrant shall, as for fund of the premium part, issue negative VAT special invoice and net off against output tax, and the canceler shall, by means of the obtained special invoice, impair input tax, and warrant canceler shall not issue special VAT invoice to the warrant registrant.
The registrant shall, when issuing negative special invoice, obtain Standard Warrant Registration Premium Bill or Standard Warrant Cancellation Premium Bill (its form is shown in Appendix 2, Appendix 3) and issue the special invoice hereof in accordance with the noted premium or discount sum and retain them for the supervision and check by the taxation authorities in charge.

III. The Notice shall come into effect as for December 1, 2005, the collection and administration of VAT of forward business warrant registered prior to December 1 shall be governed and implemented in accordance with Notice of the State Administration of Taxation on Printing Measures for Collection of Value-added Tax for Forward Goods (GuoShui Fa [1994] No. 244) and otherwise relevant rules.

IV. Premium, as mentioned in the Notice, refers to the sum difference paid by the bourse via premium or discount account to the registrant provided that the grade, weight, sort and warrant position of the benchmark and of benchmark warrant are superior in accordance with the prescribed forward business rule. In case that premium occurs, if the standard warrant holder withdraws goods cancellation warrant bill after several dealing, the bourse shall, via premium or discount account, withdraw the sum equivalent to the amount of premium.
Discount, as mentioned in the Rule refers to the sum difference paid by the bourse via premium or discount account to the registrant provided that the grade, weight, sort and warrant position of the benchmark and of benchmark warrant are inferior in accordance with the prescribed forward business rule. In case that discount occurs, if the standard warrant holder withdraws goods cancellation warrant bill after several dealings, the bourse shall, via premium or discount account, provide to the canceler the sum equivalent to the amount of premium.

V. In case that problems occur in the process of implementing the Notice, please report to the State Administration of Taxation (Turnover Tax Department).

Appendix:

1. Standard Warrant Holding Certificate of × Commodity Exchange (model)
2. Standard Warrant Registration Premium Bill of × Commodity Exchange (model) (omitted)
3. Standard Warrant Cancellation Premium Bill of × Commodity Exchange (model) (omitted)

The State Administration of Taxation.

November 9, 2005.

Appendix 1:

Standard Warrant Holding Certificate of × Commodity Exchange (model)

In accordance with articles of commodity exchange, rules of transaction and provisions in rules of implementation, the Certificate representing ownership of the listed commodity, shall be protected by law. The original Standard Warrant Holding Certificate shall be null and void automatically as of the date of the signature of the Certificate. Any alteration or forgery shall be punished by law.

Circular of MOF, SAT, and PBC on the Issues concerning the Relevant Budget Management after the Adjustment of Export Tax Refund Bearing Mechanism.

No. 438, August 22nd, 2005.

The finance offices or bureaus, state taxation bureaus and local taxation bureaus of all provinces, autonomous regions, municipalities directly under the Central Government, and cities under separate state planning, all branches and business administration departments of the People's Bank of China as well as central sub-branches thereof in capital cities and in Shenzhen, Dalian, Qingdao, Xiamen, and Ningbo, the finance bureau of Xinjiang Production and Construction Corps.

With a view to implementing the Circular of the State Council on Improving Central and Local Export Tax Refund Bearing Mechanism (Guo Fa [2005] No. 25) and ensuring that the all kinds of work for export tax refund progress smoothly, you are hereby notified of the relevant matters on budget management after the adjustment of export tax refund bearing mechanism:

I. Since January 1st, 2005 (the date of examination and approval of tax refund shall be referred to, the same hereinafter), the amount of value added tax refund for export goods calculated within the tax base (including the amount of export value-added tax that is exempted or offset, the same hereinafter) of all regions shall continue to be borne by the state treasury; the amount of tax refund calculated beyond the tax base shall be shared by central and local treasuries according to the proportion of 92.5–7.5 instead of the former proportion of 75–25. The base of export tax refund of every region as approved and verified by the State Council shall remain unchanged.

II. Since January 1st, 2005, the value-added tax refund for export goods shall be handled in the following ways:

1. Since September 1st, 2005, the value-added tax refund for export goods to be paid by the state treasury shall be paid uniformly from the central revenue; the value-added tax exempted and offset shall be adjusted in the item of "increased value-added tax from tax exemption and offset"(Code 010151) for the central and local treasuries respectively according to the proportion of 75–25, and the item of "decreased value-added tax from tax

exemption and deduction"(Code 010302) of the central treasury shall be adjusted according to the amount of tax exemption and offset. And meanwhile, the part of 25% of the value-added tax increased from exemption and offset shall be transferred to local treasuries from the central treasury. Other measures for adjusting the state treasury for tax offset and exemption shall be implemented continuously in light of the Circular on the Relevant Issues concerning the Budget Management for the Implementation of the Measures for Tax Offset, Exemption and Refund as promulgated by the Ministry of Finance, State Administration of Taxation and the People's Bank of China (Cai Yu Zi [1998] No. 242).

2. For the value-added tax refund which has been handled for export goods before September 1st, 2005, the departments of finance, bureaus of state taxation and the state treasury departments of the people's bank at all levels shall have the related accounts adjusted. The concrete measures for account adjustment shall be separately formulated by the Ministry of Finance, State Administration of Taxation and the People's Bank of China.

III. The part of value-added tax refund, which shall be borne by the local treasuries for export goods in 2005 and the following years, shall be specially turned into the central treasury by the local treasuries at the year end.

IV. In order to reflect the changes of export tax refund, the following adjustments are made to the Subjects of Government Budget Revenue and Expenditure in 2005 and the Subjects of Government Budget Revenue and Expenditure in 2006:

1. The item of "value-added tax refund for export goods"(Code 010301) under the subject of general budget revenue shall be changed into the subject of withdrawal of central revenue, which shall reflect the value-added tax refund for export goods returned by the central treasury. The item of "decreased value-added tax after tax exemption and offset" (Code 010302) shall be changed into the subject exclusively used by the central treasury, which shall reflect the value-added tax decreased according to the amount of tax exemption and offset.
2. The item of "revenue from the return of export tax refund base" (Code 720110) under the subject of general budget revenue and the item of "expenditure from the return of export tax refund base" (Code 660110) under the subject of general budget expenditure shall be cancelled.
3. The item "special revenue turned in from export tax refund" (Code 720203) shall be added to the general item of "revenue turned in from general budget" (Code 7202) under the subject of general budget revenue, and shall reflect the export tax refund revenue turned into the central treasury by the local treasuries. The item of "special expenditure turned in from export tax refund" (Code 660203) shall be added to the general item of "expenditure turned in from general budget" (Code 6602) under the subject of general budget expenditure, and shall reflect the expenditure of export tax refund turned into the central treasury by local treasuries.

V. The local budget revenue and expenditure shall be adjusted according to the relevant adjustments of the export tax refund bearing mechanism. The public finance department at the provincial level shall report the relevant adjustment information to the government at the corresponding level, and shall, in light of the conditions of the export tax refund work of their own regions, formulate corresponding management measures so as to ensure the smooth progress of all kinds of work.

The Ministry of Finance.

The State Administration of Taxation.

The People's Bank of China.

August 22nd, 2005.

8.5 Circulars and Other Regulations from 2008 to 2009

Notes on the Taxable Scope of Some Goods for VAT.

2009-04-14.

I. Staple foods.
This is the general term for all staple foods. This taxable scope covers wheat, rice, maize (corn), kaoliang, millets, soybeans and other food crops (barley, oats, etc.) and flour, husked rice, corn flour processed therefrom, but excluding re-processed food crops (such as dried noodles, fresh noodles, yuntun peals, etc.) and all types of cooked staple foods.

II. Edible vegetable oils.
Vegetable oils are extracted from the roots, stems, leaves, fruits, flowers and embryos of plants and refined.
Edible vegetable oils include sesame oil, peanut oil, soybean oil, rape seed oil, rice bran oil, sunflower seed oil, cotton seed oil, corn embryo oil, tea oil (camellia oil), linseed oil, and mixtures of part of the oils listed above.

III. Running water.
Running water refers to water produced by waterworks after a series of processing including screening, segmentation, sterilization and provided to residents through pipelines.
Water used in agricultural irrigation or water sent by water diversion projects is not covered by this scope.

IV. Heat and hot water.
Heat and hot water refer to air and water heated warm or hot water and heat with all sorts of fuel (such as coal, rock oil and other gaseous, liquid and solid fuels) and electricity, and heat energy exploited from natural resources such as geothermal energy and solar energy.

This scope also covers the heat and hot water recovered from industrial wastes.

V. Refrigerated air refers to cool ail refrigerated by machine and provided to homes through air-conditioning systems.

VI. Gas.
Gas refers to the products through distillation or gasification of coal, coke, semi-coke and heavy oil.
Gas covers:

(1) Gas from coke ovens refers to the gas resulting from dry distillation in the coke oven.
(2) Gas from gas ovens refers to gas, mixed gas, mono-water-gas and bi-water-gas, etc.
(3) Liquefied gas refers to liquefied gas after compression.

VII. LPG refers to liquefied petrol gas produced from hydrocarbon generators liquefied through compression in the course of oil refining, the major contents of which are propane, butane and butylene etc.

VIII. Natural gas.
Natural gas, the inflammable gas of hydrocarbons deposited underground, the major contents of which are methane, ethane and others of methane series, and propane, butane and pentane and other heavy hydrocarbons.
Natural gas includes gas from gas fields, oilfields, coal deposits and other natural gas.

IX. Marsh gas.
Marsh gas is an inflammable gas with methane as its main content which is produced through natural decomposition from plant debris in sealed containers.
March gas includes both natural marsh gas and artificially produced marsh gas.

X. Coal products for civil use.
They include coal balls, coal cakes, coal cakes with perforated holes and kindling coal.

XI. Books, newspapers and magazines.
Books, newspapers and magazines are paper prints of words, pictures, graphs and tables, including:

(1) Books: those books of words and pictures printed by publishing houses with the approval of the State Press and Publication Administration and printed with internationally accepted book serial numbers.
(2) Newspapers: journals printed with the approval of the State Press and Publication Administration and registered with the press and publication administrative departments of the provinces, autonomous regions and municipalities directly under the State Council, each newspaper carrying a domestic press serial number starting with CN.
(3) Magazines: those printed with the approval of the State Press and Publication Administration and registered with the press and publication

administrative departments of the provinces, autonomous regions and municipalities directly under the State Council, each newspaper carries a domestic press serial number starting with CN.

XII. Feed.
Feed refers to products and processed products as feed for domestic animals. This scope covers:

(1) Mono feed: this refers to a product from one kind of animals, plants, microbes and products processed from one kind of them.
(2) Mixed feed: this refers to feed by mixing two or more than two types of feed.
(3) Composite feed: this refers to feed of a mixture of ingredients to maintain different proportions of nutrients to meet the need of different animals at different stages of growth and made into specific forms with the ingredients evenly mixed.
Grains, feed additives used as direct feed to animals are not covered by this scope of goods.

XIII. Chemical fertilizers.
Chemical fertilizers include:

(1) Chemical nitrogenous fertilizer, including primarily urea, and ammonium sulphate, ammonium nitrate, ammonium bicarbonate, ammonium chloride, calcium ammonium, and ammonia liquor, etc.
(2) Phosphate fertilizer, mainly including phosphorous fertilizer, calcium super phosphate (including calcium super phosphate and concentrated super phosphate), calcium magnesium phosphate, cinder phosphate fertilizer, etc.
(3) Potash fertilizer, primarily including potassium sulphate, muriate of potash, etc.
(4) Composite fertilizer, mainly composite fertilizer containing two or more types of elements of nitrogen, potash and phosphate produced through chemical or mechanical processes. Those containing two elements are called bi-component fertilizer and those containing three elements are called triple-component fertilizer, and those containing more than three are termed multi-component fertilizer, primarily including Nitra phosphate fertilizer, ammonium sulphate, phosphate potash fertilizer, calcium magnesium phosphate fertilizer, di-ammonium phosphate fertilizer, tri-ammonium phosphate powder, nitrogen, phosphate and potash composite fertilizer, etc.
(5) Micro-element fertilizer, mainly fertilizers that contain boron, manganese, zinc, copper, molybdenum or other trace elements needed for plant growth.
(6) Other fertilizers: fertilizers other than those cited above.

XIV. Pesticides.
Pesticides include chemicals for the control of pests to farming, forestry and chemicals for the control of the growth of grass, such as pesticides, germicide, herbicide and plant auxin, which may be made from herbs, microorganic pesticide, health drugs, other farm-use chemicals and chemical preparations.

XV. Farm-use plastic sheets.
Plastic sheets to be used to cover seedbeds and hothouses.

XVI. Farm machinery.
They include machines, semi-mechanized tools and tools used in all branches of agriculture including also forestry, animal husbandry, side-line production, fish farming, etc.
Farm machinery includes:

(1) Tractors: They include tractors driven by diesel engines for farming activities and field transportation, including wheel tractors, caterpillar tractors, hand tractors and mechanical farming vessels.
(2) Land working machines: They include machine-drawn ploughs, harrowers, disc ploughs, compressors, combine tillers, soil mixers, and other farm work machines.
(3) Machines for field construction, specifically those machines to be used in capital construction on crop land, including ditch diggers, pipeline layers, bulldozers, land levellers, etc.
(4) Planting machines: They include speeders, rice translators, planters, plastic sheet spreaders, complex speeders, crop sprouts preparing machines, etc.
(5) Machines for plant protection and field management, including powder dusting machines, chemical-spraying machines, fog sprayers, pruning machines, cultivators, cultivator-speeders, fertilizer applying machines, etc.
(6) Harvesting machines: including harvesters of cereals, cotton, tubers, sugarcanes, tealeaves, oil-bearing crops, etc.
(7) Machines on farmyards: including threshers, screens, driers, seed selectors, etc.
(8) Irrigation and drainage machines: all types of machines for irrigation and drainage on farm land and stock farms, also including well diggers, water sprinklers, semi-mechanical water pumping equipment, etc.
This scope does not cover machinery made with farm and side-line produce as raw material.
This scope does not cover machinery that processes industrial products with farm produce and farm side-line products as raw material.
(9) Machines for processing farm produce and agricultural side-line products: machines for the primary processing of farm products which after primary processing remain farm produce and products of agricultural side-line products, including tea processing machines, husking

machines, cotton ginning machines and balers, edible fungi cultivators, small grain processors, etc.
This category does not include those machines using farm products as raw material to produce industrial products.

(10) Farm transport machines: all sorts of machines and equipment used for transport purpose on the farm, including carts drawn by tractors, draft animals and manual power, but excluding three-wheel trucks.

(11) Animal husbandry machines: all types of machines used in the production on dairy and stock farms, including grassland building machines, domestic animal feeding equipment, animal products collecting machines and equipment, etc.

(12) Fishery and fish farming machines: they include all types of fishing equipment and machinery, oxygenizing machines, bait makers, etc.
This category does not include mechanized fishing vessels.

(13) Forestry machines and equipment: they include forestry planting and nursing equipment, sapling planters, machines used in tree nurseries, etc. but excluding tree felling and logging machines.

(14) Small farm tools, including animal drawn ploughs and harrowers, spades, sickles, and other small farm tools.
This category does not cover auxiliary parts of farm machines.

Provisions on Some Specific Issues Regarding Value-added Tax.

2009-04-13.

I. Scope of Taxation.

(1) The goods futures (including commodity futures and precious metal futures) are subject to value-added tax.
(2) The selling of gold and silver by banks is subject to value-added tax.
(3) The financial leasing is not subject to value-added tax, no matter whether the ownership of the leased goods has been transferred to the leasee.
(4) If the cement prefabrications, other components or building materials produced in the factories and workshops attached to the units engaged in capital construction or to the enterprises engaged in construction and installation are used for the construction projects of these units or enterprises, value-added tax shall be levied when they are moved for use. However, if the prefabrications produced at the construction sites are directly used for the construction projects of these units or enterprises, they are not subject to value-added tax.
(5) The selling of dead pawns by the pawn-broking industry and the selling of consigned goods by the consignment industry on behalf of the consignors are all subject to value-added tax.

(6) The selling of master films, master videos and master cassettes arising from the transfer of copyrights and also the selling of computer software products arising from the transfer of the ownership of patented and unpatented technologies are not subject to value-added tax.
(7) The supply or extraction of unprocessed natural water (for example, the reservoirs supply water for agricultural irrigation and the factories extract groundwater for production) are not subject to value-added tax.
(8) The selling of collectible stamps and first-day covers by the postal departments is subject to value-added tax.
(9) Sewing is subject to value-added tax.

II. Bases for Taxation.

(1) If the deposits charged by the taxpayers when leasing or lending the packing articles for selling goods are separately booked and accounted, they shall not be included into the value of sales for tax collection. However, if the deposits are not refunded because the packing articles are not returned after the time limit, value-added tax shall be collected at the tax rates applicable to the packed goods.
(2) When the taxpayers sell goods at discount, value-added tax shall be collected according to the discounted value of sales if the value of sales and the discounted amount are separately marked in the same invoice. But if a separate invoice is issued for the discounted amount, the discounted amount shall not be deducted from the value of sales no matter how they are financially treated.
(3) If the taxpayers use the trade-in method to sell goods, the value of sales shall be determined according to the selling prices of the new goods in the same period.
If the taxpayers sell goods through principal repayment, the expenditure on principal repayment shall not be deducted from the value of sales.
(4) If the selling prices of the taxpayers are obviously low or the taxpayers have no selling prices and if the taxable prices shall be formed as required to determine the value of sales, the cost-profit ratio in the price-forming formula shall be 10%. But if the consumption tax of the goods shall be collected according to the ad valorem ratio, the cost-profit ratio in the pricing-forming formula shall be the cost-profit ratio specified in the Regulations on Some Specific Issues regarding Consumption Tax.

III. Standards for Small Taxpayers.

(1) The value of sales mentioned in the provisions on the standards for small taxpayers specified in Article 24 of the Regulations on Value-added Tax refers to the value of sales of the small taxpayers specified in Article 25 of the same Regulations.
(2) The taxpayers specified in Article 24 of the above Regulations who are mainly engaged in the production of goods or the provision of taxable labour and also engaged in the wholesale or retail of goods refer to the

taxpayers whose value of sales for goods or taxable labour exceeds 50% of the total annual taxable value of sales or whose value of sales of the wholesale or retail goods is below 50%.

IV. When the fixed businesses sell goods outside their native counties (cities), they shall apply to the competent tax authorities in the places where their institutions are located for issuing the tax management certificates on outside economic activities and return to the places where their institutions are located for making tax reports to the tax authorities. If these businesses do not have the tax management certificates on outside economic activities issued by the competent tax authorities in the places where their institutions are located, the competent tax authorities in the places of sales must collect tax at the rate of 6%. With regard to the value of sales occurred in the places of sales, these businesses shall still make tax declarations as required after they return to the places where their institutions are located and the tax paid by them at the places of sales shall not be deducted from the payable tax in the period.

Detailed Rules for Implementing the Interim Regulations of the People's Republic of China on Value-added Tax.

No. 50 Decree of the Ministry of Commerce and the State Administration of Taxation.

December 15, 2008.

Article 1

The Detailed Rules are formulated according to the provisions of the Interim Regulations of the People's Republic of China on Value-added Tax (hereinafter referred to as the Regulations).

Article 2

The "goods" mentioned in Article 1 of the Regulations refers to tangible movables, including electric power, thermal power and gas.

The "processing" mentioned in Article 1 of the Regulations refers to commissioned processing of goods, a business where the entrusted party produces goods with the raw materials and principal materials provided by the entrusting party according to the requirements of the entrusting party and receives processing fees.

The "repair and replacement" mentioned in Article 1 of the Regulations refers to the businesses of being entrusted to restore the damaged or malfunctioned goods to their original conditions and functions.

Article 3

The "sales of goods" mentioned in Article 1 of the Regulations refers to the transfer of the ownership of goods with compensations.

The "provision of processing, repair and replacement services" (hereinafter referred to as taxable services) mentioned in Article 1 of the Regulations refers to the provision of services of processing, repair and replacement with compensations.

The provision of processing, repair and replacement services by the employee of a unit or an individual industrial and commercial household to their unit or employer are excluded.

The term "compensation" herein refers to the obtaining of money, goods or any economic benefit from the purchasers.

Article 4

The following activities of a unit or an individual industrial and commercial household shall be deemed as sale of goods:

(1) Consignment of goods to other units or individuals for sale;
(2) Sale of goods on a commission basis;
(3) Transfer of goods from one agency to another agency for sale by the taxpayer that has two or more agencies and adopts unified accounting, unless the relevant agencies are located in the same county (or city);
(4) Use of self-produced goods or goods processed on commission for non-VAT taxable items;
(5) Use of self-produced goods or goods processed on commission for collective welfare or personal consumption;
(6) Provision of self-produced or purchased goods or goods processed on commission to other units or individual industrial and commercial households as investments;
(7) Distribution of self-produced or purchased goods or goods processed on commission to shareholders or investors; and
(8) Donation of self-produced or purchased goods or goods processed on commission to other units or individuals without compensation.

Article 5

A sales activity involving both goods and non-VAT taxable services shall be deemed as a mixed sales activity. Except otherwise stipulated in Article 6 herein, the mixed sales activities of enterprises, enterprise units and individual industrial and commercial households engaged in production, wholesale and retail of goods shall be deemed as sale of goods, for which VAT shall be paid. The mixed sales activities of other units and individuals shall be deemed as sale of non-VAT taxable services, for which no VAT shall be paid.

The non-VAT taxable services mentioned in the first paragraph of this Article refer to the services subject to business tax within the scope of the taxable items of industries including transportation, construction, finance and insurance, communication, culture and sport, recreation and services.

The enterprises, enterprise units or individual industrial and commercial households engaged in production, wholesale or retail of goods as mentioned in the first paragraph of this Article include units and individual industrial and commercial households mainly engaged in the production, wholesale or retail of goods and concurrently engaged in non-VAT taxable services.

Article 6

If taxpayers have the following mixed sales activities, separate accountings of the sales amounts of goods and the turnovers of non-VAT taxable services shall be made with calculation of the payable VAT according to the sales amounts of goods and no VAT shall be paid for the turnovers of non-VAT taxable services. If they fail to make separate accountings, the sales amounts of their goods shall be calculated and checked by the tax authorities:

(1) Activities of sale of self-produced goods and provision of services in construction industry concurrently; and
(2) Other circumstances prescribed by the Ministry of Finance and the State Administration of Taxation.

Article 7

Taxpayers engaged in non-VAT taxable items concurrently shall have separate accountings of the sales amounts of goods or taxable services and the turnovers of VAT taxable items; and if they fail to make separate accountings, the sales amounts of goods or taxable services shall be calculated and checked by the tax authorities.

Article 8

The sale of goods or provision of processing, repair and replacement services in the territory of the People's Republic of China (hereinafter referred to as within the territory) as mentioned in Article 1 of the Regulations means:

(1) The starting place for shipping or the location of the sold goods is within the territory; or
(2) The taxable services provided take place within the territory.

Article 9

The units mentioned in Article 1 of the Regulations refer to the enterprises, administrative units, institutions, military units, social communities and other units.

The individuals mentioned in Article 1 of the Regulations refer to the individual industrial and commercial households and other individuals.

Article 10

For enterprises leased or contracted out to other units or individuals for operation, the lessee or contractor shall be the taxpayers.

Article 11

The amount of VAT returned to purchasers due to the return or rebate of the sold goods by taxpayers other than small scale taxpayers (hereinafter referred to as the general taxpayers) shall be deducted from the amount of output tax of the period when the return or rebate of sold goods took place; and the amount of VAT withdrew due to the return or rebate of sold goods shall be deducted from the amount of input tax of the period when the return or rebate of sold goods took place.

In any circumstance where the return or rebate of sold goods takes place or there is anything wrong about invoices after the issuance of VAT special invoices for sold goods or taxable services from general taxpayers, they shall issue special VAT invoices in red characters in accordance with the provisions of the State Administration of Taxation. If they fail to issue the said invoices, the amount of VAT shall not be deducted from the amount of output tax.

Article 12

The other fees mentioned in Paragraph 1 of Article 6 of the Regulations include handling fees, subsidies, funds, fund raising fees, profits sharing, bonuses, penalties, delinquency charges, interests on deferred payments, damages, collections for others, advance money for others, packing charges, rentals on packing materials, reserve charges, quality charges, transportation expenses, loading and unloading charges and any charges of various natures, exclusive of the following items:

(1) Consumption tax collected or withheld on taxable consumer goods processed on commission;
(2) Advance transportation expenses for others that satisfy both conditions as follows:

    a. Where the invoices of the transportation department for transportation expenses have been issued to the purchaser; and
    b. Where the taxpayers have delivered the same invoices to the purchasers.

(3) Collection of governmental funds or administrative charges for others that satisfy all the following conditions:

    a. Governmental funds established upon approval of the State Council or the Ministry of Finance or administrative charges established upon approval of the State Council or People's governments at provincial level as well as their financial or price authorities;
    b. Financial invoices printed by treasury departments above provincial level have been issued upon collection; and
    c. The money collected will be handed over to the treasury departments in full.

(4) Premiums collected from purchasers for insurance handled on behalf of the purchasers when the goods are sold, and the tax on purchasing vehicles and charges on vehicle licenses paid on behalf of the purchasers that shall be collected from the purchasers.

Article 13

Where the mixed sales activities are subject to VAT in accordance with Article 5 herein, the sales amounts shall be the sum of the sales amounts of goods and the turnovers of the non-VAT taxable services.

Article 14

Where the pricing method of combining the sales amounts and output tax is adopted for the sold goods or taxable services of general taxpayers, the sales amounts shall be calculated according to the following formula:

$$\text{Sales amounts} = \text{Sales amounts including tax} \div (1 + \text{Tax rate}).$$

Article 15

Where a taxpayer settles its/his sales amounts in currencies other than Renminbi, the Renminbi conversion rate for the sales amounts to be selected may be the medium price of Renminbi exchange rate on the day or on the first day of the month when the sale took place. Taxpayers shall determine the conversion rate to be adopted in advance and no change is permitted within one year once determined.

Article 16

For taxpayers whose prices are obviously low without due reasons as mentioned in Article 7 of the Regulations or who have activities that shall be deemed as sale of goods as mentioned in Article 4 herein but without sales amounts, the sales shall be determined according to the following order:

(1) Determined according to the average sale price of the taxpayer on the same goods in the latest period;
(2) Determined according to the average sale price of other taxpayers on the same goods in the latest period; and
(3) Determined according to the composite taxable value. The formula of the composite taxable value shall be:

$$\text{Composite taxable value} = \text{Cost} \times (1 + \text{Cost profit rate}).$$

For goods subject to consumer tax, the composite taxable value shall include consumer tax payable.

The "cost" in the formula refers to the actual production cost of sale of self-produced goods or the actual purchasing cost of sale of purchased goods. The cost profit rate in the formula shall be determined by the State Administration of Taxation.

Article 17

The purchase price mentioned in Paragraph 2 (3) of Article 8 of the Regulations includes the price indicated in the invoices for purchase or sale of agricultural produces when the taxpayers purchase such produces and the tobacco tax paid according to provisions.

Article 18

The transportation expenses mentioned in Paragraph 2 (4) of Article 8 of the Regulations refer to the transportation expenses indicated on the settlement documents of transportation expenses (including transportation expenses of interim regulatory railway lines and special railway lines) and construction funds, excluding loading and unloading charges, premiums and other charges.

Article 19

The deduction vouchers of VAT mentioned in Article 9 of the Regulations refer to special VAT invoices, special bills of payment of customs import VAT, invoices for purchase and sale of agricultural products and documents of settlement of transportation expenses.

Article 20

For any mixed sales activity which is subject to VAT according to Article 5 herein, the input tax on goods purchased for use in non-VAT taxable services involved in the mixed sales activity that satisfies the provisions of Article 8 of the Regulations is permitted to be credited against the output tax.

Article 21

The goods purchased as mentioned in Article 10 (1) of the Regulations exclude fixed assets used for VAT taxable items (excluding VAT exempt items) and non-VAT taxable items and VAT exempt items (hereinafter referred to as tax-free items), collective welfare or individual consumption.

The fixed assets mentioned in the preceding paragraph refer to machinery, mechanical equipment, means of transport and other equipment, tools and apparatus related to production or operation with the useful life exceed 12 months.

Article 22

The individual consumption mentioned in Article 10 (1) of the Regulations includes the social intercourse expenses of the taxpayers.

Article 23

The non-VAT taxable items mentioned in Article 10 (1) of the Regulations and herein refer to provision of non-VAT taxable services, transfer of intangible assets, sale of real estate and real estate under construction.

The real estate mentioned in the preceding paragraph refers to property's immovable or whose nature or shape will be changed after moving, including buildings, structures and other attachments to land.

The real estate of taxpayers which is newly built, reconstructed or expanded or under restoration or decoration belongs to real estate under construction.

Article 24

The abnormal losses mentioned in Article 10 (2) of the Regulations refers to the losses due to theft, spoilage or deterioration resulting from improper management.

Article 25

The input tax of the motorcycles, autos and yachts subject to VAT that are used by taxpayers themselves shall not be credited against output tax.

Article 26

Where the input tax of the general taxpayers engaged in tax-free items or non-VAT taxable services is unable to divide to credit against output tax, the following formula shall be adopted to calculate the non-deductible input tax:

$$\begin{aligned}\text{Non-deductible input tax} = {} & \text{Total undivided input tax of the month} \\ & \times \text{Sum of the sales amounts of tax} \\ & - \text{free items of the month and the} \\ & \ \text{turnovers of non-VAT taxable services} \\ & \div \text{Sum of the total sales amounts and} \\ & \quad \text{turnovers of the month}\end{aligned}$$

Article 27

Where the purchased goods or taxable services with input tax deducted are in any of the circumstances prescribed in Article 10 of the Regulations (excluding tax-free items and non-VAT taxable services), the input tax of the purchased goods or taxable services shall be deducted from the input tax of the same period; if the said input tax cannot be determined, the deductible input tax shall be calculated according to the actual costs of the same period.

Article 28

The standards for the small-scale taxpayers as mentioned in Article 11 of the Regulations are as follows:

(1) A taxpayer engaged in production of goods or provision of taxable services and a taxpayer mainly engaged in production of goods or provision of taxable services and in wholesale or retail of products at the same time, whose annual sales amount subject to VAT (hereinafter referred to as the taxable sales amount) is less than RMB 500,000 (inclusive, the same below); and
(2) Any taxpayers other than the taxpayers prescribed in Paragraph 1 (1) of this Article, whose annual taxable sales amount is less than RMB 800,000.

The "taxpayers mainly engaged in production of goods or provision of taxable services" prescribed in Paragraph 1 of this Article means the sales amount of the annual production of goods or provision of taxable services of the taxpayers account for more than 50% of their annual taxable sales amount.

Article 29

Other individuals with annual taxable sales amount exceeding the standards of small-scale taxpayers pay taxes as small-scale taxpayers; and non-enterprise units and enterprises which do not have taxable activities regularly may choose to pay taxes as small-scale taxpayers.

Article 30

The sales amount of small-scale taxpayers excludes taxes payable.

For small-scale taxpayers adopting the pricing method of combining the sales amount and tax payable for its or his sale of goods or provision of taxable services, the sales amount shall be calculated according to the following formula:

$$\text{Sales amount} = \text{Sales amount including tax} \div (1 + \text{Levy rate}).$$

Article 31

The sales amount returned to purchasers by the small-scale taxpayers due to the return or rebate of the sold goods shall be deducted from the sales amount of the period when the return or rebate of sold goods took place.

Article 32

The sound accounting as mentioned in Article 13 of the Regulations and the Detailed Rules herein refers to the capability of setting up account books according to the national unified accounting system and carrying out accounting according to valid and effective vouchers.

Article 33

Except as otherwise stipulated by the State Administration of Taxation, taxpayers that once have been confirmed as general taxpayers shall not turn to be small-scale taxpayers.

Article 34

General taxpayers in any of the following circumstances shall calculate its/his tax payable based on the sales amount and according to the VAT rates, but no input tax can be credited against output tax and special VAT invoices shall not be used:

(1) The accounting systems of general taxpayers are unsound or fail to provide accurate tax information; or
(2) Except as otherwise stipulated in Article 29 herein, the sales amount of a taxpayer exceeds the standards of small-scale taxpayer, but the taxpayer has not applied for the procedures of confirmation as general taxpayers.

Article 35

The scopes of the part of tax-free items stipulated in Article 15 of the Regulations are prescribed as follows:

(1) The agriculture mentioned in Paragraph 1 (1) refers to plant production, livestock breeding, forestry, animal husbandry and aquatic products industry.

The agricultural producers including units and individuals engaged in agricultural production.

The agricultural products refer to primary agricultural products, the specific scopes of which shall be determined by the Ministry of Finance and the State Administration of Taxation.

(2) The antique books as mentioned in Paragraph 1 (3) refer to the ancient books and used books purchased from the public; and
(3) The goods which have been used as mentioned in Paragraph 1 (7) refer to the goods that have been used by other individuals.

Article 36

Where the sold goods or taxable services provided by taxpayers are applicable to the provisions on exemption of taxes, the taxpayers may give up the said exemption and pay VAT according to the Regulations. The taxpayers shall not apply for exemption of tax within 36 months after its/his waiver of such exemption.

Article 37

The scope of application of VAT minimum threshold is limited to individuals.

The ranges of the VAT minimum threshold are stipulated as follows:

(1) The minimum threshold for sale of goods shall be monthly sales amount of RMB 2000–5000;
(2) The minimum threshold for sale of taxable services shall be monthly sales amount of RMB 1500–3000; and
(3) The minimum threshold for the payment of tax on transaction-by-transaction basis shall be the sales amount per transaction (or per day) of RMB 150–200.

The sales amount mentioned in the preceding paragraphs refers to the sales amount of small-scale taxpayers as mentioned in Paragraph 1 of Article 30 herein.

The treasury departments (bureaus) of all provinces, autonomous regions and municipalities directly under the Central Government and national tax bureaus shall determine the minimum threshold applicable locally within the prescribed range according to actual conditions and report to the Ministry of Finance and the State Administration of Taxation for filing.

Article 38

The date on which the sales amount is received or the vouchers for collecting the sales amount are obtained as prescribed in Paragraph 1 (1) of Article 19 of the Regulations is specified according to the different methods of settlement for sale as follows:

(1) For sale of goods by method of direct payment, it shall be the date on which the sales amount is received or the vouchers for collecting the sales amount are obtained, regardless whether the goods are delivered;
(2) For sale of goods by method of collection and acceptance and entrustment of banks to collect payment, it shall the date on which the goods have been delivered and collection procedures have been handled;
(3) For sale of goods on credit or collection by instalments, it shall be the date of collection as agreed in written contracts; and if there is no written contract or there is no agreed date of collection in the written contracts, it shall be the date on which the goods are delivered;
(4) For sale of goods with payment received in advance, it shall be the date on which the goods are delivered, but for goods including large machinery, ships and airplanes, the period of production and sale of which exceeds 12 months, it shall be the date on which the advance payment is received or the collection date stipulated in written contracts;
(5) For sale of goods on a commission basis by other taxpayers, it shall be the date on which the lists of goods sold on commission issued by the consignee are received or sales amount are received wholly or partly. If the lists of goods sold on commission or sales amount are not received, the date shall be the date that 180 days from the delivery of such goods;
(6) For sale of taxable services, it shall be the date on which the services are provided, and the sales amount is received or the vouchers for collecting sales amount is obtained; and
(7) For the activities of taxpayers that are deemed as sale of goods listed in Article 4 (3)–(8) herein, it shall be the date on which the goods are transferred.

Article 39

The provision on one quarter as payment period in Article 23 of the Regulations is only applicable to small-scale taxpayers. The specific period for payment of taxes by small-scale taxpayers shall be determined by the tax authorities according to the amount of tax payable separately.

Article 40.

The Detailed Rules shall enter into force on January 1, 2009.

Ministry of Finance.

State Administration of Taxation.

December 15, 2008.

Circular on Several Issues Concerning the Implementation of Transformation and Reform of Value-added Tax in China.

No. 170 of Dec. 19, 2008.

Financial departments (bureaus) and state administration of taxation of provinces, autonomous regions, municipalities directly under the Central Government and separately planning cities, and financial bureau of Xinjiang Production and Construction Corp.

For the purpose of improving the VAT system and promoting the stable and fast development of national economy, the State Council has decided to transform and reform VAT in China since January 1, 2009. For full implementation of the reform, the relevant issues are hereby notified as follows:

Article 1

Since January 1, 2009, the input tax incurred on purchase (including acceptance of donation and investment in kind, the same below) or self-production (including reconstruction and expansion and installation, the same below) of fixed assets (hereinafter referred to as the input tax of fixed assets) by general taxpayers of VAT (hereinafter referred to as taxpayers) may be credited from the output tax against special VAT invoices, special bills of payment of customs import VAT, and documents of settlement of transportation expenses (hereinafter referred to as the deduction vouchers of VAT) in accordance with the relevant provisions of the Interim Regulations of the People's Republic of China on Value-added Tax (No. 538 Decree of the State Council, hereinafter referred to as the Regulations) and the Detailed Rules for Implementing the Interim Regulations of the People's Republic of China on Value-added Tax (No. 50 Decree of the Ministry of Finance and the State Administration of Taxation, hereinafter referred to as the Detailed Rules), and the input tax shall be credited under the item of "taxes payable—VAT payable (input tax)".

Article 2

The deductible input tax of fixed assets of taxpayers refers to the amount of VAT of taxpayers occurred on and after January 1, 2009 and indicated on the deduction vouchers of VAT issued on and after January 1, 2009 or calculated according to the deduction vouchers of VAT.

Article 3

No tax refund will be applied to the input tax of fixed assets occurred on and after January 1, 2009 of taxpayers in the old industrial bases in northeast China, the old industrial base cities in the six provinces of central China and the eastern area of Inner Mongolia Autonomous Region which have implemented the pilot expansion of VAT credit scope, and the ending balances of the input tax of fixed assets of the said taxpayers occurred on and before Dec. 31, 2008 that are to be credited shall be transferred to under the item of "tax payable—VAT payable (input tax)" in January 2009 on lump-sum basis.

Article 4

Since January 1, 2009, for sale of fixed assets used by taxpayers (hereinafter referred to as the used fixed assets), the VAT shall be imposed by different circumstances:

(1) For sale of the self-used fixed assets that were purchased or self-produced on and after January 1, 2009, VAT shall be imposed according to applicable tax rates;
(2) For sale of the self-used fixed assets that were purchased or self-produced on and before Dec. 31, 2008 by taxpayers who are not in the places that implement the pilot expansion of VAT deduction scope on and before Dec.31, 2008, the VAT shall be imposed at half of 4% tax rate; and
(3) For sale of the self-used fixed assets that were purchased or self-produced before the expansion of the pilot scope by the taxpayers who are in the places that implement the pilot expansion of VAT deduction scope on and before Dec. 31, 2008, the VAT shall be imposed at half of 4%; and for sale of used fixed assets purchased or self-produced by the said taxpayers after the expansion of the pilot scope, the VAT shall be imposed at the applicable tax rates.

The used fixed assets mentioned herein refer to the fixed assets after depreciation accrued by taxpayers according to the financial accounting system.

Article 5

If the fix assets of taxpayers with credit of input tax are in any of the circumstances prescribed in Articles 10 (1)–(3) of the Regulations, the amount of the non-deductible input tax of the same month shall be calculated according to the following formula:

$$\begin{aligned}&\text{The amount of the non - deductible input tax}\\&\quad = \text{Net value of the fixed assets} \times \text{Applicable tax rate.}\end{aligned}$$

The net value of the fixed assets mentioned herein refers to the net value of the fixed assets calculated by taxpayers according to the financial accounting system after the depreciation is accrued.

Article 6

Where taxpayers have any of the activities concerning fixed assets that shall be deemed as sale of goods as prescribed in Article 4 of the Detailed Rules and it is hard to determine the sales amount of the used fixed assets, the sales amount shall be the net value of the fixed assets.

Article 7

The implementation of the VAT exemption policy on import equipment and the VAT refund policy on purchase of Chinese equipment by foreign-invested enterprises shall be stopped since January 1, 2009, the specific measures of which shall be separately specified by the Ministry of Finance and the State Administration of Taxation.

Article 8

The Circular shall enter into force on January 1, 2009, and the following documents shall be repealed simultaneously: the Circular of the Ministry of Finance and the State Administration of Taxation on Printing and Issuing of the Provisions on Several Issues Concerning the Expansion of Value-added Tax Deduction Scope in Northeast China (Cai Shui [2004] No. 156), the Circular of the Ministry of Finance and the State Administration of Taxation on Printing and Issuing of the Interim Measures for Expansion of Value-added Tax Deduction Scope in Northeast China in 2004 (Cai Shui [2004] No. 168), the Urgent Circular of the Ministry of Finance and the State Administration of Taxation on Further Implementing the Expansion of Value-added Tax Deduction Scope of Value-added Tax in Northeast China (Cai Shui [2004] No. 226), the Circular of the Ministry of Finance and the State Administration of Taxation on Issues Concerning the Implementation of Expansion of Value-added Tax Deduction Scope in Enterprises Engaged in Producing Military and High-tech Products in Northeast China (Cai Shui [2004] No. 227), the Circular of the State Administration of Taxation on Recognition of the Enterprises for the Program of Expansion of Value-added Tax Deduction Scope (Guo Shui Han [2004] No. 143), the Circular of the Ministry of Finance and the State Administration of Taxation on Issues Concerning the Expansion of Value-added Tax Deduction Scope in Northeast China in 2005 (Cai Shui [2005] No. 28), the Circular of the Ministry of Finance and the State Administration of Taxation on Issues Concerning the Tax Refund of Input Tax on Fixed Assets for the Northeast China in the Expansion of Value-added Tax Offset and Deduction Scope in 2005 (Cai Shui [2005] No. 176), the Circular of the Ministry of Finance and the State Administration of Taxation on Issues Concerning the Implementation of Expansion of Value-added Tax Deduction Scope in Enterprises Engaged in Producing Military and High-tech Products in Northeast China (Cai Shui [2006] No. 15), the Circular of the Ministry of Finance and the State Administration of Taxation on Issues Concerning the Refund of Input Tax on Fixed Assets in Northeast China in 2006 (Cai Shui [2006] No. 156), the Circular of the Ministry of Finance and the State Administration of Taxation on Printing and Issuing the Interim Measures on the Expansion of Value-added Tax Deduction Scope in Central China (Cai Shui [2007] No. 75), the Supplementary Circular of the Ministry of Finance and the State Administration of Taxation on Issues Concerning the Tax Credit (Refund) of Fixed Assets for the Places in Expansion of Value-added Tax Deduction Scope in 2007 (Cai Shui [2007] No. 128), the Circular of the State Administration of Taxation on Printing and Issuing the Interim Administration Measures on Expansion of Value-added Deduction Scope (GuoShui Fa [2007] No. 62), the Circular of the Ministry of Finance and the State Administration of Taxation on Printing and Issuing of the Interim Measures on the Expansion of Value-added Tax Deduction Scope in Eastern Area of Inner Mongolia (Cai Shui [2008] No. 94), the Circular of the Ministry of Finance and the State Administration of Taxation on Printing and Issuing of the Interim Measures on the Expansion of Value-added Tax Deduction Scope in Areas Heavily Hit by Wenchuan Earthquake (Cai Shui [2008] No. 108) and the Circular of the Ministry of Finance and State Administration of Taxation on Issues Concerning

Refund of Input Tax on Fixed Assets for Northeast China, Central China and the Eastern Area of Inner Mongolia in the Expansion of Value-added Tax Credit Scope in 2008 (Cai Shui [2008] No. 141).

Ministry of Finance.

State Administration of Taxation.

Dec. 19, 2008.

Bibliography

Ainsworth, Avi-Yonah, et al. The VAT Reader: What Federal Consumption Tax Would Mean for America. (Tax Analysts, 2011)
Anderson & Co, China: Perspectives (1993)
Art and Gu, China Incorporated: The First Corporation Law of the People's Republic of China, 20 Yale J. Int'l L. 273 (1995)
Asia Law & Practice, Commercial Banking Law in the PRC (1995)
Asia Law & Practice, Forex Management for FIEs in the PRC (1996)
Asia Law & Practice, China Investment Manual (1994)
Asia Law & Practice, Establishing Representative And Branch Offices In The PRC (1996)
Asia Law & Practice, Life And Death Of a Joint Venture (1996)
Asia Law & Practice, Obtaining PRC Approvals For FIEs And Infrastructure Projects (1996)
Asia Law & Practice, PRC Joint Ventures: Drafting And Negotiating Contracts (1997)
Asia Law & Practice, The China Tax And Accounting Manual (1996)
Bachner, Regulating Pollution in the People's Republic of China: An Analysis of the Enforcement of Environmental Law, 7 Colo. J. Int'l Envtl. L. & Pol'y 373 (1996)
Bai: Chinese Constitutional Law, 26 Bracton L.J. 77 (1994)
Beaumont and Marcus, Chinese International Commercial Arbitration (Simmonds & Hill Publishing, Ltd., 1994)
Beaumont, Choi, Luk, Commentary On The Chinese Arbitration Act (Simmonds & Hill Publishing, Ltd., 1995)
Beijing Municipal Foreign Economic and Trade Commission, Beijing Municipal Planning Commission, and the Information Office of Beijing Municipal Government, Beijing Investment Guide (1995)
Berkman, Intellectual Property Rights in the PRC: Impediments to Protection and the Need for the Rule of Law, 15 Ucla Pac. Basin L.J. 1 (1996)
Bersani, Enforcement of Arbitration Awards in China: Foreigners Find the System Sorely Lacking, CHIN. BUS. REV., May-June 1992, at 6
Bing: Assessing China's Legal System of Judicial Review of Administrative Actions, 8 China L. Rep. 1 (1994)
Birden, Technology Transfers to China: An Outline of Chinese Law, 16 Loy. L.A. Int'l & Comp. L.J. 413 (1994)
Bloodworth, The Profile Of An Opportunity: The Risks And Rewards Of Investing In China (D., ed.) (Times Academic Press, 1995)
Bodde And Morris, Law And Imperial China (Harvard Univ. Press, 1967)
Brachner And Fu, Commercial Laws In The People's Republic Of China: Regulation And Reform (Michie, 1995)
Brahm, Banking and Finance in China (Michie, 1997)

L. Riccardi and G. Riccardi, *China VAT*,
https://doi.org/10.1007/978-981-15-5967-9

Brown, Understanding Chinese Courts And Legal Process: Law With Chinese Characters (Kluwer Law Tax Publications, 1997)
Cai and Harrison. The Value-Added Tax Reform Puzzle. (NBER, 2011).
Campbell, A Coming Of Age: Developments In Sino-Foreign Joint Ventures, Advances in Chinese Industrial Studies, Vol. 5,(Jai Press, 1997)
CCH Asia Pacific, China Labor And Social Security Law: Essential Facts Explained (1998)
Chang, American Business In China, 1998–1999 (Caravel, 1998)
Chaput, An Introduction to Insurance Law and Coverage in the People's Republic of China, 30 Tort & Ins. L.J. 871 (1995)
Chen, Changing Patterns In Chinese Foreign Trade Law And Institutions (Oceana, 1992)
Chen, From Administrative Authorization To Private Law: A Comparative Perspective Of The Developing Civil Law In The People's Republic Of China (Martinus-Nijhoff Publishers, 1994)
Chen: An Introduction To The Legal System Of The People's Republic Of China (Michie, 1992)
Chen: The Chinese Criminal Legal System and Its Impact on the Foreign Investor, 10 Chin. L. News 1 (1998)
Chen: The Criminal Justice System in China: Present Position and Development Trends, 1 China L.Q. 42 (1996)
China Hand, vol. 1–2 (The Economist Intelligence Unit)
China International Economic Consultants, Inc. China Investment Guide (CITIC Publishing House, and Longman, 1989)
China Law and Practice, 10 issues per year (Asia Law & Practice)
China Law Reference Service, vol. 1–8 (CCH International)
China Laws for Foreign Business, Business Regulation, vol. 1–4 (CCH International)
China Laws for Foreign Business, Customs (CCH International)
China Laws for Foreign Business, Special Zones and Cities, vol. 1–3 (CCH International)
China Laws for Foreign Business, Taxation (CCH International)
China Master Tax Guide 2008/09. 6th Edition. (CCH Hong Kong, 2008)
China Publishing House of Law, Accounting Standards for Business Enterprises (1993)
China Publishing House of Law, General Rules on Financial Affairs for the Enterprises (1993)
China Publishing House of Law, A Collection Of Tax Laws And Regulations Of The People's Republic Of China (1994)
China's Foreign Economic Legislation, vol. I-IV (China Foreign Language Press, 1979–85)
Chui and Yang, The Value-Added Tax in China: Identifying Important Issues, 23 Int'l Tax J. 71 (1997)
Cohen: The Criminal Process In The People's Republic Of China: 1949–1963 (Harvard Univ. Press 1968)
Collection Of Laws And Regulations Of China Concerning Import/Export Commodity Inspection (American Overseas Book Company, 1994)
Commission of the Standing Committee of the National People's Congress of the People's Republic of China)
Copenhagen Economics. Study on reduced VAT applied to goods and services in the Member States of the European Union: Final Report. (2007).
Corne, Foreign Investment In China: The Administrative Legal System (Transnational Publishers, Inc., 1997)
Cui. China's Business-Tax-To-Vat Reform: An Interim Assessment. (Allad School of Law at the University of British Columbia, 2014)
Curley and Fortunato, Tax Considerations for Investors in China: A Preliminary Look, 20 N.C.J. Int'l L. & Com. Reg. 531 (1995)
Cutshaw And Zhang, Corporate Counsel's Guide To Doing Business In China (Business Laws, Inc., 1995)
Dauchez and Vernay, Tax Treatment of FIE Reorganizations, 11 China L. & Prac. 55 (July/Aug. 1997)

David, A Review and Analysis of Enterprise Bankruptcy Laws in China, 2 Insolvency L.J. 164 (1994)

Dejun, Moser, Shengchang, International Arbitration In The People's Republic Of China: Commentary, Cases and Materials, Second Edition (Butterworths, 2000)

Dellapenna: The Role of Legal Rhetoric in the Failure of Democratic Change in China, 2 Buff. J. Int'l L. 231 (1995/96)

Fei, Copyright Practice in the Two Regimes of One Country: A Prospective Harmonization Process in Hong Kong and the PRC, 19 Eur. Intell. Prop. Rev. 360 (1997)

Finder: The Supreme People's Court of the People's Republic of China, 7 J. Chin. L. 145 (1993)

Folsom, Minan, And Otto, Law And Politics In The People's Republic Of China In A Nutshell (West Publishing, 1992)

Foreign Enterprise Services Corporation, Procedures For The Establishment Of Representative Offices Of Foreign Enterprises (1996)

Foreign Investment Administration, the China Economic and Trade Consultant Corporation, and the Ministry of Foreign Trade and Economic Cooperation, Investment in China (1993)

Fu, Select Bibliography on Chinese Business Law: Companies, Joint Venture, Banking, Insurance and Consumer Laws, 4 Canberra L. Rev. 257 (1997/1998)

Garland, Basic Concepts Of Chinese Law (T. Lee, ed.) (1996)

Gates, An Investor's Guide To China's Provinces And Cities, U.S.-China Business Council, Second Edition (2003)

Gelatt: Lawyers in China: The Past Decade and Beyond, 23 N.Y.U. J. Int'l L. & Pol. 751 (1991)

Gensler, The 1994 Consumption Tax of the People's Republic of China, 13 Ucla Pac. Basin L.J. 293 (1995)

Gensler, The 1994 Individual Income Tax Law of the People's Republic of China, 26 Cal. W. Int'l L.J. 115 (1995)

Gensler, The People's Republic of China Business Tax of 1994, 8 Transnat'l Law. 103 (1995)

Gongshang Publishing House, Guide To Trading And Investing In Shanghai (1994)

Grub and Lin, Foreign Direct Investment in China (Quorum Books, 1991)

Han, China's Company Law: Practicing Capitalism in a Transitional Economy, 5 Pac. Rim L. & Pol'y J. 457 (1996)

Harmer, Insolvency Law and Reform in the People's Republic of China, 64 Fordham L. Rev. 2563 (1996)

Hayward, China: Registration and Enforcement Procedures: Practical Steps for Doing Business in the PRC, 76 Trademark World 29 (1995)

Hecht: Opening To Reform?: An Analysis Of China's Revised Criminal Procedure Law (Lawyers Committee on Human Rights, 1996)

Hein, The 1997 Criminal Code Of The People's Republic Of China (1998)

Hill and Evans, Chinese Patent Law: Recent Changes Align China More Closely with Modern International Practice, 27 GW. J. Int'l L. & Econ. 359 (1993–94)

Hom, Legal Education in the People's Republic of China: A Select Annotated Bibliography of English-Language Materials, 6 China L. Rep. 73 (1989)

Hsu, The Common Law In Chinese Context (Hong Kong University Press, 1992)

Huang and Hua, An Overview of China's Real Estate Law, 28 J. Marshall L. Rev. 393 (1995)

Huang, An Introduction to Foreign Investment Laws in the People's Republic of China, 28 J. Marshall L. Rev. 593 (1995)

Huang, Civil Justice In China: Representation And Practice In The Qing (Stanford University Press, 1996)

Jan, How To Do Business With China (American Institute of Technology, 1997)

Jia, Metamorphosis Of Chinese Foreign Investment Laws And Policies: Implications For Economic Development In The 1990s And Beyond (Quorum Books, 1994)

Jianduan, A Milestone of Air Legislation in China: Some Thoughts on the Civil Aviation Law of the People's Republic of China, 62 J. Air L. & Com. 823 (Feb./March 1997)

Johnson, Chinese Law: A Bibliography Of Selected English-Language Materials (Diane Publications, 1995)
Jones, The Great Qing Code: A New Translation (Oxford University Press, 1994)
Josephs, Defamation, Invasion of Privacy, and the Press in the People's Republic of China, 11 UCLA Pac. Basin L.J. 191 (1993)
Josephs, Labor Law in a "Socialist Market Economy": The Case of China, 33 Colum. J. Transnat'l L. 559 (1995)
Josephs, Labor Law In China: Choice And Responsibility (Michie, 1990)
Kaplan, Spruce, Moser, Hong Kong and China Arbitration: Cases and Materials (Michie, 1994)
Keith, China's Struggle For The Rule Of Law (St. Martin's Press, 1994)
Kerzner, The Commercial Real Estate Laws of the People's Republic of China and Shenzhen: An Overview, 26 Vand. J. Transnat'l L. 581 (1993)
Khan, Patterns Of Direct Foreign Investment In China (World Bank, 1991)
Khu, Selected Bibliography of English-Language Materials on the Law of the People's Republic of China, 28 Colum. J. Transnat'l L. 531 (1990)
King and Tong: Consumer Protection In China: Translations, Developments and Recommendations (Rothman, 1991)
Krever, Li, Teoh. VAT Reform in China Reaches a Critical Turning Point. International Volume 82, Number 4. (Tax Notes Int'l, 2016)
KPMG International. Asia Pacific Indirect Taxes on The Rise. (KPMG International 2011)
Lam and Kan, Impact of Recent Changes in China's Foreign Security Measures in China Lending, 12 J. Int'l Banking L. 367 (1997)
Lange and Ross, New Project Finance Measures Further Limit Lenders' Room for Maneuver, in China Law & Practice 51–54 (June 1997)
Lapres and Yuejiao, Business Law In China: Trade Investment And Finance (International Chamber of Commerce, 1997)
Laws of the People's Republic of China, vol. 1–5 (Lubrecht& Cramer, 1996) (Legislative Affairs
Lees And Liaw, Foreign Participation in China's Banking and Securities Market (Quorum Books, 1996)
Lee. China Accounting 101: What is VAT Tax in China? . (Hongda, 2018).
Lehman, Lee & Xu. Value Added Tax Reform in China.
Li, Legal Aspects of Labor Relations in China: Critical Issues for International Investors, 33 Colum. J. Transnat'l L. 522 (1995)
Li, Na & Teoh, Jonathan & Krever, Richard. VAT Reform in China Reaches a Critical Turning Point. Tax Notes International. 82. 387–398. (2016).
Li, Walker, Fox, Lau, and Leung, Foreign Exchange Reform in the PRC: Impact on Foreign Direct Investment and State-Owned Enterprises, 11 J. Int'l Banking L. 228 (1996)
Li: Teaching, Research, and the Dissemination of International Law in China: The Contribution of Wang Tieya, 31 Can. Y.B. I. 189 (1993)
Lin, Chinese Law Past And Present (Columbia Univ. 1966)
Lo, Labor and Employment in the People's Republic of China: From a Non-Market-Driven to a Market-Driven Economy, 6 Ind. Int'l & Comp. L. Rev. 337 (1996)
Lu And Tang, State Intervention And Business In China: The Role Of Preferential Policies (Elgar, 1997)
Lugang, Customs Protection in the PRC, 82 Trademark World 12 (1995)
Lung, Annotated Bibliography of Selected English-Language Literature on Chinese Law, 6 Legal Reference Services Q. 95 (1986)
Luo, How to Find the Law of the People's Republic of China: A Research Guide and Selective Annotated Bibliography, 88 Law Libr. J. 402 (1996)
Luo, International Investment Strategies in the People's Republic Of China (Ashgate, 1998)
Ma, The Chinese Concept of the Individual and the Reception of Foreign Law, 9 J. Chin. L. 207 (1995)
Maccormack, The Spirit Of Traditional Chinese Law (University of Georgia Press, 1995)

Maccormack, Traditional Chinese Penal Law (Edinburgh University Press, 1991)
Mak, The Historical Development of Income Tax Law for Domestic and Foreign Enterprises in China, 22 Int'l Tax J. 51 (1996)
Marshall, Brink and Li, A Legal and Practical Overview of Direct Investment and Joint Ventures in the "New" China, 28 L. Rev. 567 (1995)
Maugue, Tax Incentives in the People's Republic of China: Who Benefits?, 5 Tul. J. Int'l & Comp. L. 155 (1997)
Mcknight, Law And Order In Sung China (Cambridge University Press, 1995)
Min, Qin, Tian, Practical Handbook Of Laws Of People's Republic Of China Governing Intellectual Property (PRC Publishing House of Law 1994)
Minor and Stevens-Minor, China's Emerging Bankruptcy Law, 22 Int'l Law. 1217 (1988)
Moser, International Arbitration in the People's Republic of China (Michie, 1995)
Mu and Guiguo, Chinese Foreign Economic Law: Analysis And Commentary (International Law Institute, 1994)
Nagle, The Missing Chinese Environmental Law Statutory Interpretation Cases, 5 N.Y.U. ENVTL. L.J. 517 (1996)
Nanpinq: An Ignored Source of Chinese Law: The Gazette of the Supreme People's Court, 5 Conn. J. Int'l l. 271 (1990)
Ng, An Overview of the Turnover Tax System in China and the Tax-Planning Opportunities for Foreign Investors, 23 INT'L TAX J. 25 (1997)
Ng. People's Republic of China: Corporate – Other taxes. (PwC, 2018).
Norland. China Completes the Process of Replacing Business Tax with VAT. (Bloomberg BNA, 2016)
Note, "Chinese Characteristics" in Corporate Clothing: Questions of Fiduciary Duty in China's Company Law, 80 Minn. L. Rev. 503 (1995)
Note, Bankruptcy Behind the Great Wall: Should U.S. Businesses Seeking to Invest in the Emerging Chinese Market Be Wary? 8 Transnat'l L. 351 (1995)
Note, China's Choice: Tax Incentives to Fund Economic Development, 9 Temp. Int'l & Comp. L.J. 413 (1995)
Note, China's Copyright Law and the TRIPS Agreement, 5 J. Transnat'l L. & Pol'y 431 (1996)
Note, Class Action Litigation in China, 6 Harv. L. Rev. 1523 (1998)
Note, Copyright Law and the People's Courts in the People's Republic of China: A Review and Critique of China's Intellectual Property Courts, 17 U. PA. J. Int'l Econ. L. 415 (1996)
Note, Playing by a New Set of Rules: Will China's New Arbitration Laws and Recent Membership in the ICC Improve Trade with China? 12 J. Int'l Arb. 51 (1995)
Note, Protecting Ideas and Ideals: Copyright Law in the People's Republic of China, 27 Law & Pol'y Int'l Bus. 1185 (1996)
Note, Selected Bibliography: the Reintegration of Hong Kong into China, 30 Vand. J. Transnat'l L. 793 (1997)
Note, The Company Law of the People's Republic of China, 13 Ucla Pac. Basin L.J. 373 (1995)
Note, The Sleeping Giant Awakens: The Development of Intellectual Property Law in China, 9 J. China L. 93 (1995)
NYU Press, Chinese Law And Legal Theory (M. Palmer, ed.) (1996)
Ou, The Practice of Patent Law in China: Some Firsthand Observations, 15 Wis. Int'l L. J. 313 (1997)
Oxford University Press, China's Legal Reform (S. Lubman, ed.) (1996)
Park, The Special Economic Zones Of China And Their Impact On Its Economic Development (Praeger Publishers, 1996)
Peck, Kung, and Ho, Enter the VAT, The China Business Review 40–43 (Mar./Apr. 1994)
Peerenboom, Law and Morality in Ancient China: The Silk Manuscripts of Huang-Lao, 106 Yale L. J. 1885 (1997)
Perkovich, A Comparative Analysis of Community Mediation in the United States and the People's Republic of China, 10 Temp. Int'l & Comp. L.J. 313 (1996)

Pinard, The People's Republic of China: A Bibliography of Selected Annotated English Language Legal Materials, 6 China L. Rep. 11 (1989)
Pinard, The People's Republic of China: A Bibliography of Selected English-Language Legal Materials, 3 China L. Rep. 46 (1985)
Ping, Chinese Legal Reform: Achievements, Problems and Prospects, 9 J. Chin. L. 67 (1995)
Pomfret, Investing In China: Ten Years Of The Open Door Policy (Iowa State University Press, 1991)
PRC Ministry of Power, The Regulations For Utilization Of Foreign Capital In China's Power Industry (Songbin Systems Press, 1997)
Qinhuo, The Legal Protection of the Insured's Rights and Interests under the Insurance Law of China, 4 Canberra L. Rev. 189 (1997/98)
QualityInspection. VAT Rebate for Exporters in China: How Does It Work?. (2018)
Quenedey and Yongqing, King & Wood Malleson. VAT reform in China. (Globe Business Media Group, 2018).
Ramjerdi and D'Amato, The Intellectual Property Rights Laws of the People's Republic of China, 21 N.C. J. Int'l L. & Com. Reg. 169 (1995)
Reinganum, Negotiating Direct Investment in the People's Republic of China, 1995 Priv. Inv. Abroad 24:1
Ren, Copyright Law of China: Can It Effectively Protect U.S. Works?, 16 Loy. L.A. Ent. L.J. 67 (1995)
Reuvid, Doing Business With China (Kogan Page Ltd., 1997)
Reyes: The Enforcement of Foreign Court Judgments in the People's Republic of China: What the American Lawyer Needs to Know, 23 Brook. J. Int'l L. 241 (1997)
Riccardi. Chinese Tax Law and International Treaties. (Springer, 2013).
Riccardi. Guida alla fiscalità di Cina, India e Vietnam. (II Sole 21 ORE S.p.A, 2011)
Roehrig, Foreign Joint Ventures In Contemporary China (St. Martin's Press, 1994)
Ross, The Next Wave of Environmental Legislation: Tougher Rules Could Have a Significant Impact on Key Chinese Sectors, Chin. Bus. Rev., July/Aug. 1994, at 30 L. Ross, Environmental Policy In China (Indiana University Press, 1988)
Ruilan, Handbook Of Regulations On Environmental Protection In China (Resources Future, 1995)
Ryan, World-Wide Pharmaceutical In China: Investing In And Bargaining With A Socialist State In Transition (Georgetown University, 1995)
Saadat: The Lawyer's Guide To China's Technical Regulations For Imported Products (American Bar Association, 2001)
Sang: China's Civil Procedure Law: A New Guide for Dispute Resolution in China, 26 Int'l Law. 413 (1992)
Seidman, Seidman And Payne, Legislative Drafting For Market Reform: Some Lessons From China (St. Martin's Press, 1997)
Shangquan and Chi Fulin, New Progress In China's Special Economic Zones (Foreign Language Press, 1997)
Shangquan and Fulin, eds.: Chinese Securities Market, Studies On The Chinese Market Economy Series (Foreign Language Press, 1996)
Shapiro, Direct Investment And Joint Ventures In China: A Handbook For Corporate Negotiations (Quorum Books, 1991)
Sharpe, Basic Principles Of Civil Law In China (W. Jones, ed.) (1989)
Shen, Anti-Dumping and Countervailing Laws: An Emerging System in China, 2 Asian Com. L. Rev. 135 (July/Aug. 1997)
Simms, China's Insurance Law, Chin. Bus. Rev., Sept./Oct. 1996, at 30
Simone, A Stronger Front Line: New Customs Regulations May Help Enforce Intellectual Property Rights, Chin. Bus. Rev., Mar./April 1996, at 36
Smil, China's Environmental Crisis: An Inquiry Into The Limits Of National Development (East Gate Books, 1993)

Snell: The Development of Competition Policy in the People's Republic of China, 28 N.Y.U. J. Int'l L. & Pol. 575 (1996)
Sommers and Phillips, Assessing the Tax Administration Law of the People's Republic of China, 18 Loy. L.A. Int'l & Comp. L.J. 339 (1996)
Song: Competition Policy in a Transitional Economy: The Case of China, 31 Stan. J. Int'l L. 387 (1995)
Stephens, Order And Discipline In China: The Shanghai Mixed Court, 1911–1927 (University of Washington Press, 1991)
Stewart, Environmental Statutory Interpretation in China and the United States, 5 N.Y.U. Envtl. L.J. 556 (1996)
Strange, Slater, And Wang, Trade And Investment In China: The European Experience (Routledge, 1998)
Streng and Wilcox Doing Business In China (Juris Publishing, Inc., 1990)
Sun, Foreign Investment And Economic Development In China, 1979–1996 (Ashgate, 1998)
Symposium, Doing Business in China, 14 NW. J. Int'l L. & Bus. 15 (1993)
Symposium, Focus on Privatization in China, 5 Duke J. Comp. & Int'l L. 145 (1995)
Symposium, Intellectual Property Protection of Software: International Perspectives, 14 J. Marshall J. Computer & Info. L. 657 (1996)
Thompson, China's Local Councils In The Age Of Constitutional Reform, 1898–1911 (Harvard University Press, 1995)
Thomson, Liability to Tax and Transfer Pricing in the People's Republic of China: A Comparative Analysis, 4 Pac. Rim L. & Pol'y 327 (1995)
Thurston, Country Risk Management: China and Intellectual Property Protection, 27 Int'l Law. 51 (1993)
Tokley and Ravn, Banking Law in China, 2 Asian Com. L. Rev. 163 (July/Aug. 1997)
Tomasic, Company Law and the Limits of the Rule of Law in China, 4 Austl. J. Corp. L. 470 (1995)
Van Der Sprinkel, Legal Institutions In Manchu China (Athlome Press, 1962)
Wang and Tomasic, China's Company Law (Michie, 1994)
Wang, Business Law Of China: Cases, Texts, And Commentary (Michie, 1993)
Wang, China's New Foreign Trade Law: Analysis and Implications for China's GATT Bid, 28 J. Marshall L. Rev. 495 (1995)
Wang, The Chinese Traditions Inimical to the Patent Law, 14 J. Int'l L. Bus. 15 (1993)
Wang, The Judicial Explanation in Chinese Criminal Law, 43 Am. J. Comp. L. 569 (1995)
Wang: Celebrations Turn to Sorrow: Where Is China's Consumer Protection Law?, 4 Canberra L. Rev. 151 (1997/98)
Waters, China's Economic Development Strategies For The 21ST Century (Quorum Books, 1997)
Weiguo: Fraudulent Conduct and Punitive Damages in the Consumer Protection Law of China, 4 Canberra L. Rev. 111 (1997/98)
Willard, The Protection of Computer Software in the People's Republic of China: Current Law and Case Develpments in the "One-Copy" Country, 14 J. Marshall J. Computer & Info. L. 695 (1996)
Williams and Woo, The "Worthy" Unemployed: Societal Stratification and Unemployment Insurance Programs in China and the United States, 33 Colum. J. Transnat'l L. 457 (1995)
Wing-Hung Lo, China's Legal Awakening: Legal Theory And Criminal Justice In Deng's Era (Hong Kong University Press, 1995)
Wolf, The Legal Framework for Joint Development of China's Onshore Oil Resources: Negotiation Strategies and Future Prospects, 9 J. Chin. L. 141 (1995)
Wu, Joint Venture Law of the People's Republic of China, 7 Corp. & Bus. L.J. 15 (1994)
Xiangyuan and Huang, China on the Horizon: Exploring Current Legal Issues: China's New VAT System, 28 J. Marshall L. Rev. 619 (1995)
Xin, Tradition Of The Law And Law Of The Tradition: Law, State And Social Control In China (Greenwood Press, 1997)
Xu and Chew, Foreign Investment Enterprises in China, 17 East Asian Executive Rep. 9, Dec. 15, 1995

Yan, China's VAT Experience, (Tax Analysts, 2011).
Yu, The Emerging Framework of China's Business Organizations Law, 10 Transnat'l Law. 39 (1997)
Yu: An Unfair Competition Law Without a Core: An Introductory Comparison between U.S. Antitrust Law and the New Law of the People's Republic of China, 4 Ind. Int'l & Comp. L. Rev. 315 (1994)
Zee: Investing In China B Shares (American Educational Systems, 1991)
Zheng, China's Civil And Commercial Law (1988)
Zongling: The Role of Lawyers in Social Change: China, 25 Case W. Res. J. Int'l L. 163 (1993)